POSTCARD HISTORY SERIES

Warrensburg and Johnson County

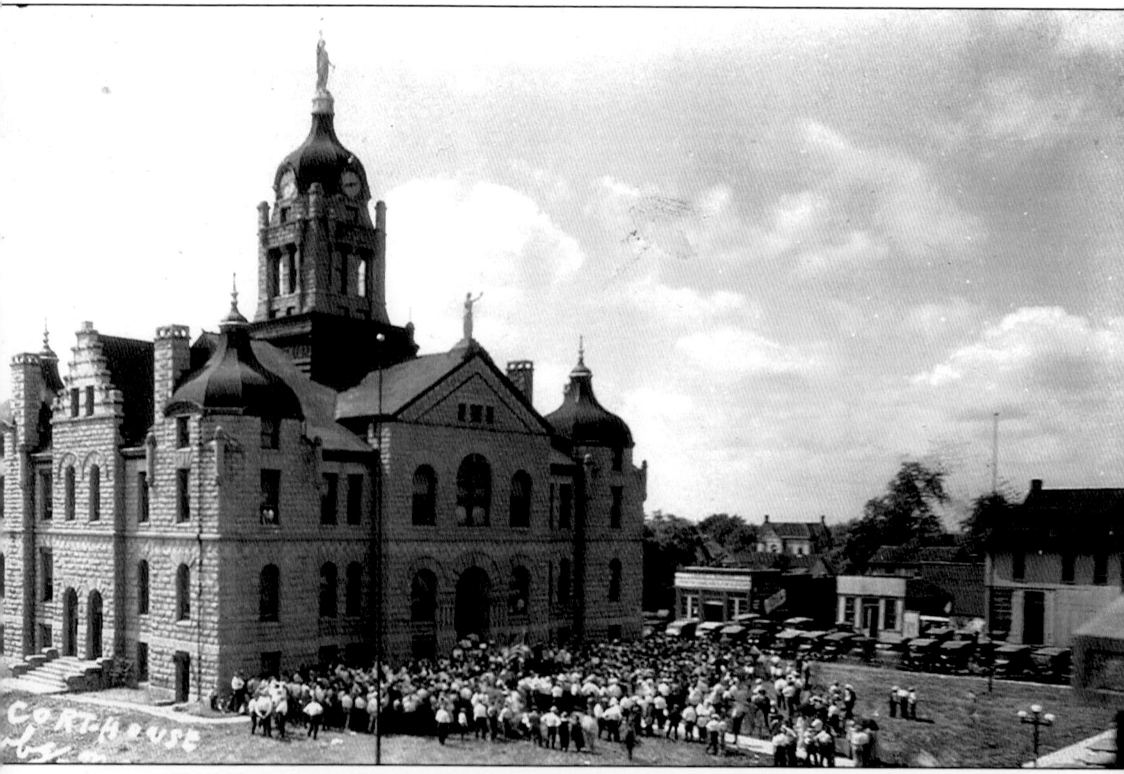

COURT HOUSE. Perhaps the most important single structure for the entire county is the court house. It was built of native Warrensburg sandstone and completed in 1898. This *c.* 1920 view, looking southwest, shows Lady Minerva standing tall atop the dome. Note the large crowd of people in the courthouse shadow and the misspelling of "Cort."

POSTCARD HISTORY SERIES

Warrensburg and Johnson County

Carol Berkland, Herb Best, and Lisa Irle

ARCADIA PUBLISHING

ISBN 978-0-7385-3251-6

Published by Arcadia Publishing
Charleston, South Carolina

Printed in the United States of America

Library of Congress Catalog Card Number: 2004105461

For all general information contact Arcadia Publishing at:
Telephone 843-853-2070
Fax 843-853-0044
E-mail sales@arcadiapublishing.com
For customer service and orders:
Toll-Free 1-888-313-2665

Visit us on the Internet at www.arcadiapublishing.com

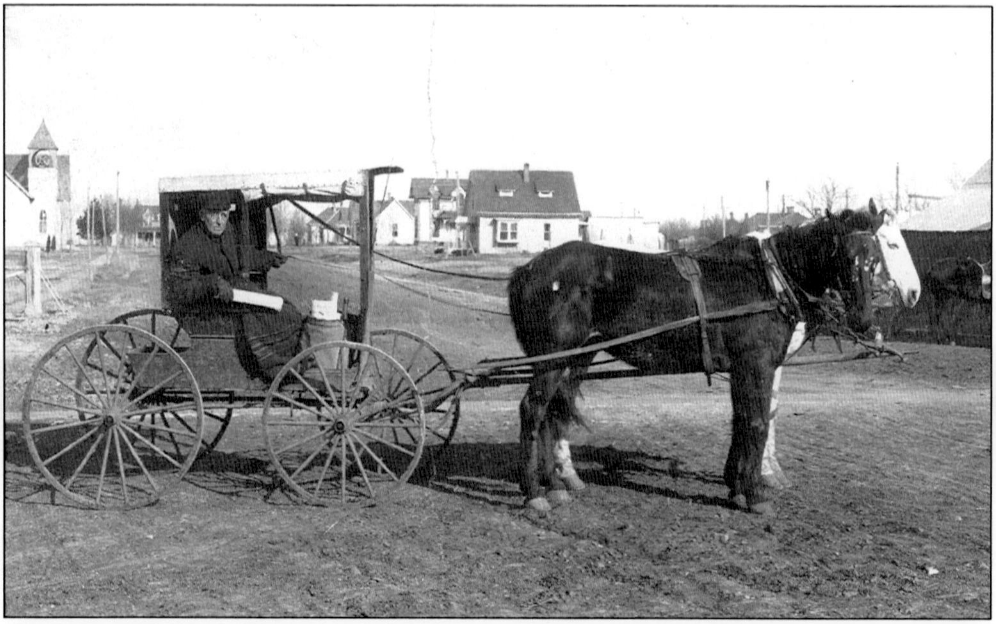

MAIL CARRIER C.C. RIDLEY. For Christmas of 1912, Carrier Ridley had these postcards made up for his patrons. E.J. Kensington and family of Chilhowee received this particular greeting wishing them a Merry Christmas and a Happy New Year. Thanks to the service of these carriers in all sorts of weather, the postcards included in this collection made it safely to their addressees. (JCHS Collection.)

Contents

ACKNOWLEDGMENTS

The authors would like to thank the Johnson County Historical Society (JCHS), its board of directors, library volunteers Donna Holt and Mary Rainey (for helping us find information) and all of the historical society members and volunteers—past and present—who work to collect, index, and preserve the holdings in the Mary Miller Smiser Heritage Library. Many of the postcards included in this journey are found in the collections of C. Berkland, C.H. Best, and L.A. Irle. Where that is not the case, it is so noted. Thanks also to Tom (Warren T.) Christopher and Marcine Pennington for sharing postcards from their personal collections. For our friends and families who have lent support in this adventure, we also are grateful.

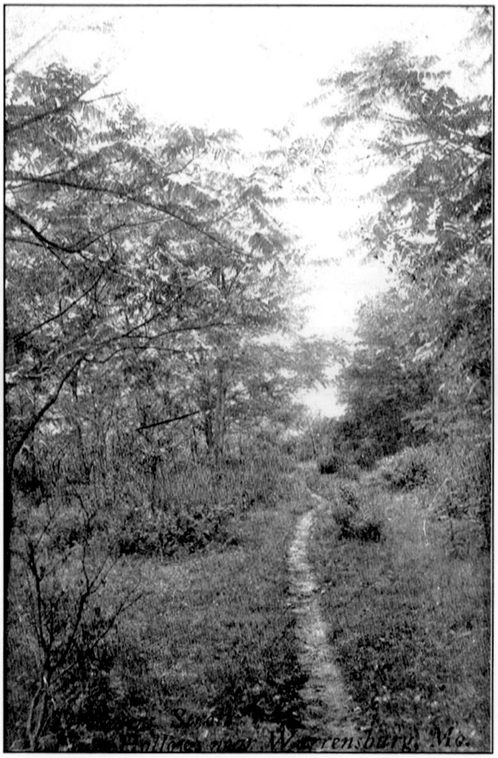

CAVE HOLLOW PATH. The path least traveled.

INTRODUCTION

Looking at Warrensburg and Johnson County history and evolution through the eye of the camera lens, using postcards as a medium, gives a glimpse of how our communities have progressed.

Around 1865, Warrensburg business owners rapidly moved several blocks east from the original town square, seeking a closer proximity to the railroad. Pine Street and Holden Street were established as the central business area, while Gay Street abounded with stately homes and churches. Among the businesses bringing economic growth and attention to Johnson County were the high quality sandstone quarries providing building materials for many courthouses throughout the state.

As the county seat of Johnson County, Warrensburg has provided 34 communities, throughout the years, with its health and educational services. Starting long ago with the Oak Hill Sanitarium and continuing with the recently remodeled Western Missouri Medical Center, excellent services have been provided to all county residents. Higher learning has been in the forefront since the Old Normal No. 2 was established in 1871. The educational opportunities ripple out to many of the county's school districts.

Churches have been a very important part of community life. Church sites were near the old town square, even using the old courthouse for a time, gradually moving east as the town expanded. Methodist, Christian, Presbyterian, Episcopalian, and Church of Christ are near the present day downtown area. The Lutheran, Baptist, and Catholic churches have relocated to accommodate growing congregations.

Two highways, U.S. 50 and Missouri 13, run through town, as well as Missouri Pacific passenger trains (now Amtrak), bringing visitors and the need for services. An immediate need for accommodations saw hotels and restaurants move to the downtown area. With automobile and private airplane travel, and visitors to Whiteman Air Base, the businesses have spread widely in the city. Mineral springs brought many people to the resort areas of Electric Springs and Pertle Springs. Now belonging to Central Missouri State University, Pertle Springs provides many recreational opportunities as well as a source for research.

Carol Berkland, a resident of Warrensburg since 1967, has been greatly interested in its history for some time. This interest led her to become a volunteer at the Johnson County Historical Society (JCHS). She is an avid collector of postcards of the City of Warrensburg, Pertle Springs, and Central Missouri State University (CMSU), including all its "ancestors." Having a passion for the past has led her interests into photography of old barns and cemetery stones and playing bluegrass music. Carol would like to thank both her mother and father for instilling in her a curiosity about the past, present, and future. She would like to thank Terry, her husband, for encouraging her to do this work and making it possible to devote time to doing the necessary research.

Also a volunteer at JCHS, a retired professor from CMSU and a longtime resident of Chilhowee, Missouri, Clarence H. (Herb) Best has a curiosity about the history of Johnson County. A collector of postcards of Chilhowee, Missouri, an interest in antique tractors, steam trains, bluegrass music, and family genealogy, he has found this book to be a labor of love.

Lisa Irle, born third generation in the 'burg, returned in 1991. She feels so fortunate, not only to be employed as curator at JCHS, but also to have met many friends and her co-authors as a result. The journey through a vaguely familiar past has been illuminating in many ways. Lisa would especially like to thank her dear late father, Roger L. Irle, for driving her mom and the reluctant little Irles to historic spots all over the country—and filming it on 8mm—back in the day. He would pretend to be mean and say, "und you vill enjoy it." She sure misses him.

Postcards provide familiar as well as rare glimpses into the towns and people's lives in these communities. While over 200 postcards have been utilized in creating this small work, the authors realize that many more, and different ones, are out there. We regret that some places may not be well represented, perhaps not at all. Though considerable effort has been made to insure accuracy, errors may occur, so please bear with us and inform us in writing if the record is to be set straight. We might also add that a hand lens was required to read some of the text recorded in these images. Try it yourself to discover more.

We invite you to take a trip through historical Johnson County, Missouri to see pictures of who we are and where we live. Hopefully, you will find the journey as exciting and enjoyable as we, your tour guides, have.

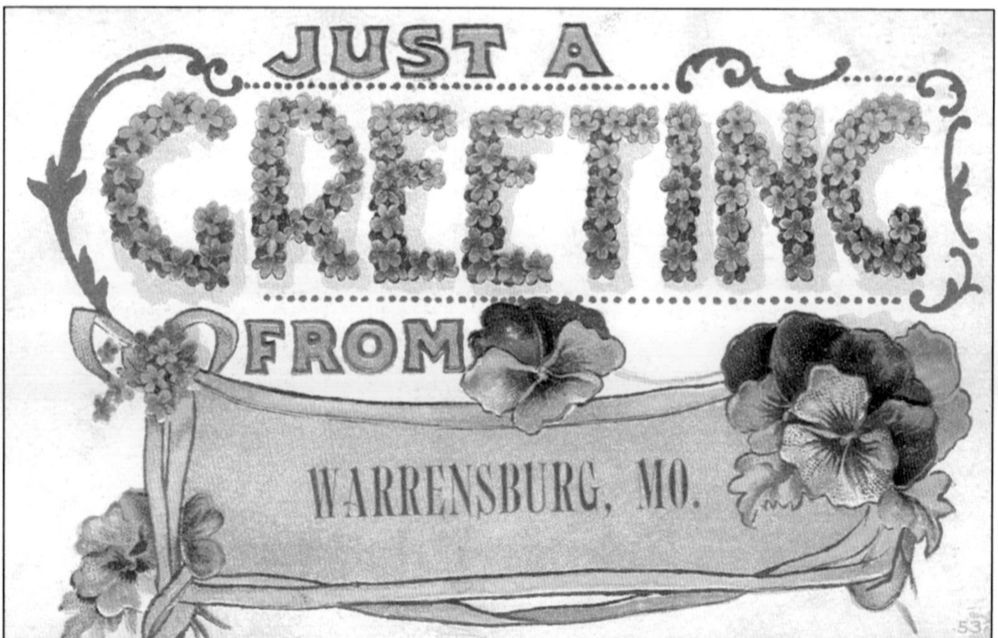

GREETINGS FROM. Warrensburg welcomes visitors in this early 1900s postcard. (A handy and inexpensive way to send a brief note, the penny postcard was used both by residents of towns throughout Johnson County and by visitors sending a few thoughts homeward.)

One

Welcome to Warrensburg

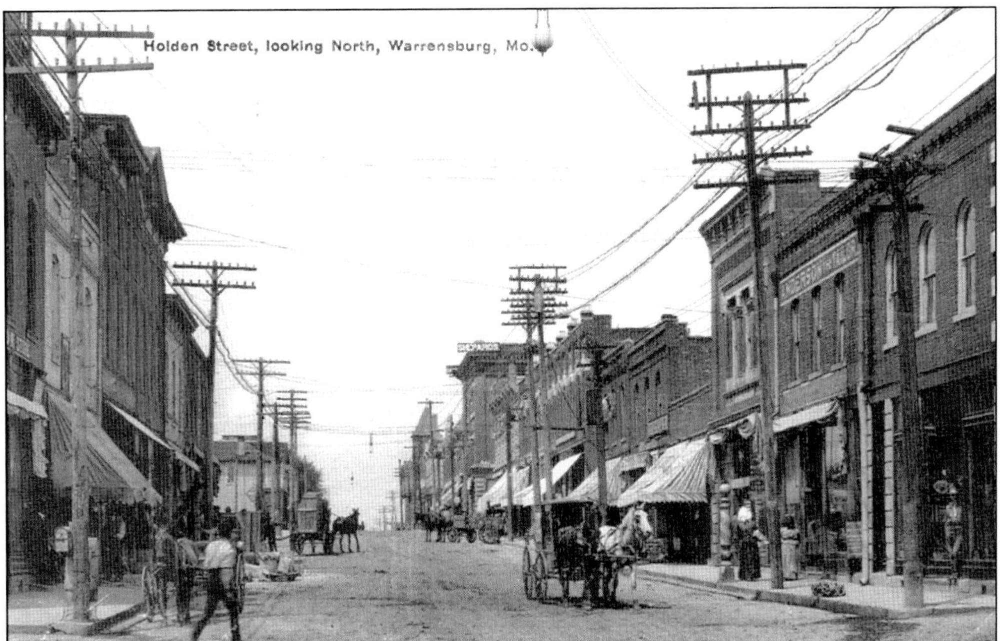

Holden Street Looking North. Horse-drawn vehicles show the early nature of this image of "new town" *c.* 1895. The telephone and power lines disappeared as improvements came. A barber pole in front of the Anderson & Taylor building welcomes customers. Shepard's store and The White House Store are evident, as is the original Christian Church steeple in the background. The gap one block up on the left is the courthouse square.

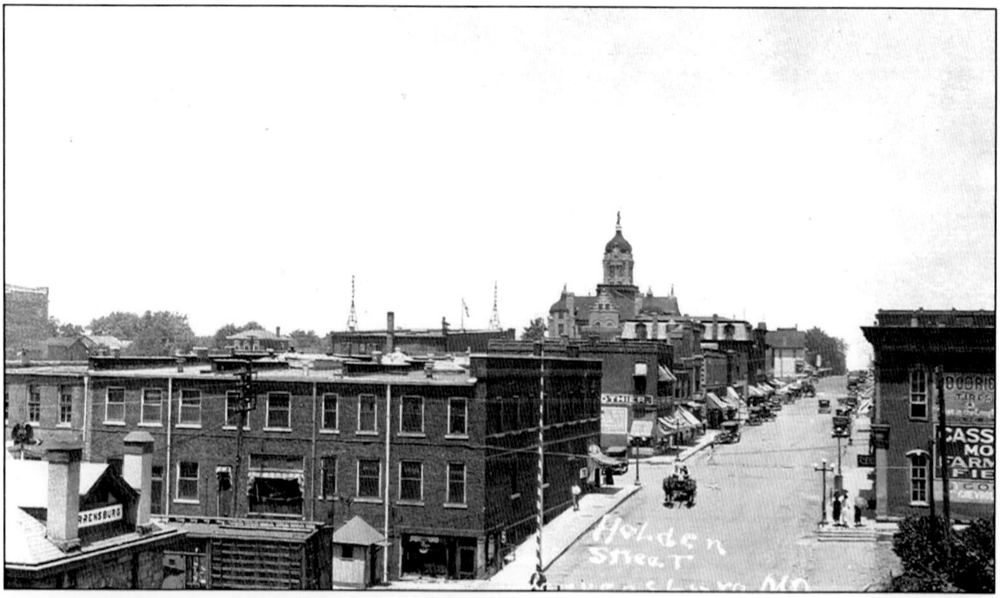

HOLDEN STREET LOOKING NORTH. Another vista, perhaps from high atop the Culp Mill, shows Warrensburg prominently welcoming trains from the east. The name Cassingham is here displayed at the corner of Railroad and Holden Streets, where the UMB currently stands. (JCHS Collection.)

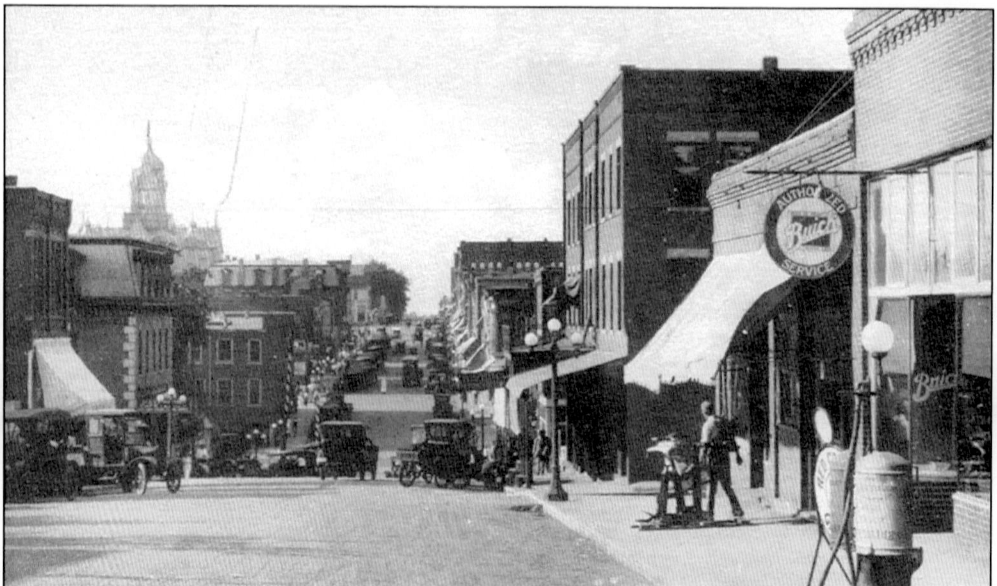

HOLDEN STREET LOOKING NORTH. Taken from the top of the hill, near Ming Street, this card seems to be from the same time period as the previous card, neither was ever posted. The authorized Buick service station on the right features a gas pump of the day, which dispensed "high proof gasoline." The sign on the building second on the left advertises the Davenport Café, an amenity of the Davenport Hotel. (JCHS Collection.)

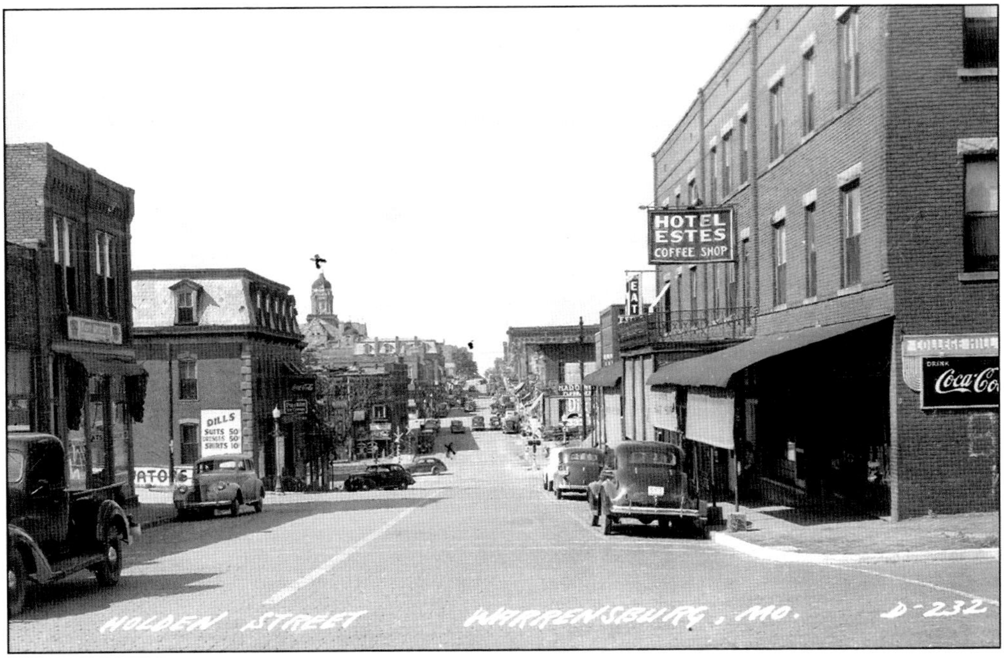

Holden Street Looking North. A bustling community can be seen in this *c.* 1941 view showing Holden Street from Grover Street. Whoever sent this card pointed out some places of particular interest to them, including the Armory Building at the center of the photo.

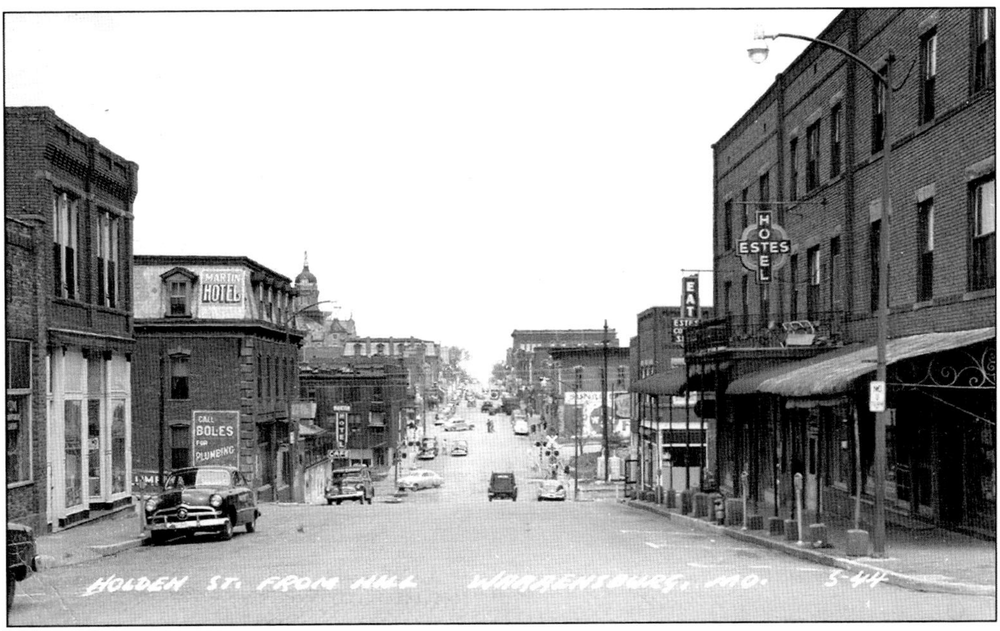

Holden Street Looking North. A *c.* 1950 image shows a Holden Street scene from Grover Street. New streetlights appeared. Warrensburg business life of the time was displayed by a new Hotel Estes sign, Martin Hotel signs, a Pay-Way feed sign on the Sunrise Feed & Seed Store at Holden and Railroad Streets, and a Vess Cola sign near the tracks at the bottling plant. The Estes Coffee Shop sign is now at Modern Mud, 111 East Culton Street.

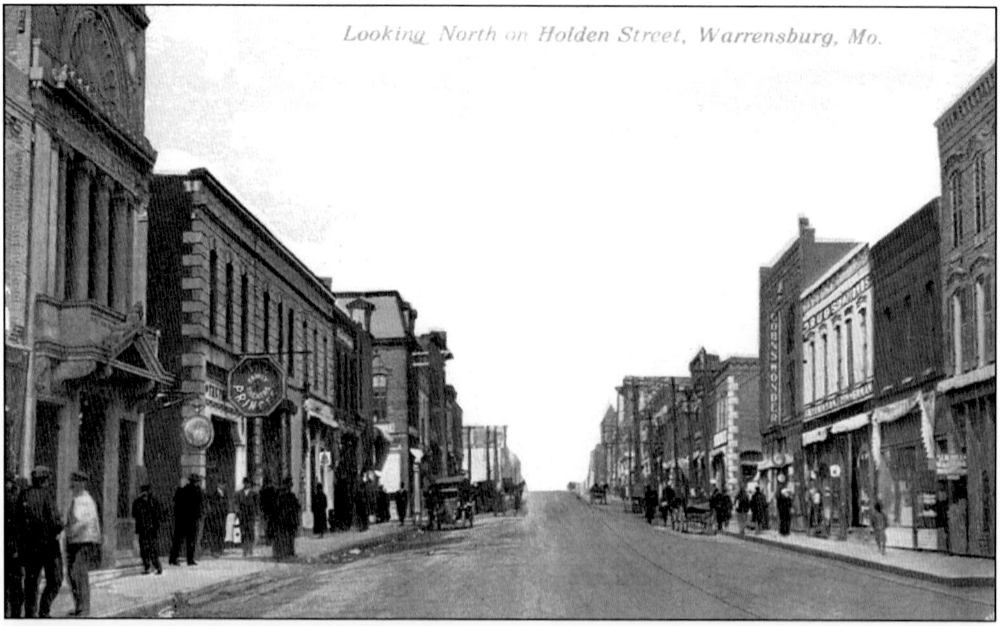

Holden Street Looking North. This early 1900s picture shows the new town with many of its new buildings along Holden Street, as seen from Pine Street. Citizen's Bank, The Princess Family Theatre with W.E. Buskirk as proprietor (now a parking lot), Cohn's Wonder Store (Trail's Regional Library today), and the mansard roof of the building now housing The Corner Café are among them.

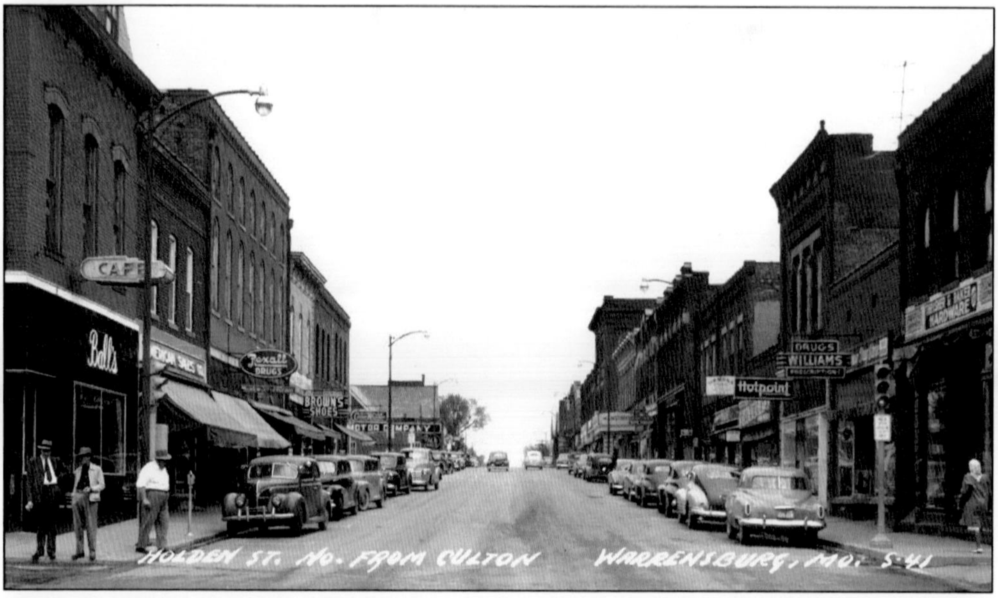

Holden Street Looking North. Neon signs line both sides of Holden in this 1940s–1950s view of the business district. Balls Café, Rexall Drugs carrying Meadow Gold Ice Cream, Brown's Shoes, Connor Wagoner's, The Main Street Theatre, Hotpoint, and Williams Drugs all exhibit their wares with this technology. Thrasher and Raker Hardware is on the corner with *the* stoplight. (JCHS Collection.)

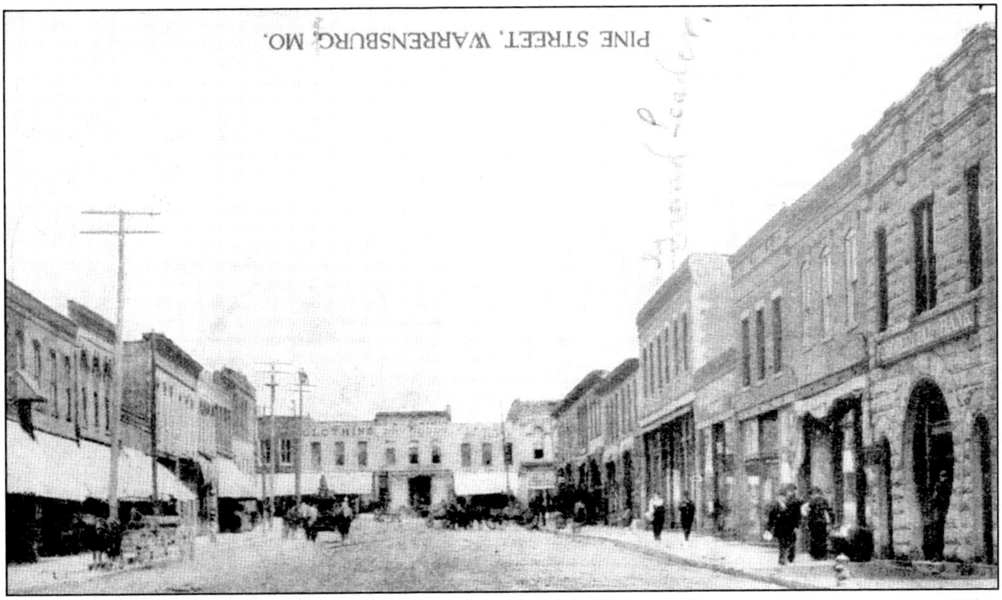

West Pine Street Looking East. In 1908, only horse-drawn vehicles are seen. The horseshoe shaped entryway of the Commercial Bank is in the far right foreground. The Grand Leader Dry Goods store, at 112-114 West Pine Street, is identified. The building to the right is J.C. Vernaz Drugs. On the north side of Pine Street the awning at the far left fronted a bakery. A clothing store, dry goods store, and druggist face the intersection on Holden Street.

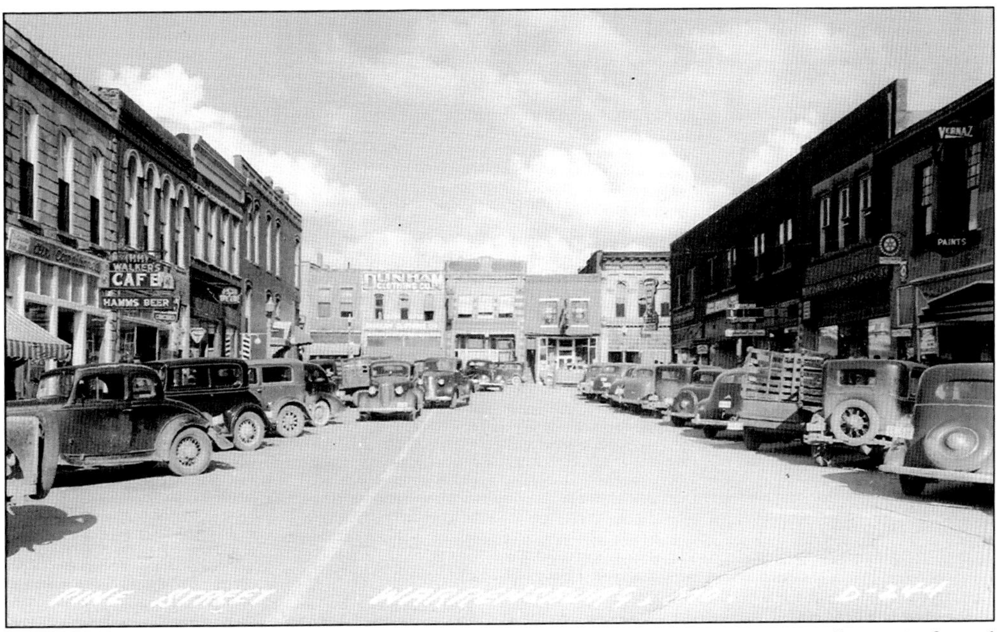

West Pine Street Looking East. In this mid- to late 1930s scene, Walker's Café and Dunham's Clothing Co. are identifiable. Many folks from rural areas came to town on Saturday—a family might bring eggs, cream, and a couple of chickens to sell for enough money to see a "picture show." That lingo didn't linger, but Hugh Reynolds says he bought the last eggs and cream direct from the farm in the early 1970s.

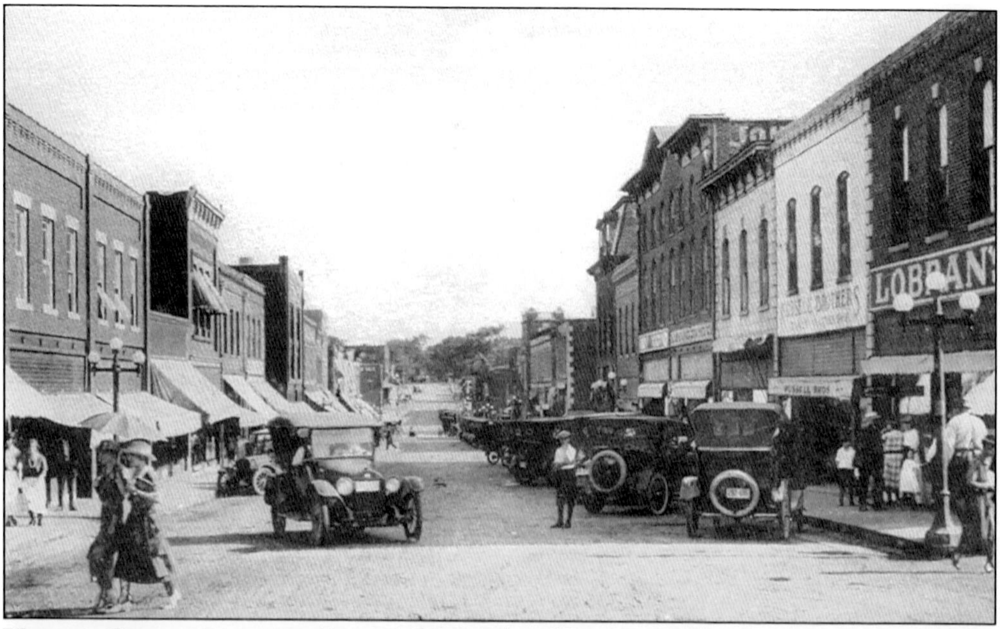

HOLDEN STREET LOOKING SOUTH. Diagonal parking on Holden Street in the mid-1920s was still acceptable. The "RUSSELL BROTHERS" sign, at 210 North Holden, reappeared in 2003 during remodeling. Russell Brothers moved to 206 North Holden Street in 1926. Lobban Dry Goods, 212 North Holden, is visible in this scene. As was Russell, Lobban was a well-known name in the 'burg. Two streets still bear the names of these clothiers.

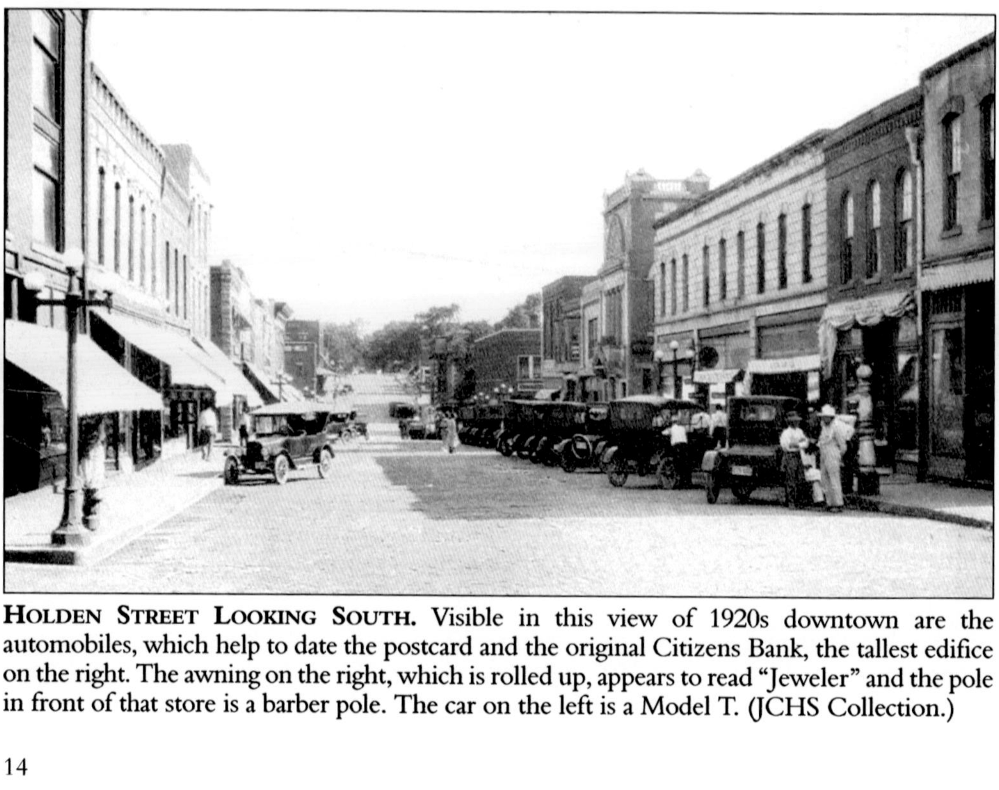

HOLDEN STREET LOOKING SOUTH. Visible in this view of 1920s downtown are the automobiles, which help to date the postcard and the original Citizens Bank, the tallest edifice on the right. The awning on the right, which is rolled up, appears to read "Jeweler" and the pole in front of that store is a barber pole. The car on the left is a Model T. (JCHS Collection.)

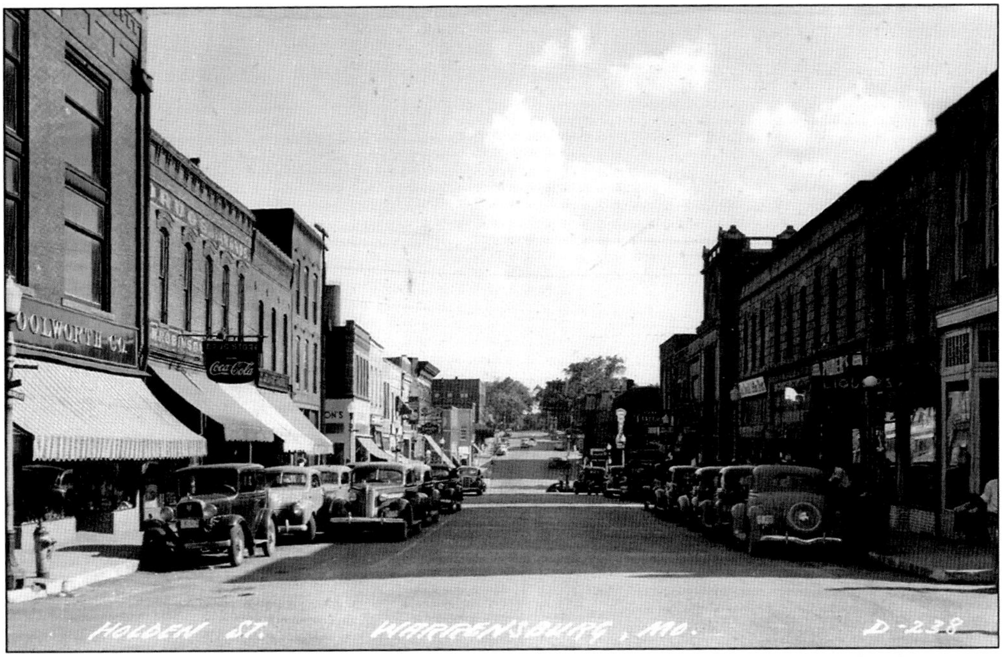

HOLDEN STREET LOOKING SOUTH. Look at the east side of Holden Street in this late 1930s shot. Ever hear of "double parking"? F.W. Woolworth Co. store and a drug store with a Coca Cola sign operated until the 1970s. What can you find?

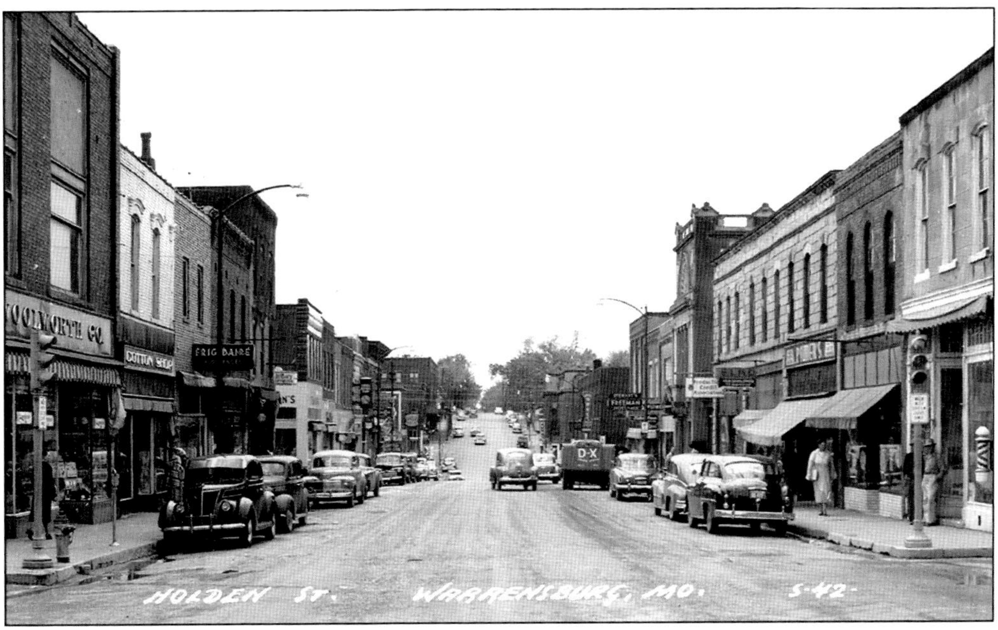

HOLDEN STREET LOOKING SOUTH. In this late 1940s view from Culton Street many of the buildings remain as they were in the early 1900s. The Cotton Shop stands next to F.W. Woolworth Co. O'Bannon's, Palmer's, Production Credit Association, The People's National Bank clock, and other signs remind us of the businesses found "down town." Note the traffic signals.

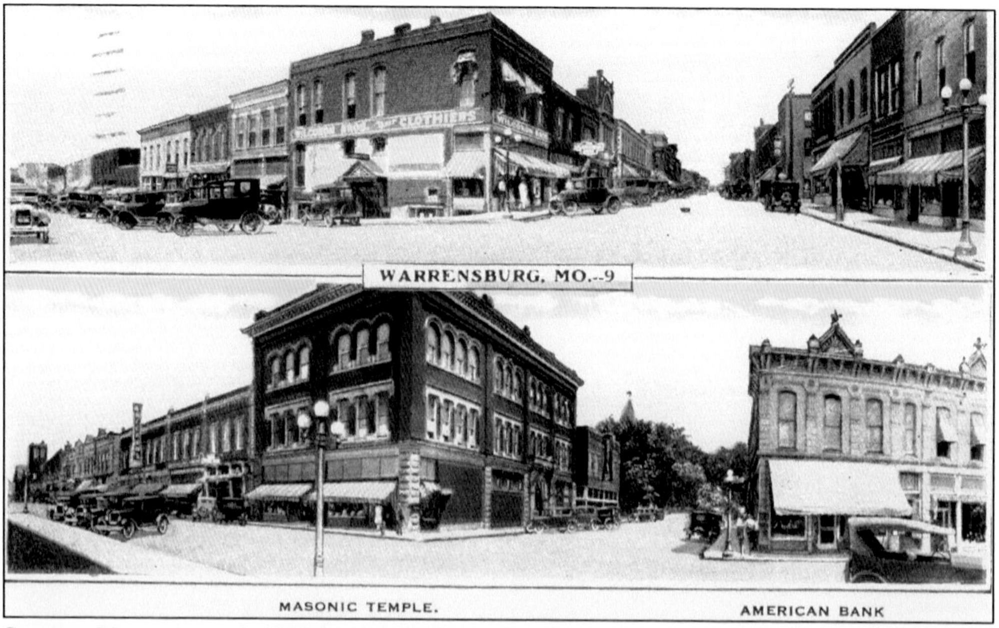

Street Multiview. A 1918 Star Journal article relates, "About 30 years ago," said Mr. G.A. Lobban, "the Masons bought the two lots on which the Masonic Temple stands. They paid $400 apiece for the lots and when it came to financing the building they got cold feet and were afraid to invest the price of a good building so far up the street." Lobban immediately purchased stock and got the ball rolling.

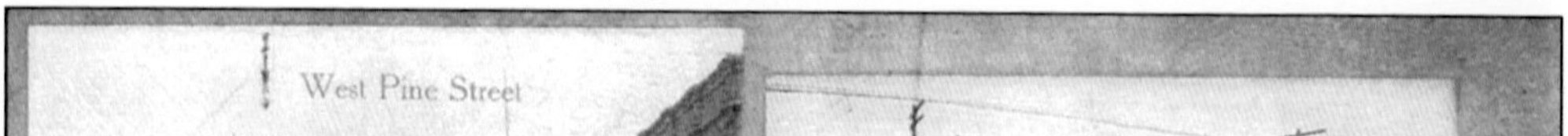

Street Multiview. Downtown buildings from various positions can be seen, such as West Pine Street (see page 13), Johnson County Abstract Block from Market Street south on Holden Street, Masonic Temple and the Cord Block from Market Street north on Holden Street, and the A. Nathan Clothiers at the corner of Holden and West Pine Streets. These cards were popular as photographers made montages of their work, when cut and paste meant just that.

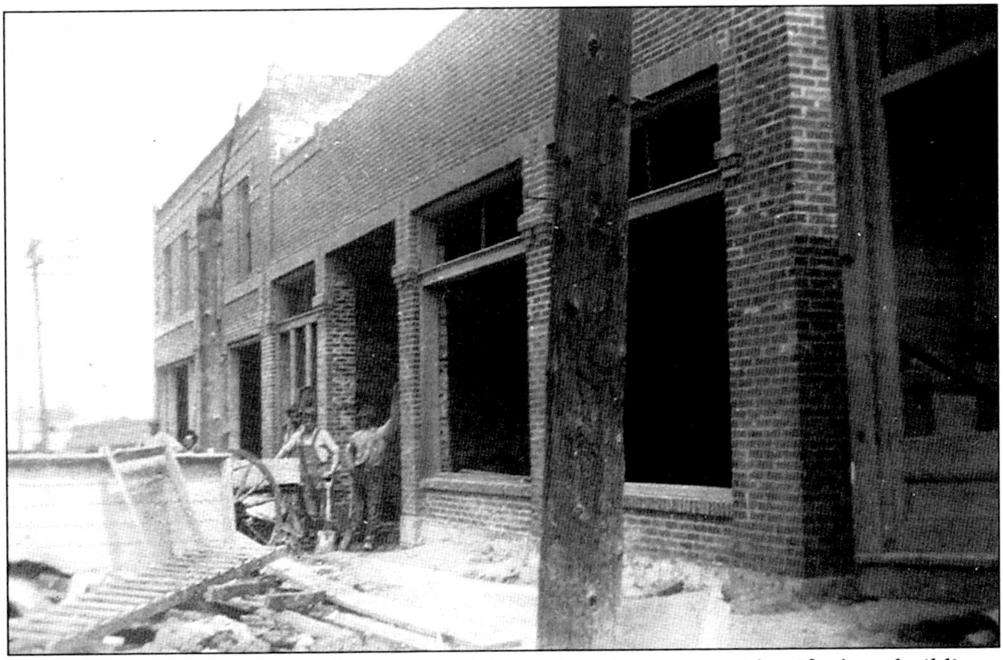

UNIDENTIFIED DOWNTOWN BUILDINGS. The authors have yet to identify these buildings, but the donor's family had always lived in Warrensburg, and she is sure this must be a local scene. This view shows part of the business district while in some state of disarray. Perhaps the buildings were under construction. (Marcine Pennington Collection.)

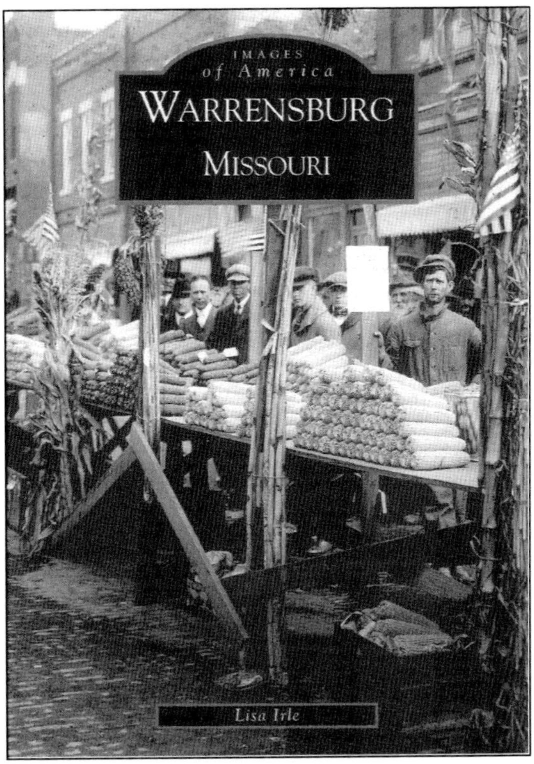

A DOWNTOWN VIEW. A promotional postcard, not the traditional 3.5" x 5.5" size, from a previous Arcadia title, shows the east side of Holden Street, in the 200 block, and lots of corn.

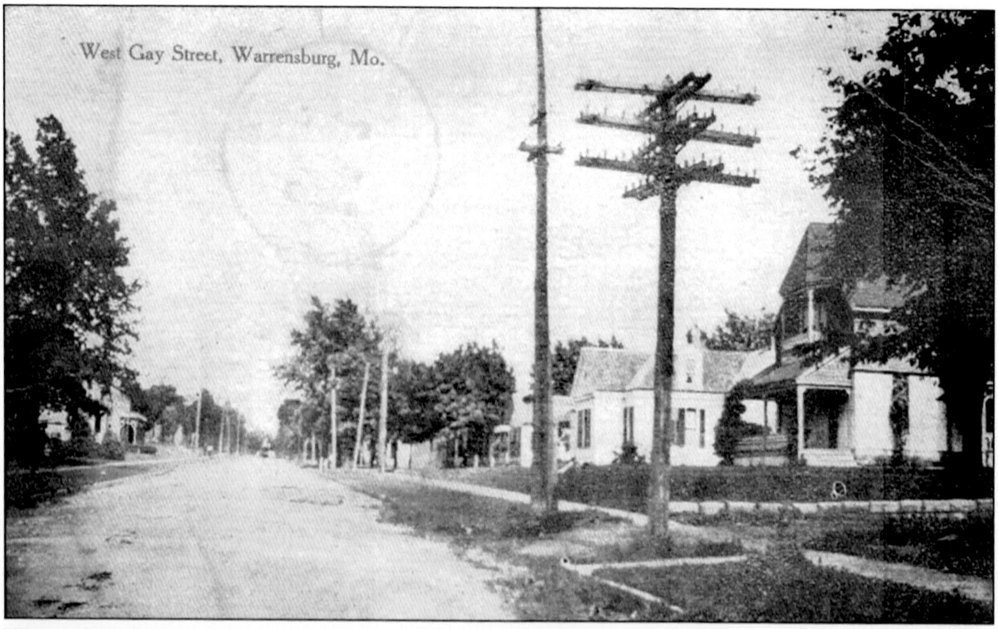

WEST GAY STREET LOOKING EAST. From Warren Street, the home at 222 West Gay Street can be seen in the right foreground. The house stands today, looking much as it did in this early scene, though the gardens of Robert and Nancy Jones add to its charm.

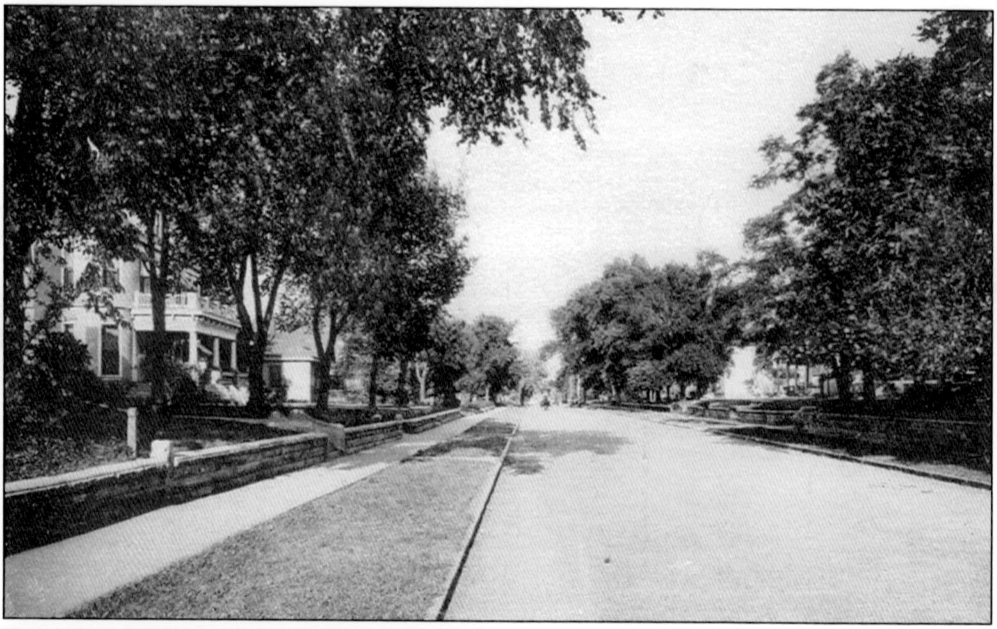

EAST GAY STREET LOOKING WEST FROM MAGUIRE. The home in the left foreground still stands today at 216 East Gay Street.

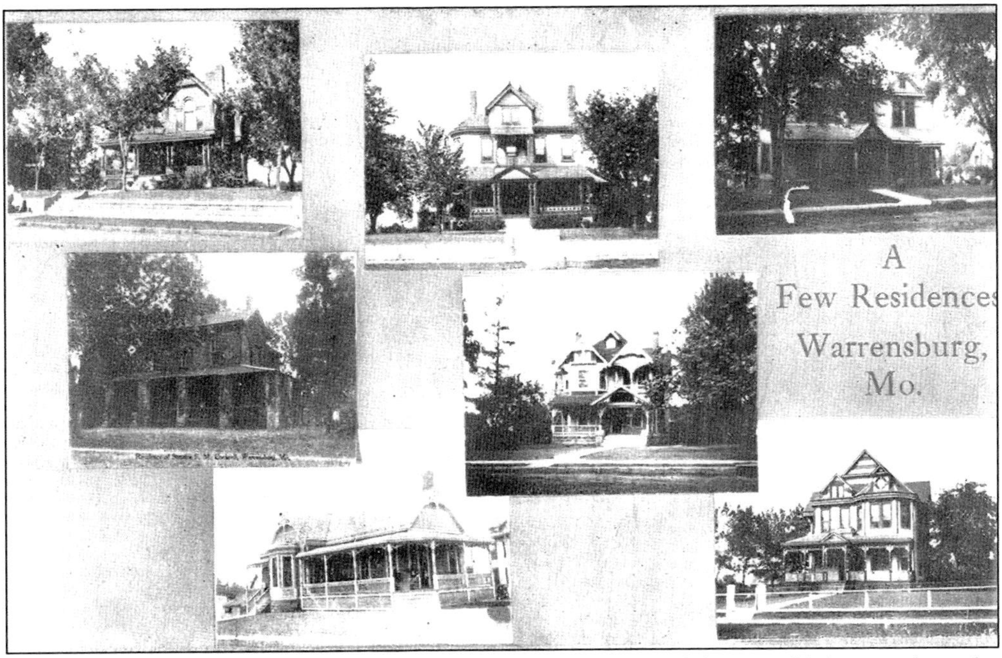

RESIDENCE MULTIVIEW. The photographer or publisher created these multiviews to show the availability of individual cards. These were some of the stately homes found in Warrensburg at the time. Some of them still exist. In the *Standard Herald*, October 1908, Stillwell Souvenir Store advertised they would photograph your house and make real photo postcards—plain or colored—for you.

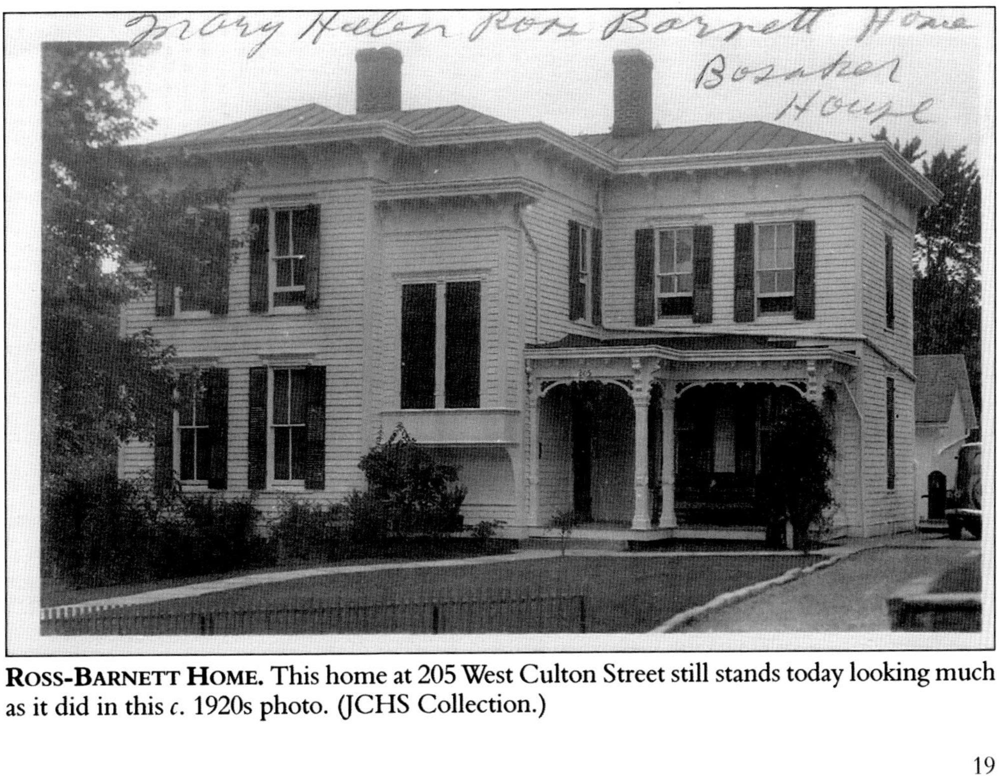

ROSS-BARNETT HOME. This home at 205 West Culton Street still stands today looking much as it did in this *c.* 1920s photo. (JCHS Collection.)

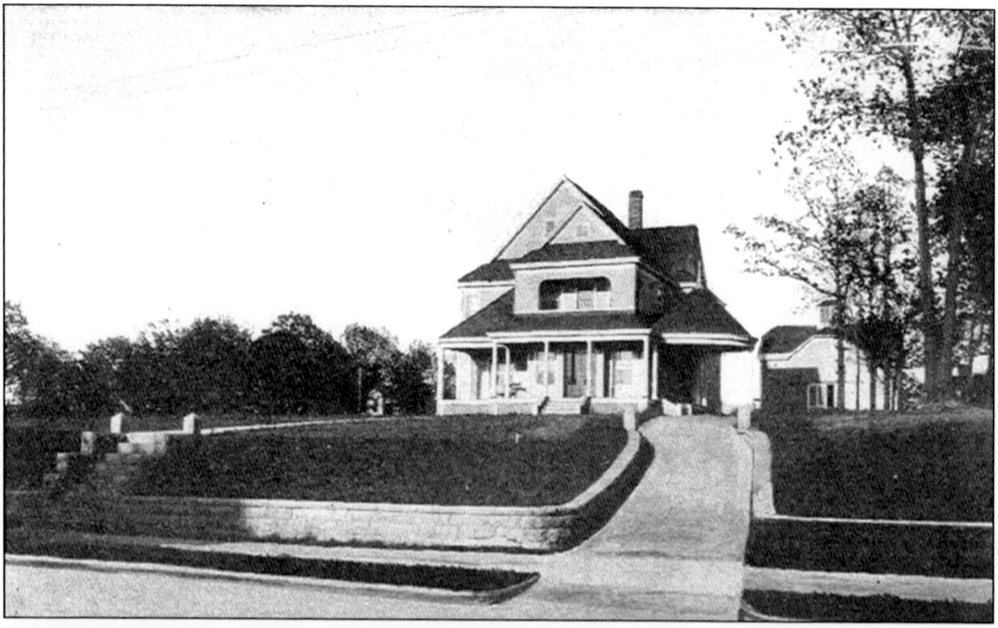

J.A. KEMPER HOME. In 1903, attorney J.A. Kemper purchased land across from C.H. Harrison on North Holden Street to build this lovely home. In 1901, he had moved to a new office over Nathan's Clothing, 112 North Holden Street. Two of Kemper's cases are mentioned in the *Star Journal's* "Backward Glances"—a battle to obtain a Dram Shop License and a personal injury, which involved the biting off of the plaintiff's earlobe. (JCHS Collection.)

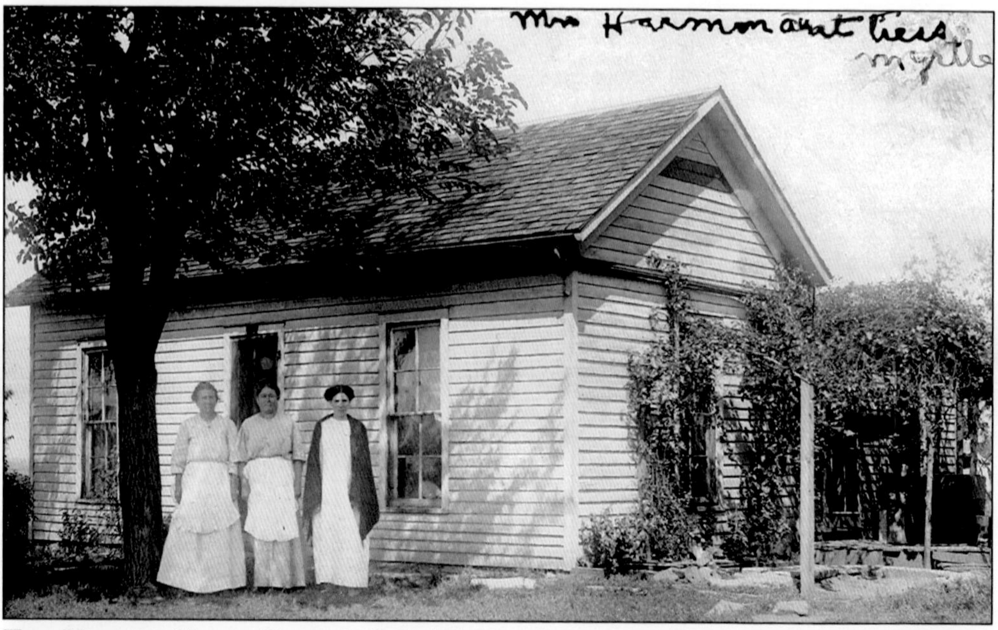

THE HARMON HOME. Pictured, from left to right, are: Mrs. Tressa Hewitt Shaw, Emma (Emily) Hewitt Harmon, and Aunt Myrtle Harmon Shaw (Uncle Charles' wife). Emma Harmon's house, on the northeast corner of Water and West Gay Streets, is adorned with a beautiful vining trellis. (Marcine Pennington Collection.)

Two

OPEN FOR BUSINESS

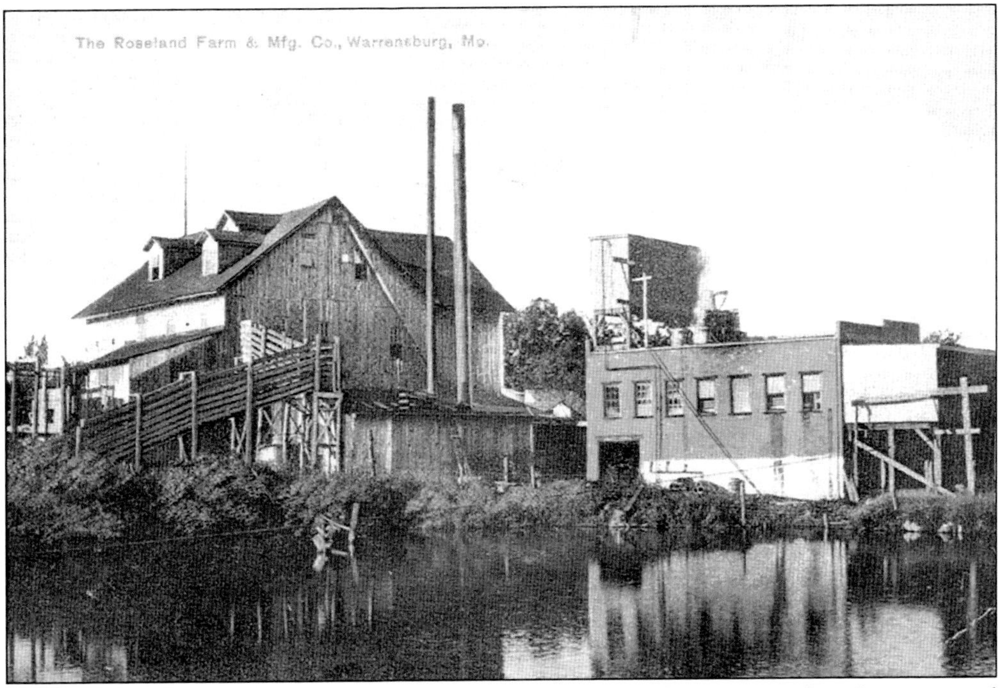

ROSELAND FARM & MANUFACTURING CO. Widely known for its "Warnsburg" sausage and country cured, hickory smoked hams and bacon, Roseland was one of the largest industries in Johnson County. Established in 1908, with William Shockey as president, it was located between East Gay and East North Streets. Roseland also operated an ice plant. This area was formerly occupied by Eureka Mills.

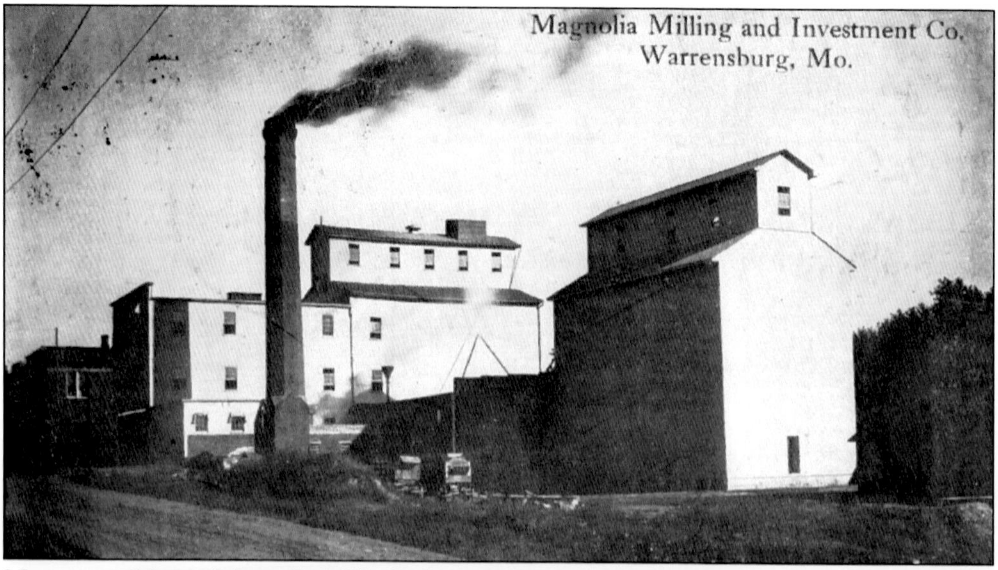

MAGNOLIA MILLS. Magnolia Mills, built in 1879, was a going agricultural concern for many years at West Pine and Washington Streets. Run by Markward and Land, the operation was ambitious and diversified, with not only the "investments" implied on the postcard, but also a foray into the entertainment field.

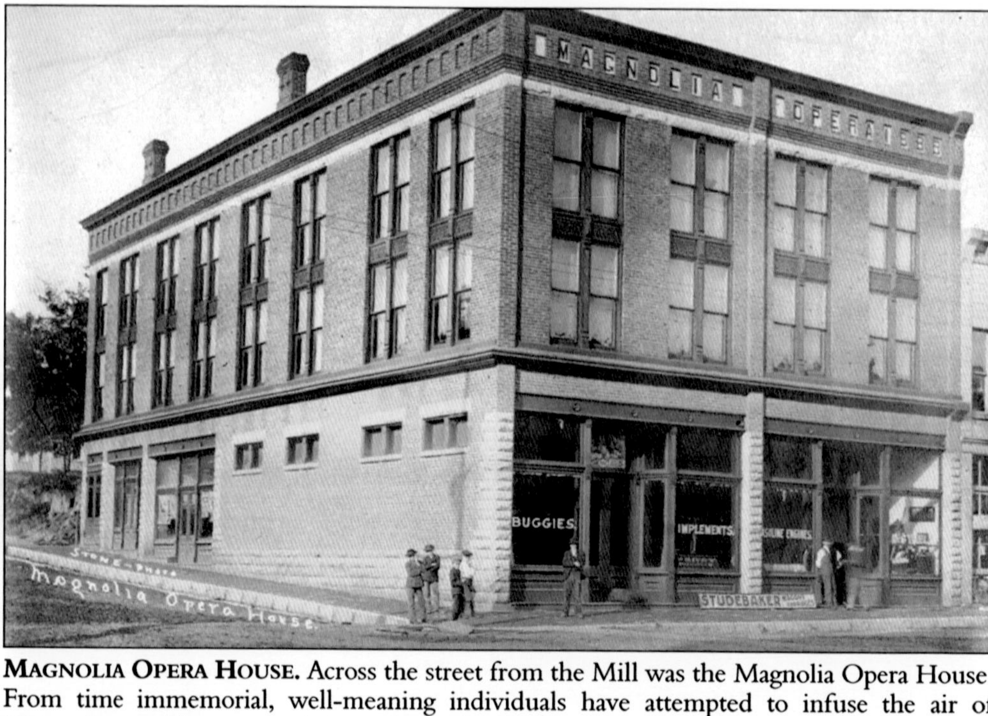

MAGNOLIA OPERA HOUSE. Across the street from the Mill was the Magnolia Opera House. From time immemorial, well-meaning individuals have attempted to infuse the air of Warrensburg with an appreciation of culture and the arts. The Opera House struggled from its opening in 1890, finally becoming a hall for graduations and other community functions. In truth, the town seems to have always been home to the talented and creative artistic soul. (JCHS Collection.)

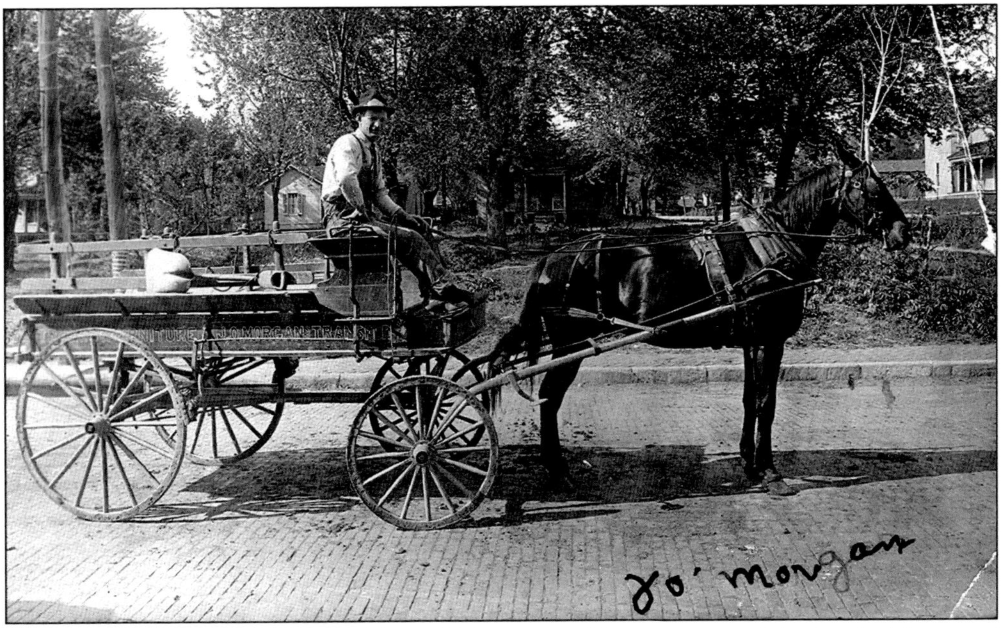

J.O. MORGAN. Mr. J.O. Morgan delivered his wares to his customers with a fine looking steed and a cart. Along with other ventures, he also moved houses. This photo is from the late 1800s or very early 1900s. (Marcine Pennington Collection.)

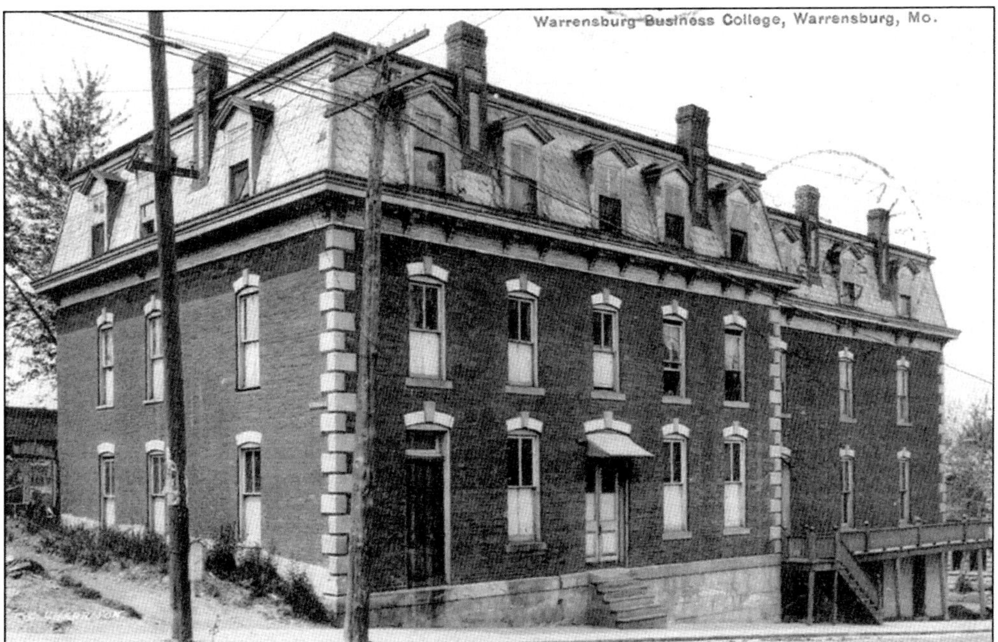

WARRENSBURG BUSINESS COLLEGE. In 1868, the second hotel in town, Simmons Hotel, was built south of the depot. The building had been the Commercial Hotel from 1888 until it was sold by S.M. VanCleave to Mr. Parker in 1906. This building was the Warrensburg Business College from that time until 1912 when it became the Martin Hotel. Warrensburg's Municipal Building has occupied this area since 1976.

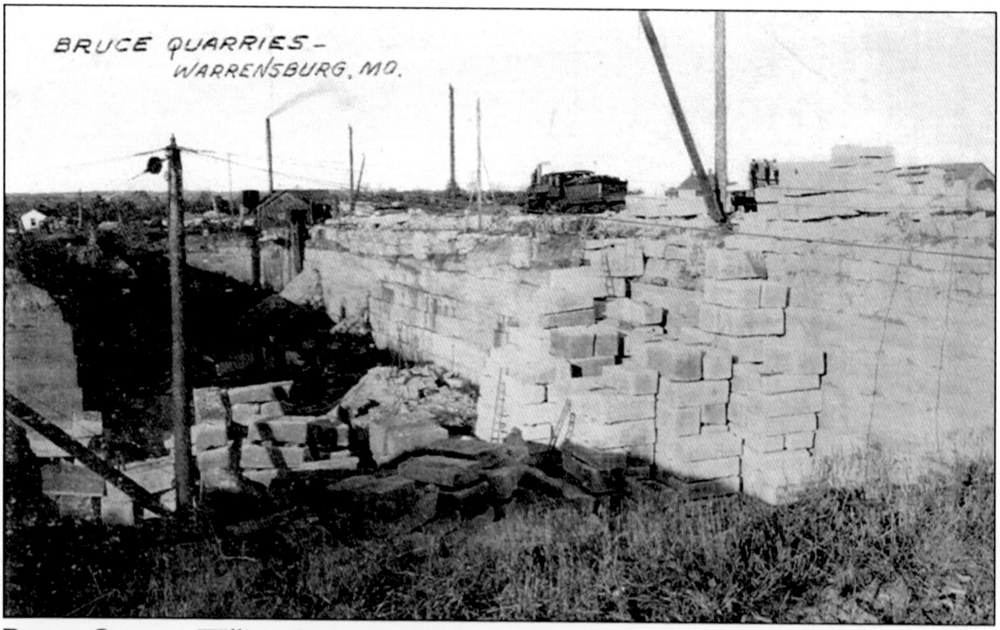

BRUCE QUARRY. William Bruce opened his sandstone quarry in 1871. It was the second quarry in the area. He leased the land from General Cockrell until 1880. The Pickel Brothers then bought and operated it. In 1881, Mr. Bruce opened the third quarry, which was later operated by brothers James B. and John W. Millar. This is one of several sandstone quarries just north of Warrensburg that furnished stone for building material.

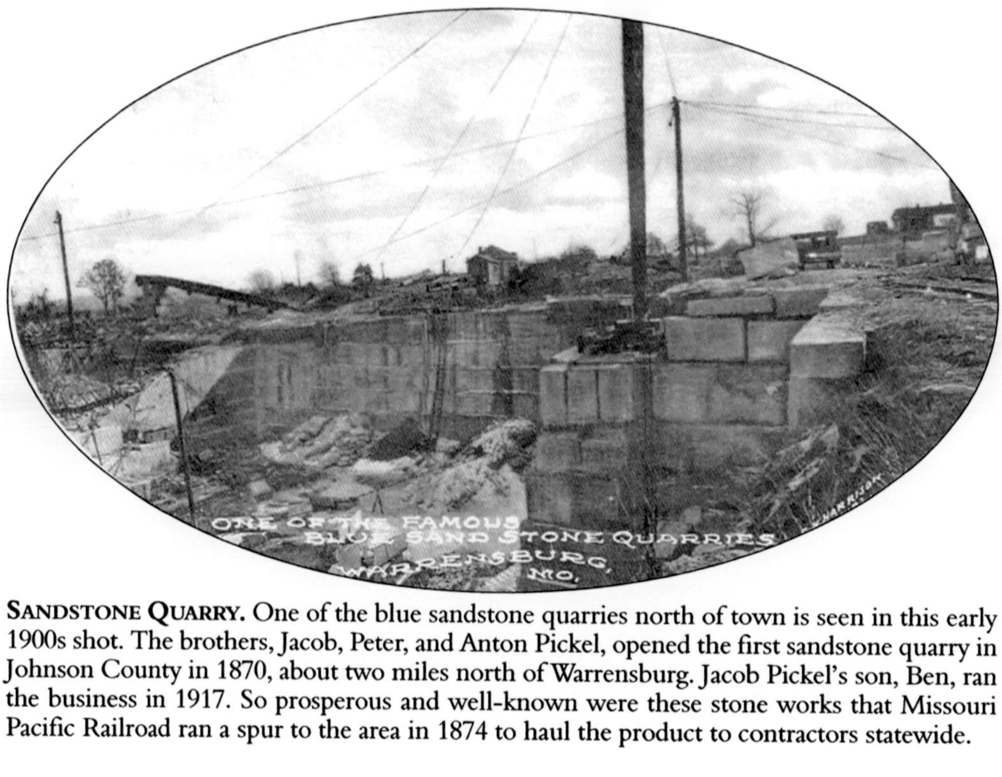

SANDSTONE QUARRY. One of the blue sandstone quarries north of town is seen in this early 1900s shot. The brothers, Jacob, Peter, and Anton Pickel, opened the first sandstone quarry in Johnson County in 1870, about two miles north of Warrensburg. Jacob Pickel's son, Ben, ran the business in 1917. So prosperous and well-known were these stone works that Missouri Pacific Railroad ran a spur to the area in 1874 to haul the product to contractors statewide.

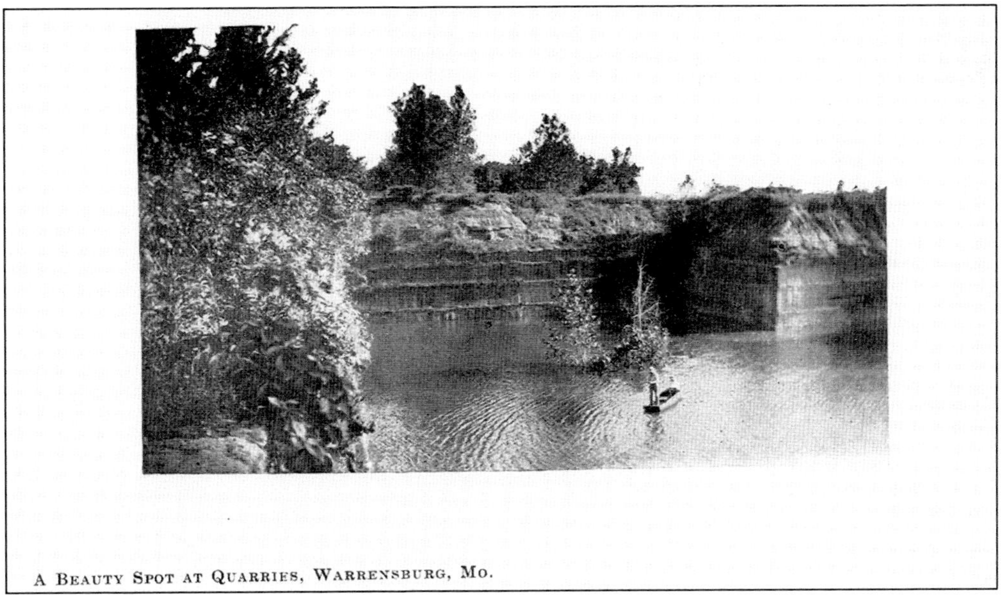

QUARRY LAKE RECREATION. When sandstone was no longer being carved from the earth, the quarry became a lake. A fishing boat is seen here in this 1920s view.

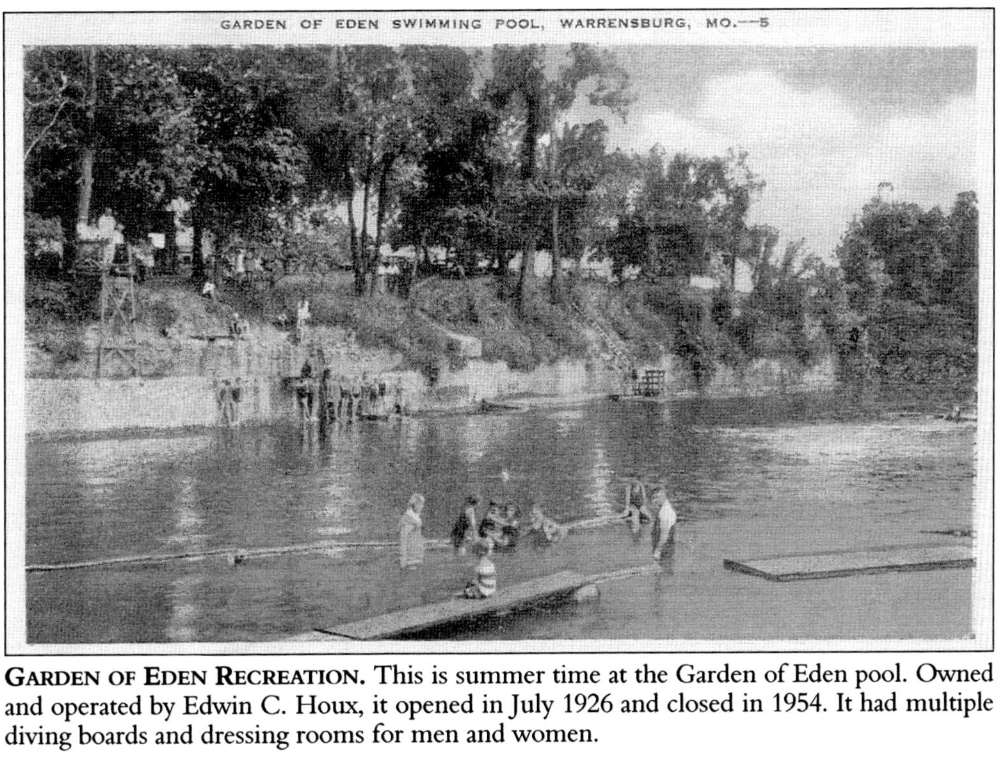

GARDEN OF EDEN RECREATION. This is summer time at the Garden of Eden pool. Owned and operated by Edwin C. Houx, it opened in July 1926 and closed in 1954. It had multiple diving boards and dressing rooms for men and women.

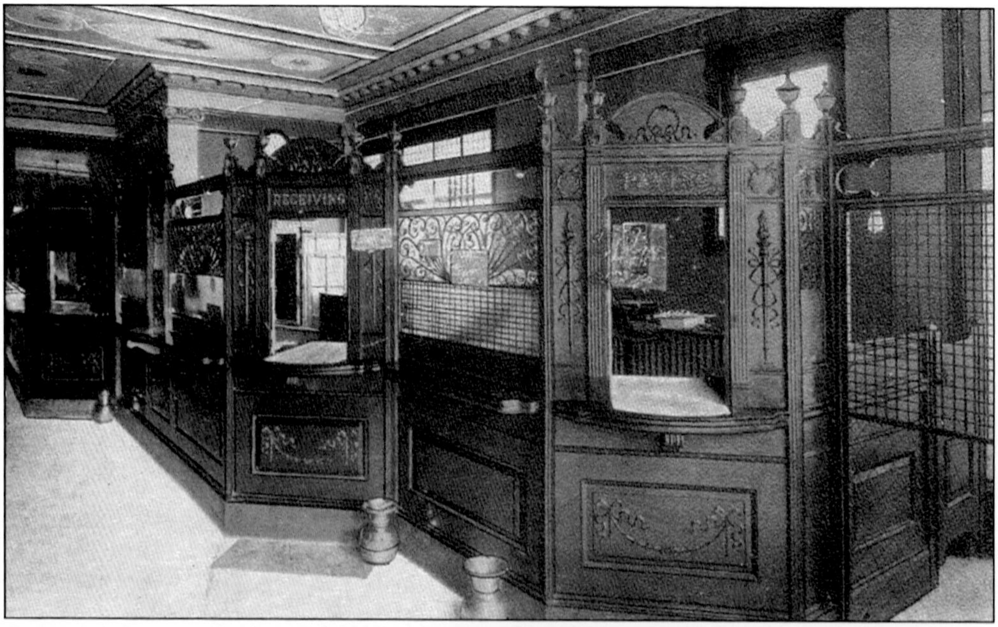

Citizen's Bank. The beautiful teller cages of the Citizen's Bank were genuinely in keeping with the ornate style of the front façade. Intricate filigree separated the customers from the actual money and personnel. Spittoons were cordially provided. (JCHS Collection.)

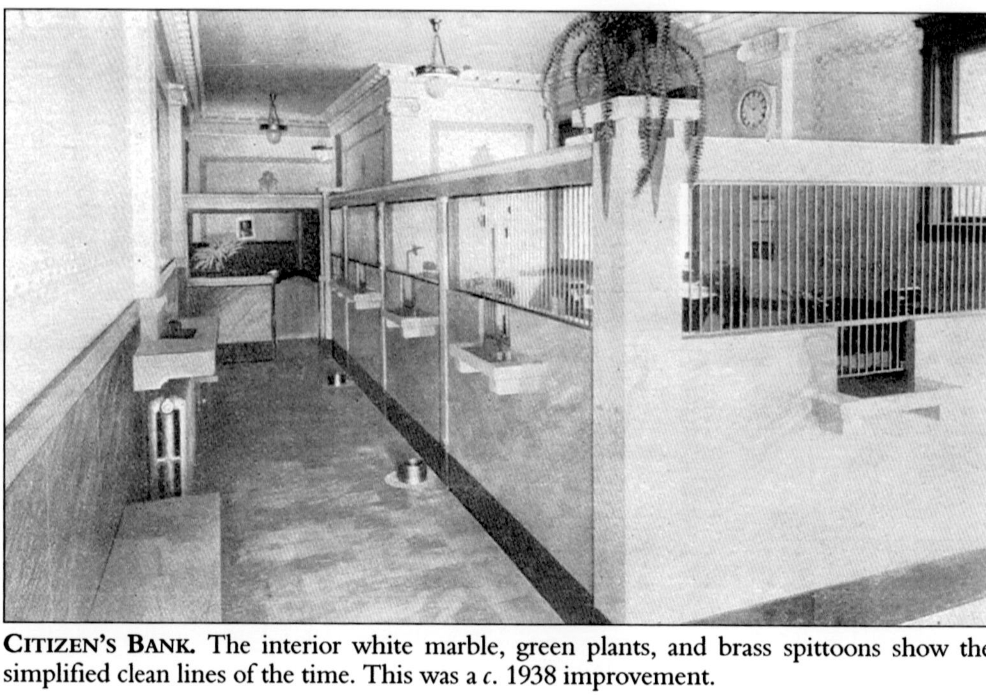

Citizen's Bank. The interior white marble, green plants, and brass spittoons show the simplified clean lines of the time. This was a *c.* 1938 improvement.

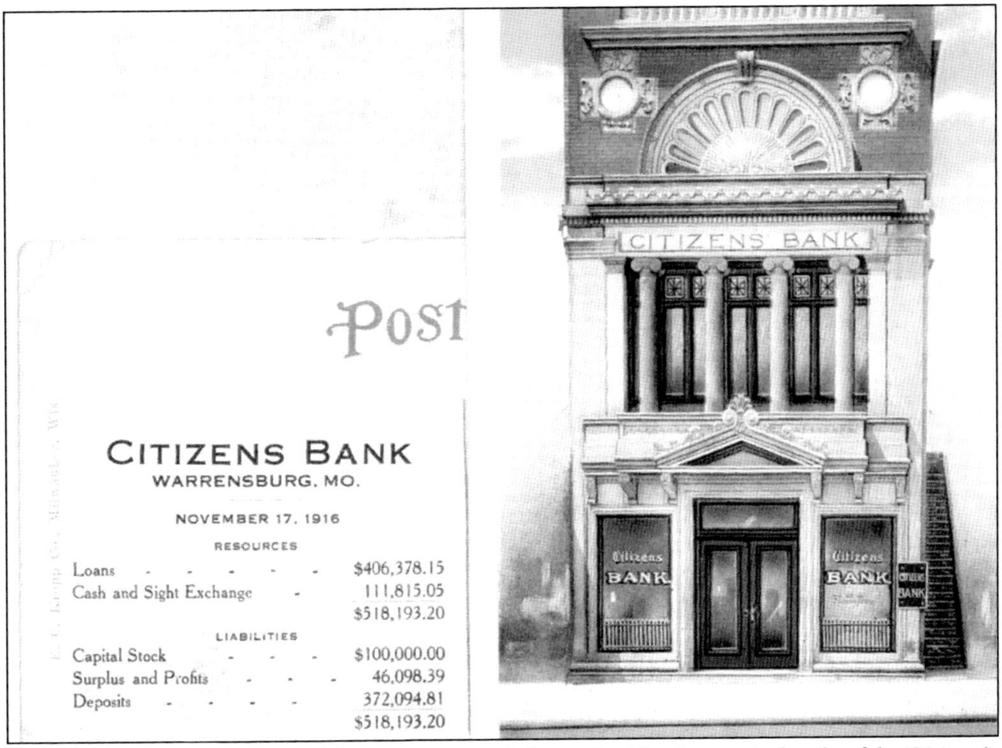

CITIZEN'S BANK. The front of this 1916 postcard shows the Greek temple façade of the Citizen's Bank, while the back describes its financial condition. The bank opened on October 19, 1888, with deposits of $35,000. The exterior was remodeled in 1954. (JCHS Collection.)

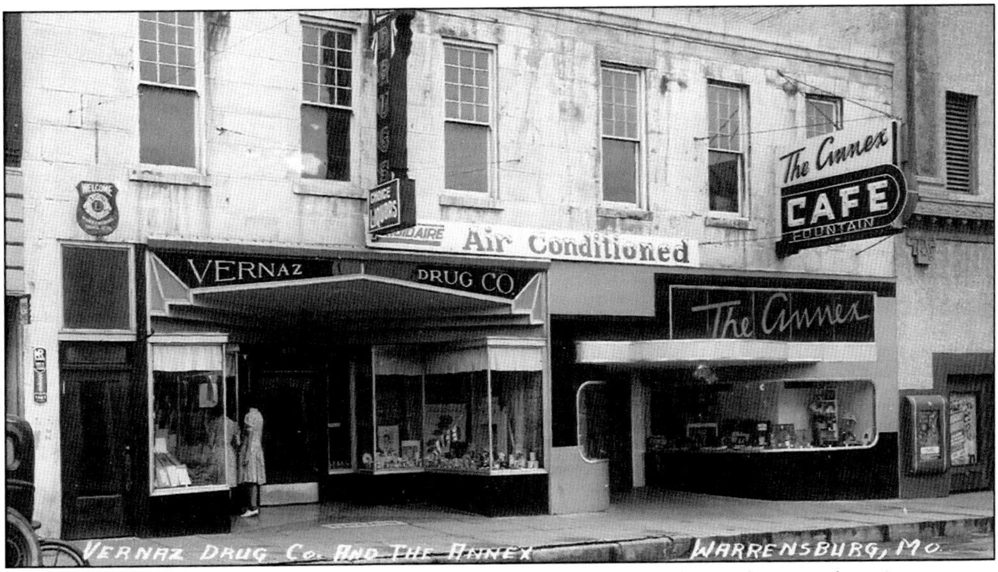

VERNAZ DRUG STORE. On West Pine Street, looking south/southwest, the viewer sees Vernaz and The Annex Café in 1943. Down the street, on the front of the Star Theater, "Now Showing" is *Stormy Weather*, starring Lena Horne and "Coming Soon" is *Du Barry Was a Lady* with Lucille Ball, Red Skelton, and Gene Kelly.

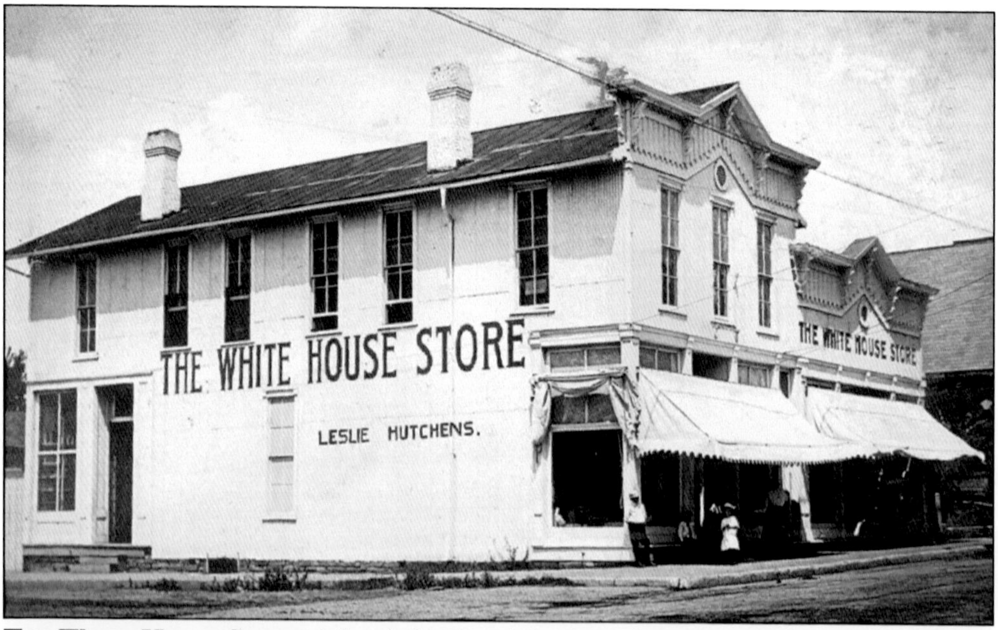

THE WHITE HOUSE STORE. A "cool place" to do business, because of its location and superb ventilation, The White House Store, owned by Leslie Hutchens, began operations around 1910. Located on Holden Street at the courthouse square and dealing in groceries and general merchandise, it did a brisk business. (Tom Christopher Collection.)

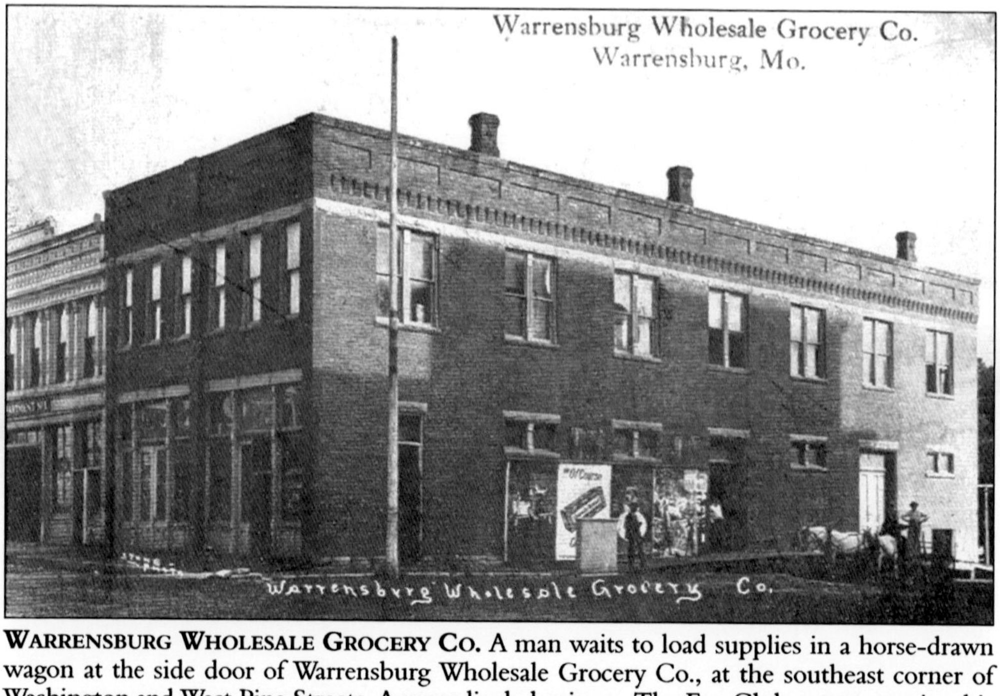

WARRENSBURG WHOLESALE GROCERY CO. A man waits to load supplies in a horse-drawn wagon at the side door of Warrensburg Wholesale Grocery Co., at the southeast corner of Washington and West Pine Streets. A more lively business, The Fan Club, now occupies this spot. The Warrensburg Fire Department No. 1 is just to the east of the grocery in this *c.* 1910 postcard. (Tom Christopher Collection.)

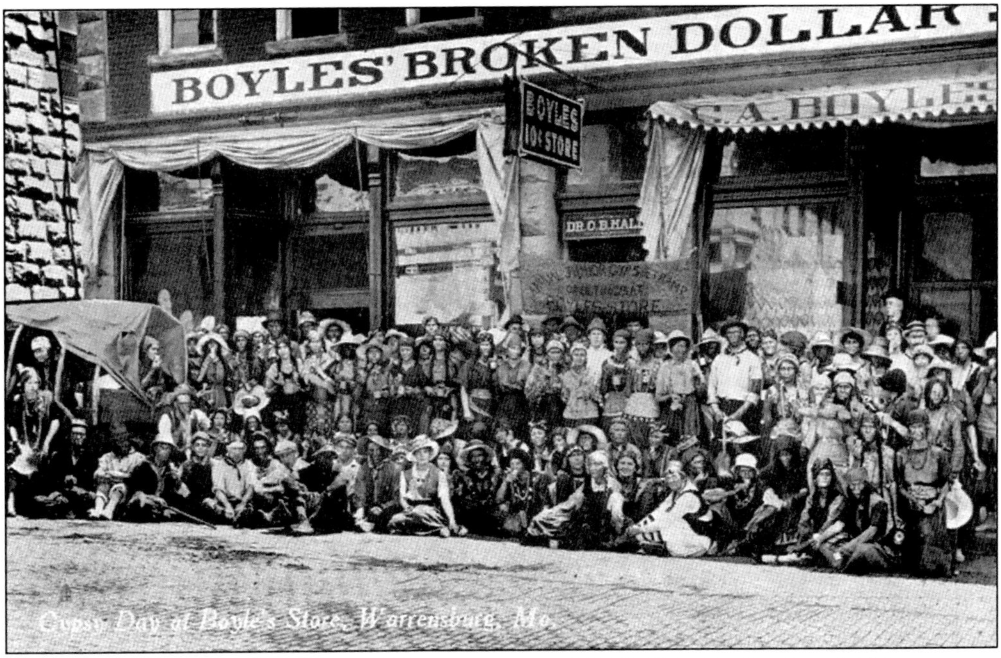

"GYPSY DAY AT BOYLE'S STORE, WARRENSBURG, MO." C.A. Boyles 5 and 10¢ store was a great seller of postcards. This building at 126 North Holden Street no longer stands. The native sandstone wall seen at the left foreground was the north wall of Citizen's Bank. The brick paved street in front of the store was once a common sight around Warrensburg. No brick streets remain downtown today. (Tom Christopher Collection.)

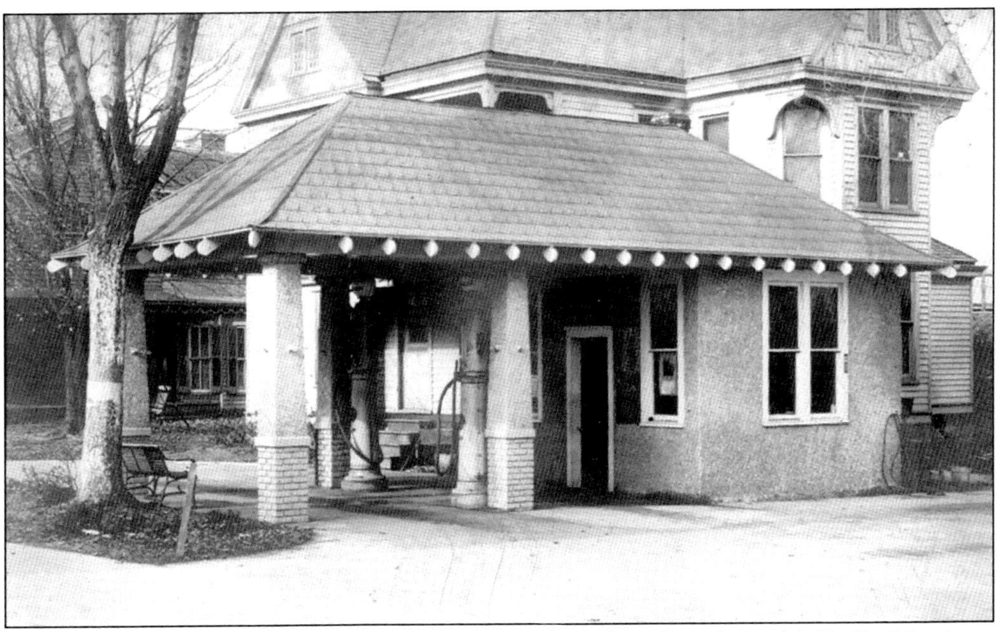

LESLIE HUTCHENS' STATION. Jaeger's Tire Store stands today where this Leslie Hutchens owned station stood *c.* 1920s. At the northwest corner of Holden and Gay Streets the large two-story house in the background is still present. (Tom Christopher Collection.)

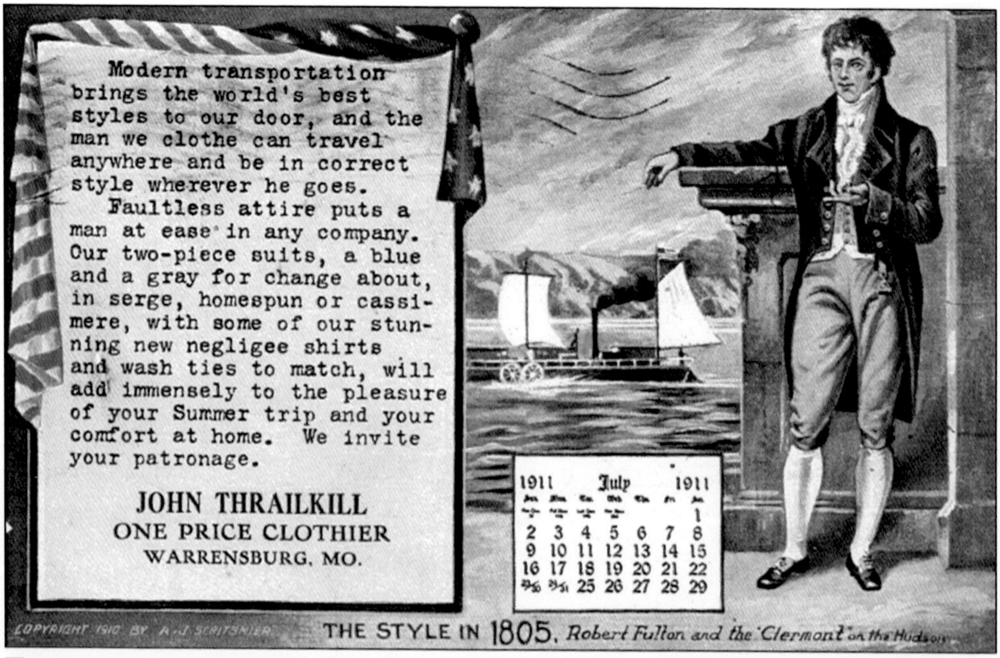

Thrailkill Clothier. John Thrailkill Clothier, 109 North Holden Street started business in 1901. He advertised his goods with the help of postcards. Each card showed a monthly calendar for a particular year and a clothing style from the past. This card illustrates the style of 1805.

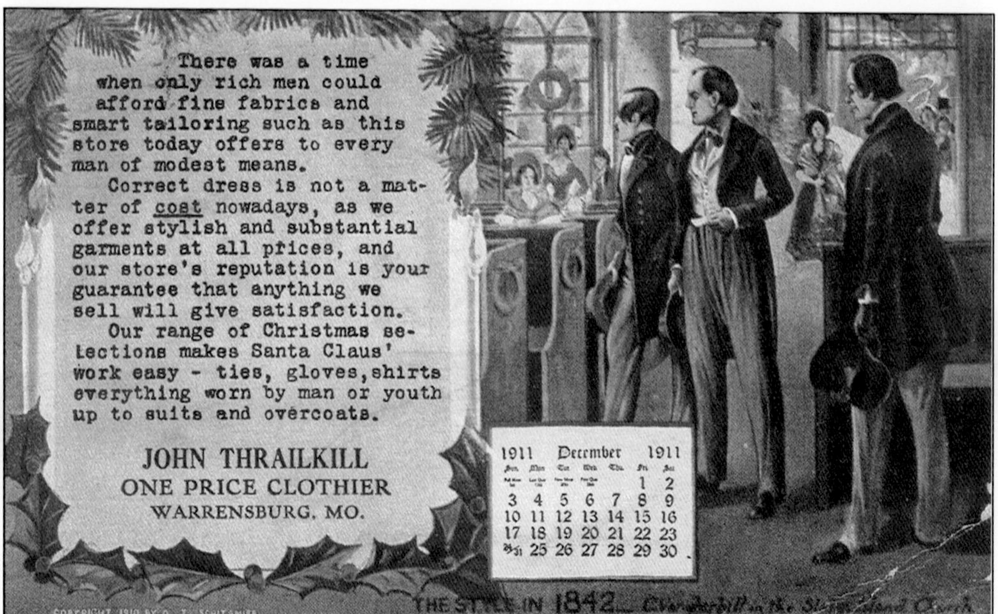

Thrailkill Clothier. In 1903, he advertised men's suits and overcoats for $10. "We show the best line of young men's, boy's and children's clothing in Johnson County. Up-to-date stock in shirts, underwear, half-hose, suspenders, handkerchiefs, neckwear, collars, cuffs and gloves." The style shown on this card is of 1842. The Depression was the undoing of the store. It closed on October 20, 1932.

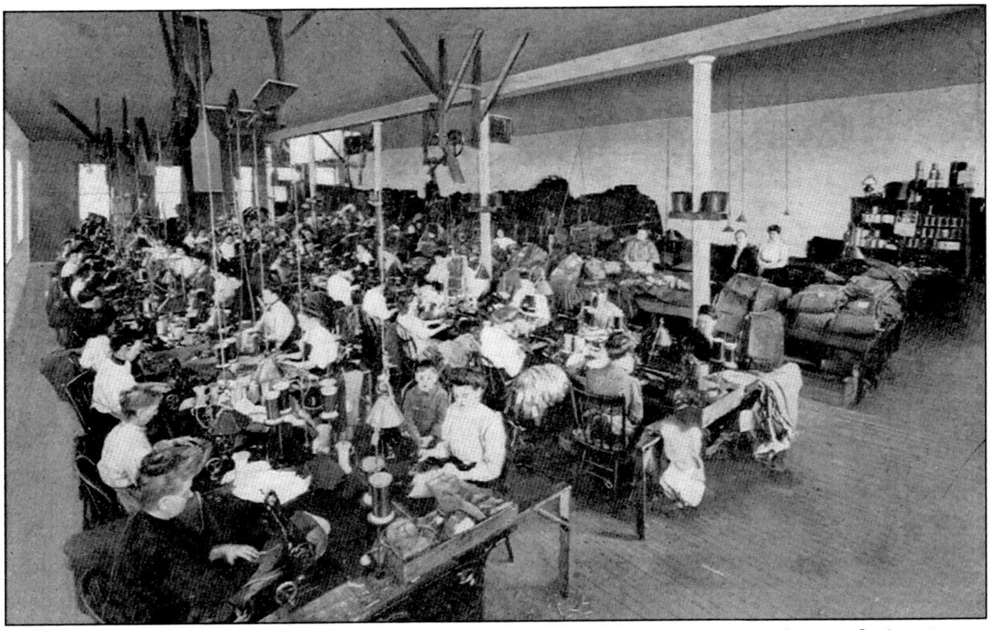

Lamy Overall Factory. In late August, 1906, J.A. Lamy, president of the Lamy Manufacturing Co. of Sedalia, contracted with the Warrensburg Board of Trade to open a factory here, having 30 days to raise the funds. Workers perform their tasks at the new factory, which commenced operations on October 8, 1906 at 321-323 North Holden Street.

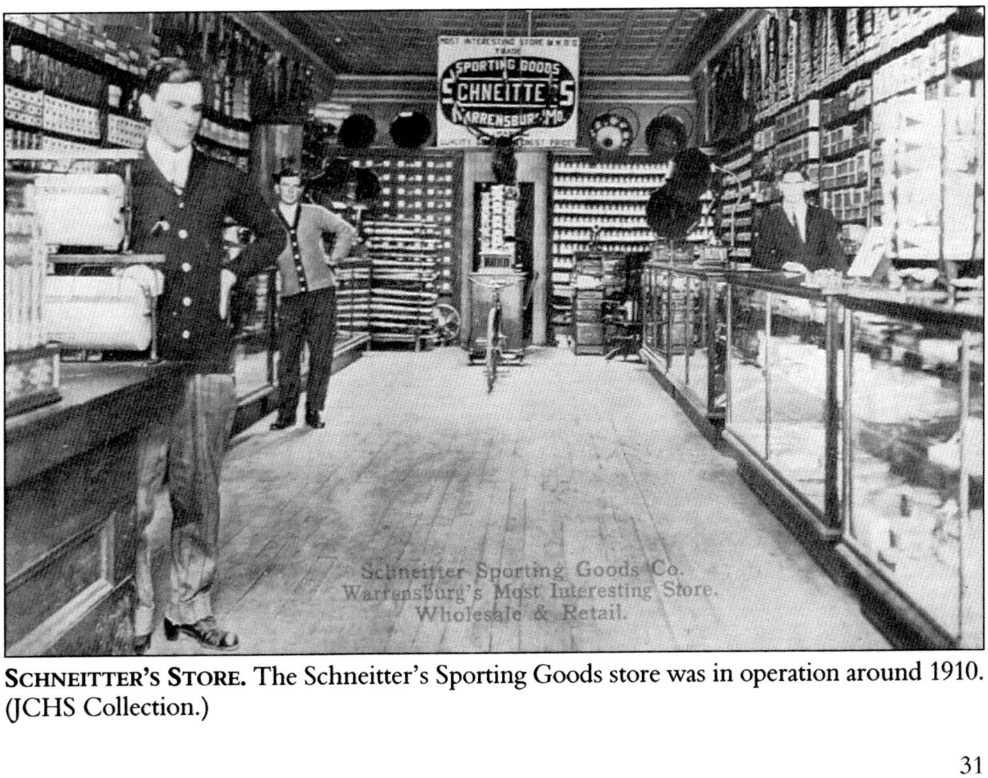

Schneitter's Store. The Schneitter's Sporting Goods store was in operation around 1910. (JCHS Collection.)

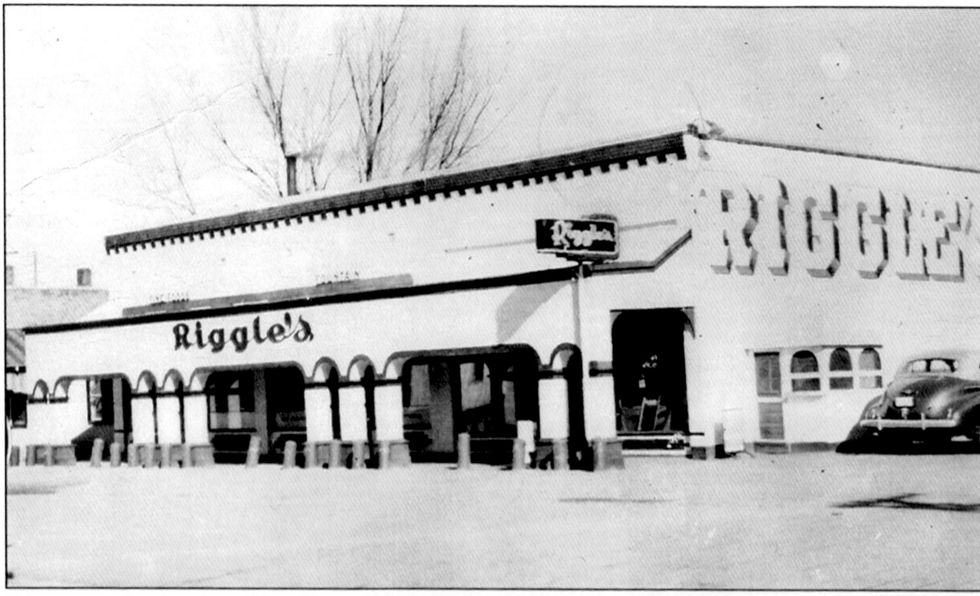

RIGGLES. A popular place for townspeople and college traffic, Riggles was located on the east side of Maguire Street, just north of the intersection with Clark Street. This area was known as "Buente Town." Steel reinforced concrete posts protect the storefront from auto traffic. (*c*. 1940s.)

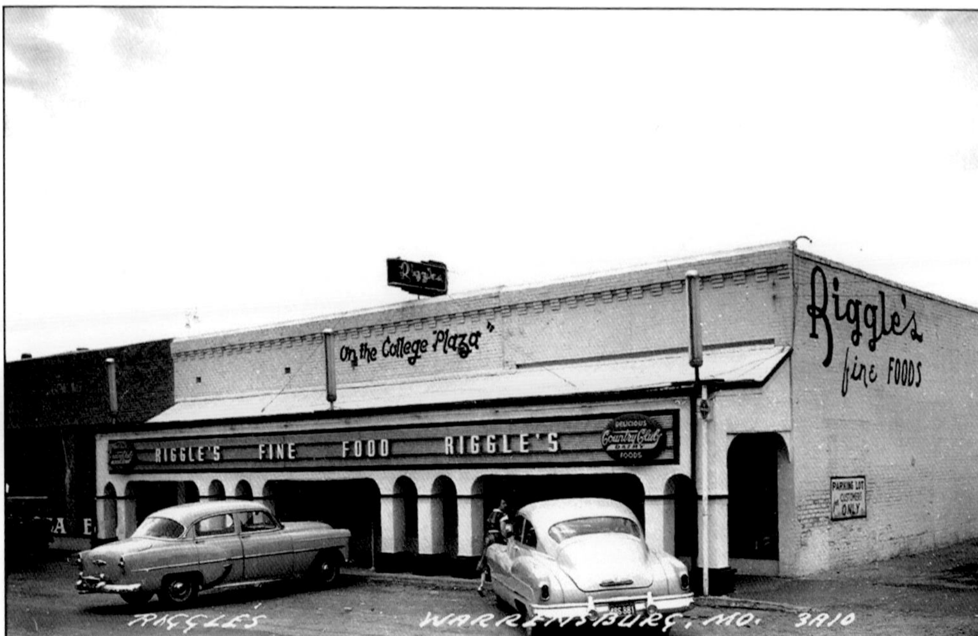

RIGGLES. The protective concrete posts are gone and some of the signs have changed in this mid- 1950s view. The area has become known as "The College Plaza." Besides the building's basic look and shape, the Riggles neon sign is still the same, though moved to the roof. The drive-up service has been discontinued.

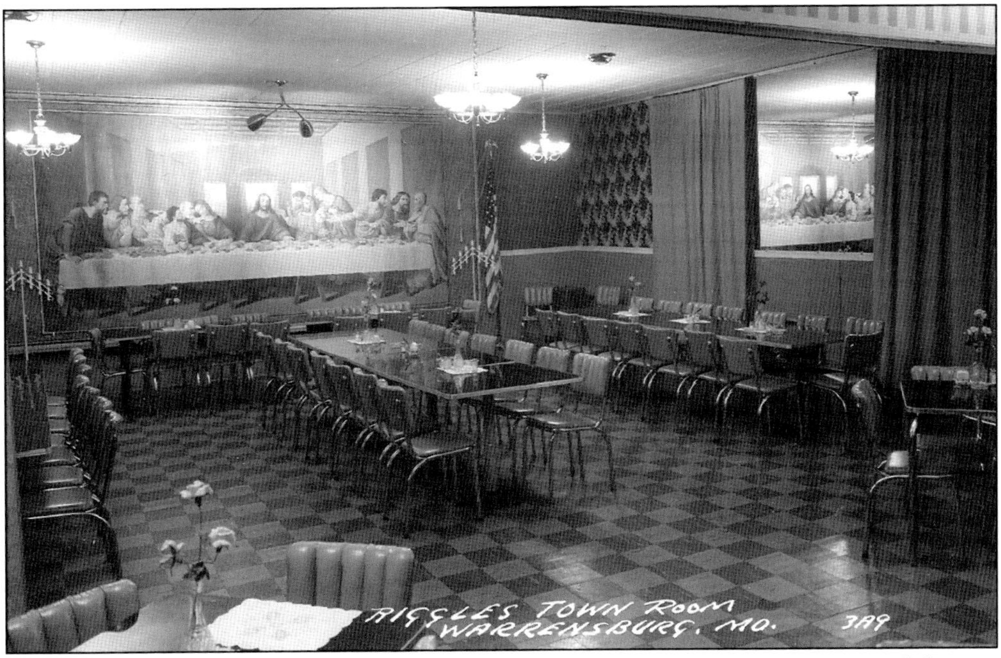

RIGGLES INTERIOR. Flowers adorn the tables in the sparkling dining area. Well-known resident of the time, Walter Hout, entrepreneur and scenic painter, created the "Last Supper" painting on the wall. (JCHS Collection.)

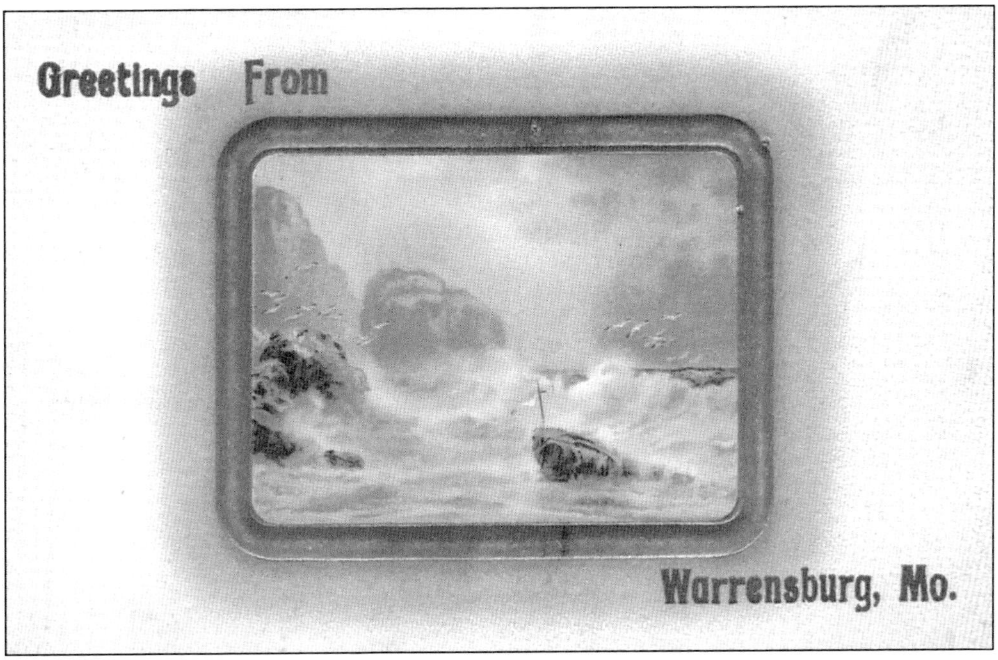

GREETINGS FROM. Generic greeting postcards were very common and could sport any town's name—but an ocean near Warrensburg? Oh well, Riggles had to get their seafood somewhere!

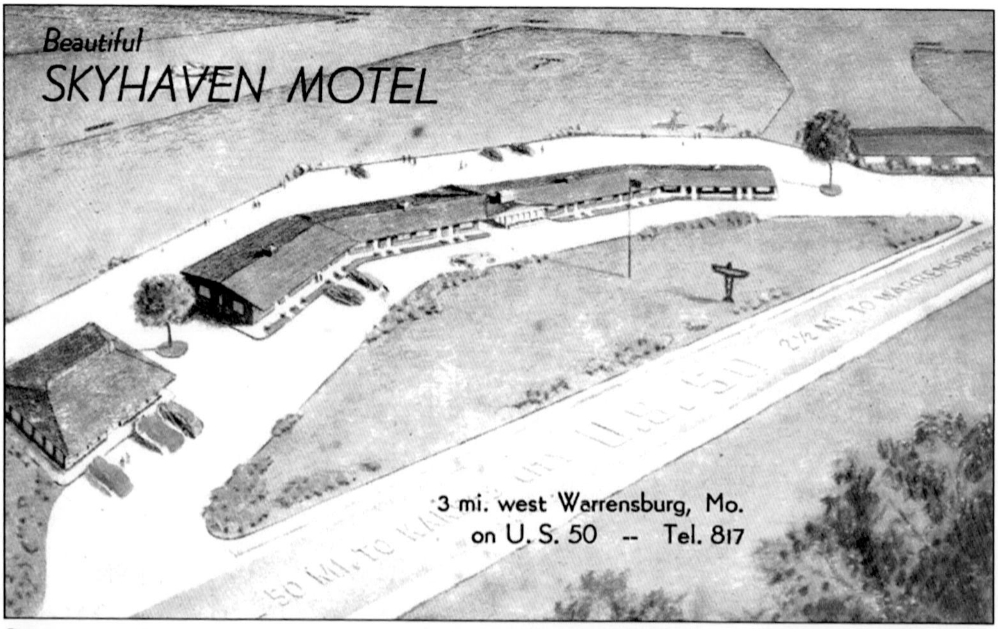

SKYHAVEN MOTEL. An aerial view drawing, in color, locates Skyhaven, built *c.* 1958, on U.S. 50, 3 miles west of town. The airplane-shaped sign near the highway displayed "Skyhaven Motel 34 Units."

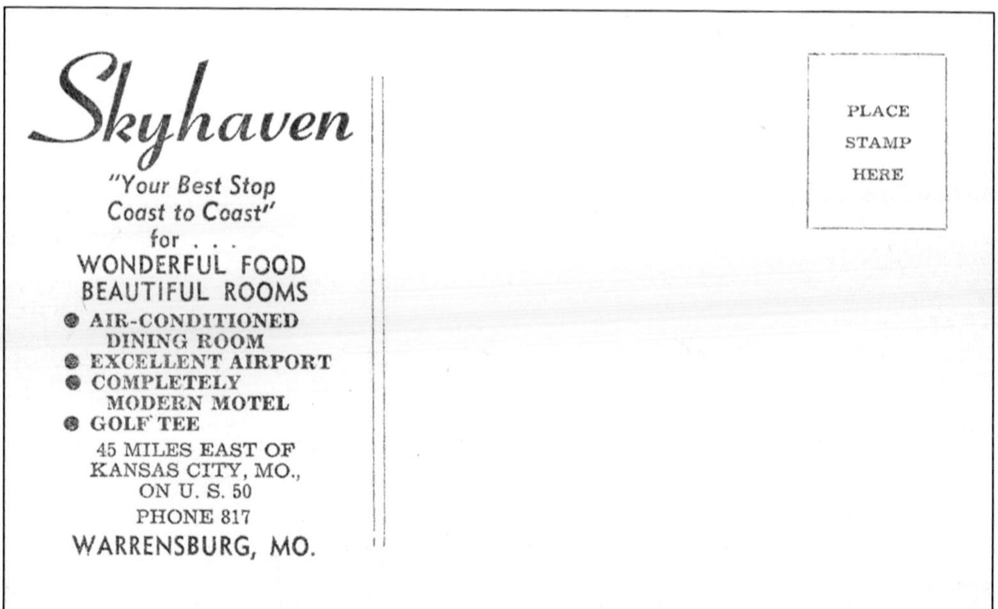

SKYHAVEN MOTEL. "Phone 817" tells us this card, of similar vintage, precedes the era of area codes and helps to date the card to around 1960. One wonders where the "golf tee" was located.

Three

SERVING THE COMMUNITY

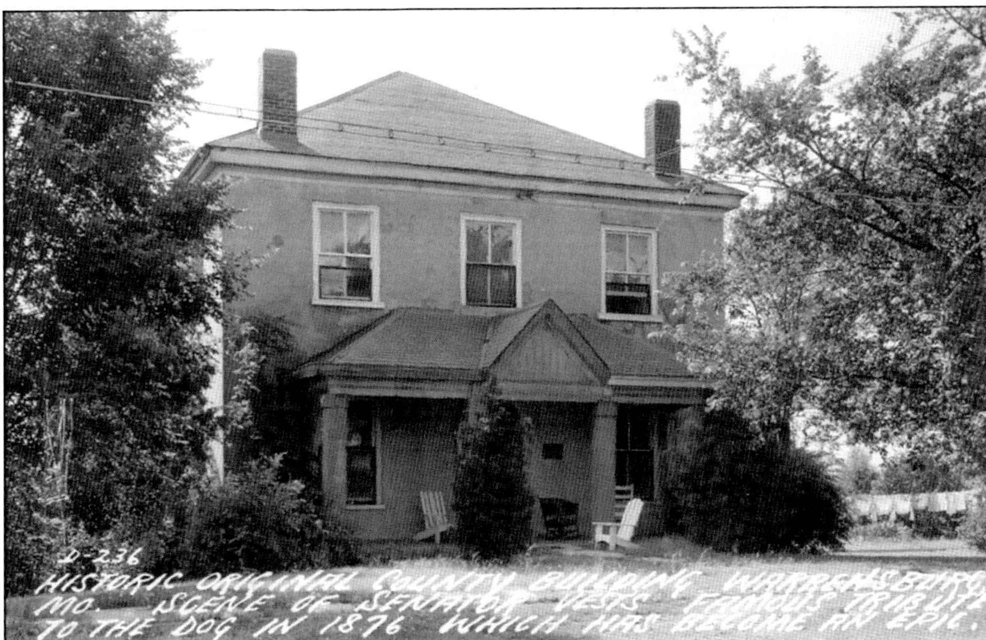

OLD COURTHOUSE. An inviting porch welcomes friends to the *c.* 1950 home of the Coles, the owners of the hub of the original town, the Old Courthouse of Johnson County, Missouri. At the junction of Main and Gay Streets, this square was once surrounded by livery stables, hotels, provisions stores, and much more. One correction must be made, however. Vest's "Tribute to the Dog" was delivered in 1870. (JCHS Collection.)

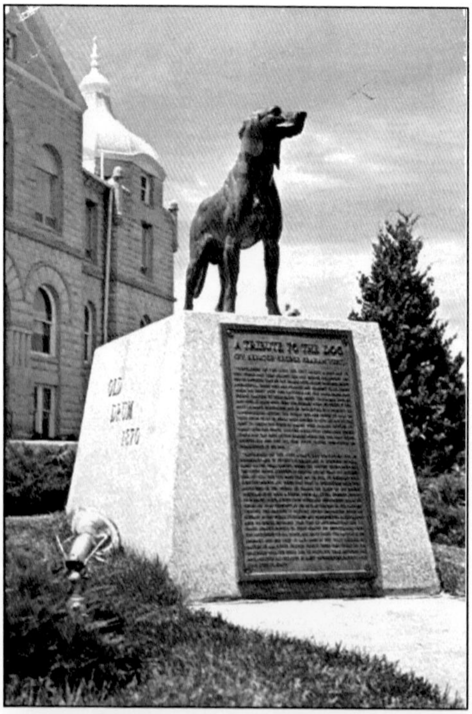

Courthouse with Old Drum. To that speech, memorialized now on the lawn of the 1898 courthouse, we can attribute the survival of the old town square. Drum, the beloved hunting dog of Charles Burden, was killed one night near the western edge of Johnson County. The blame lay squarely on the man who wanted the dog dead due to loss of livestock, Leonidas Hornsby. Both men hired lawyers and there were several trials. The original courthouse (*below*) is now the location of the Johnson County Historical Society. (JCHS Collection.)

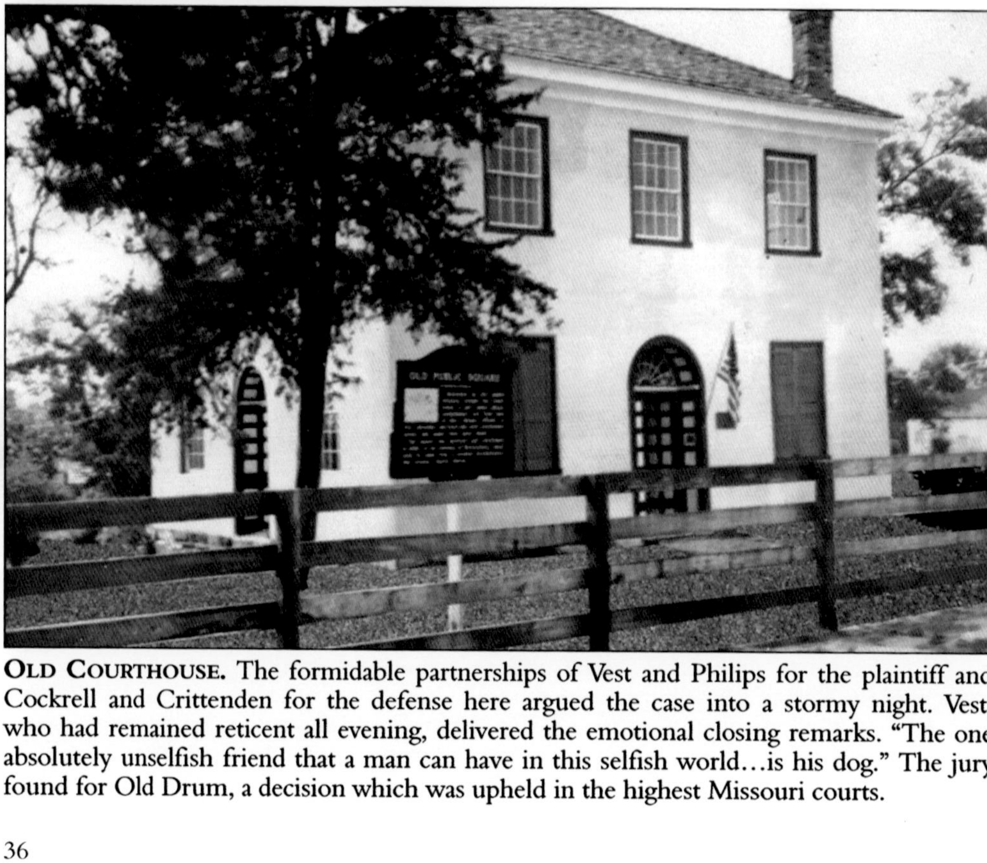

Old Courthouse. The formidable partnerships of Vest and Philips for the plaintiff and Cockrell and Crittenden for the defense here argued the case into a stormy night. Vest, who had remained reticent all evening, delivered the emotional closing remarks. "The one absolutely unselfish friend that a man can have in this selfish world…is his dog." The jury found for Old Drum, a decision which was upheld in the highest Missouri courts.

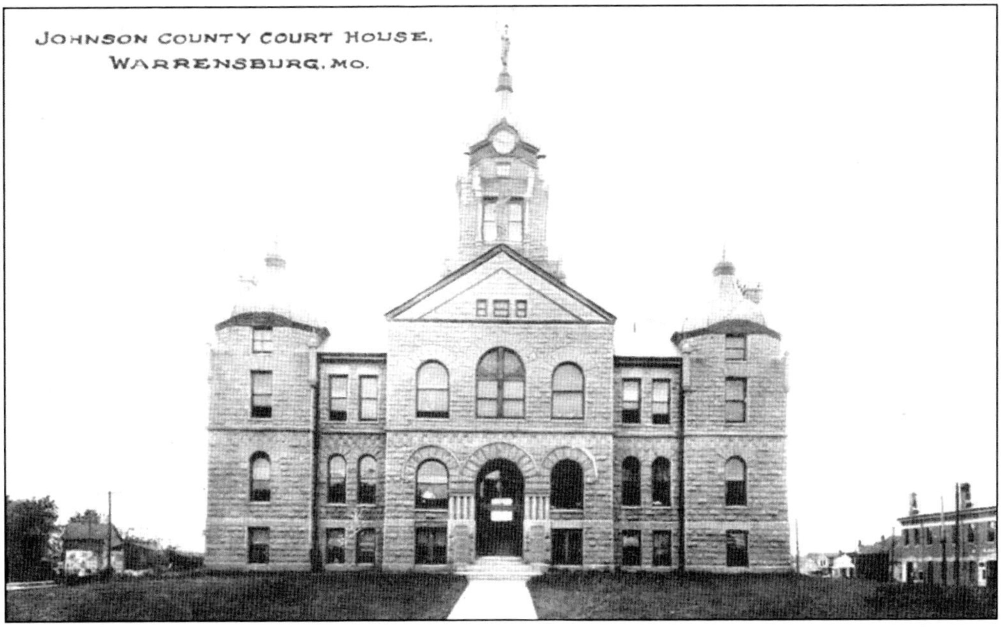

COURTHOUSE. This unusual straight-on view of the county court graces an Albertype Postcard. To the right one is treated to a view of the old city hall, which stood on West Market. To the left one notices that trees grew close to the new town square. (JCHS Collection.)

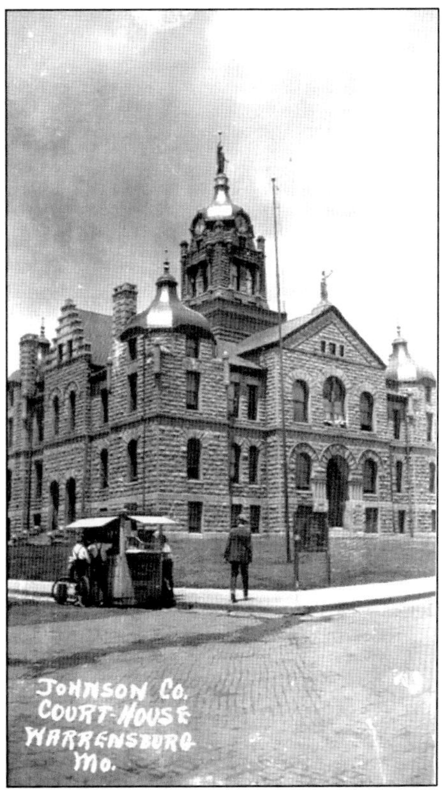

COURTHOUSE. Perhaps you did not know that there was once a hot dog stand on the corner of North Holden and Hout Streets. This is also the best picture of the metal roofing that was part of the original design. It gleams majestically over the city in a display not provided by the current shingling method. (JCHS Collection.)

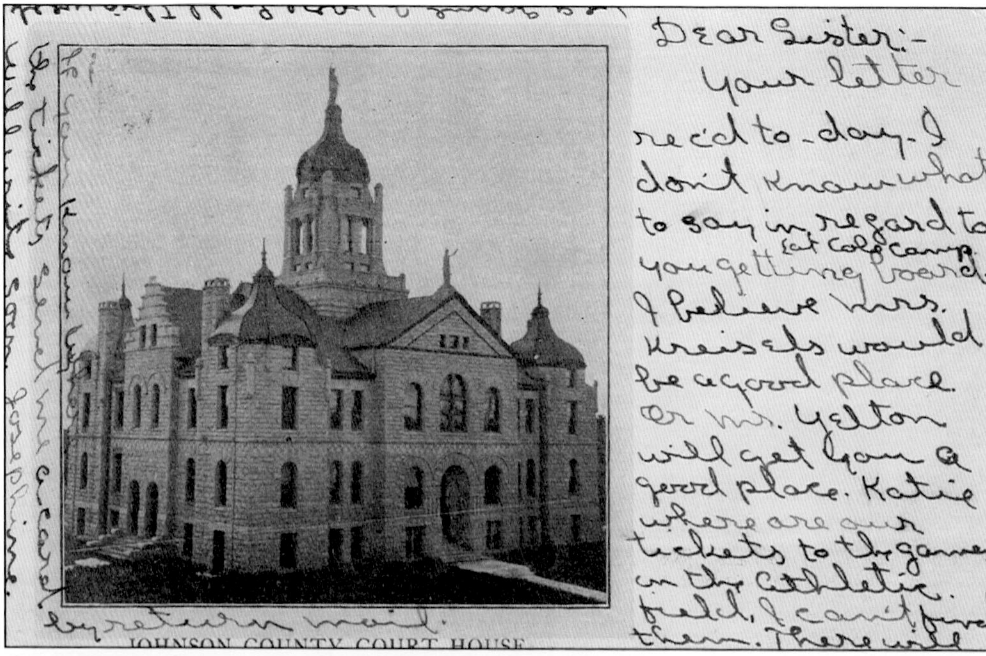

COURTHOUSE. Sent to Miss Fern Veercamp of Nevada, Missouri, the message written on a similar card was a little more cryptic, "This is *our* Court House. See that yours is as pretty when it is finished."

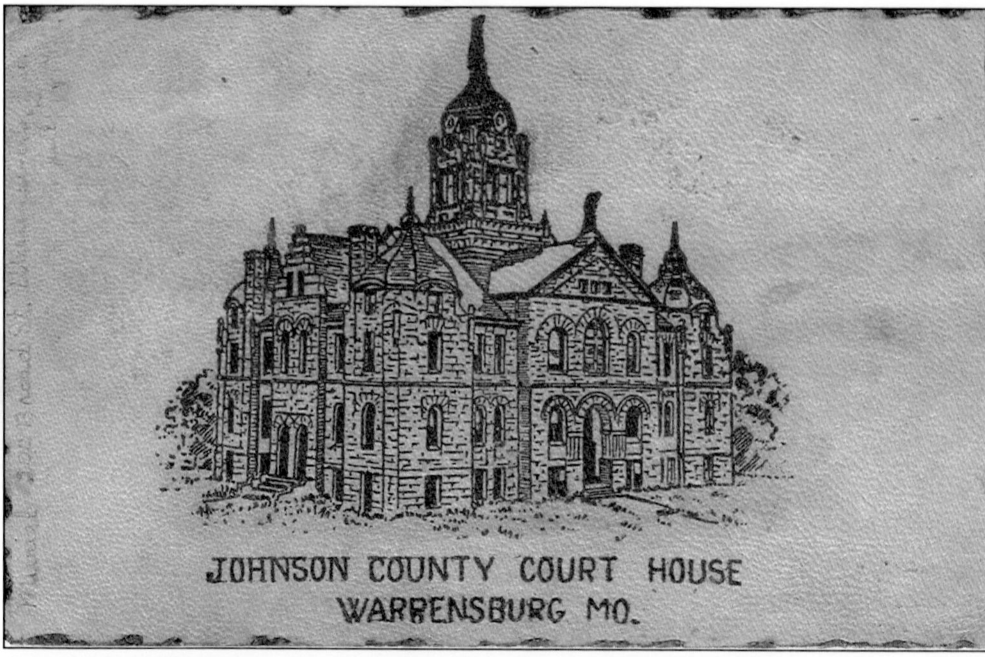

COURTHOUSE. Sporting a drawing rather than a photograph, this card has another interesting aspect. The view is from a favorite vantage point and is black ink printed on soft tan leather with distressed edges. The card is postmarked 1907.

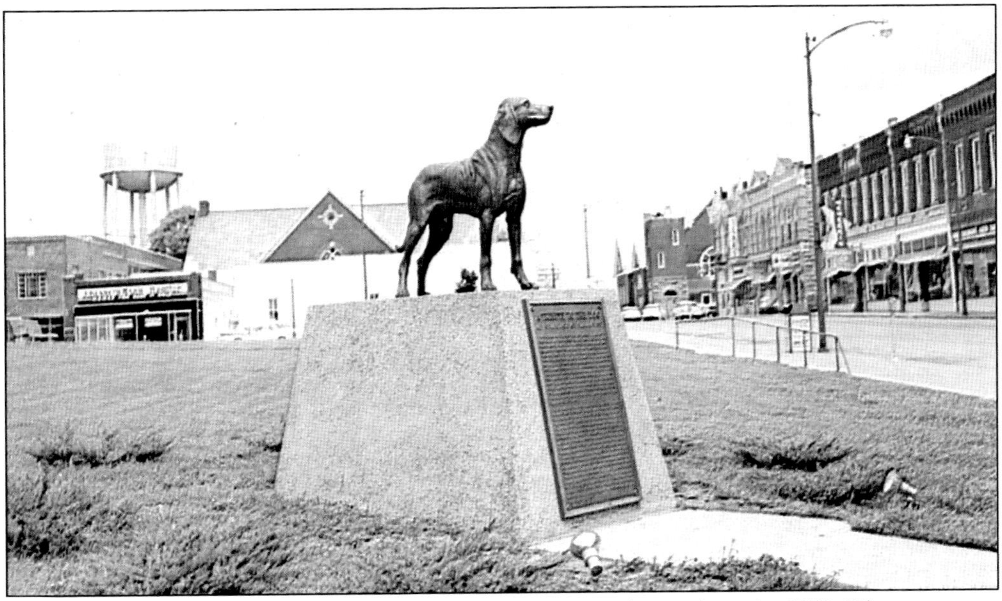

OLD DRUM. The statue of Drum was erected on the courthouse lawn in 1958. The event was recognized nationally and notable people contributed to the fund. The chamber of commerce publicized the story widely and people still make pilgrimages to the statue to remember the famous hound. Around 1999, columnist William Safire called Vest's tribute the, "best speech [of its type] of the millennium." The original postcard is in color.

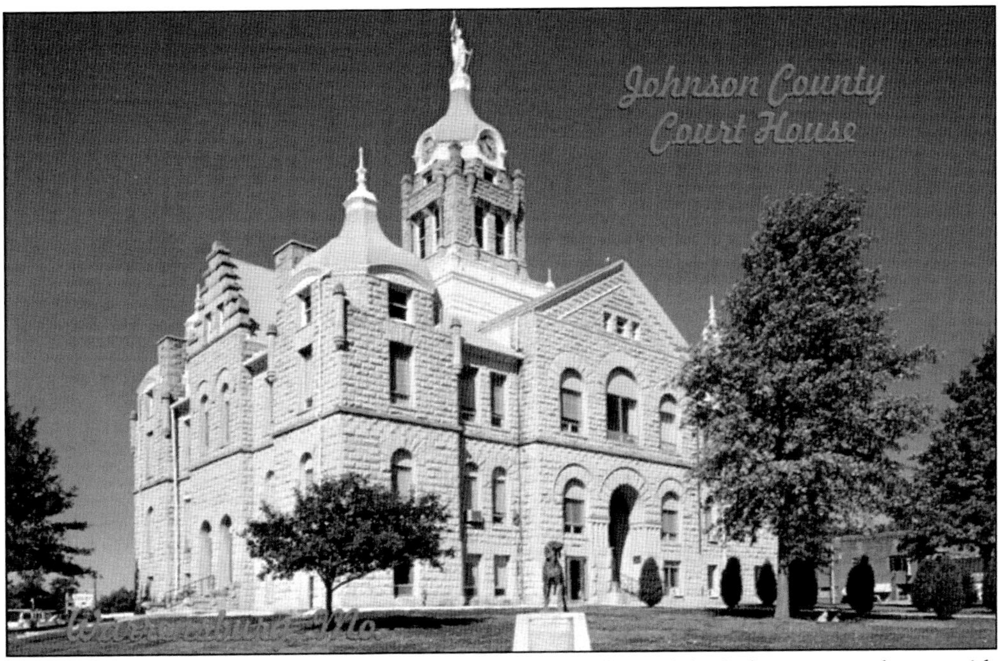

COURTHOUSE. This modern postcard, printed in color, framed the light gray courthouse with brilliant blue sky and green, green grass in a photograph by Rick Young. Its exact vintage is uncertain, but must be 1980s or so. A new courtroom addition built in 2000 on the opposite side of Market Street now houses the judicial chambers.

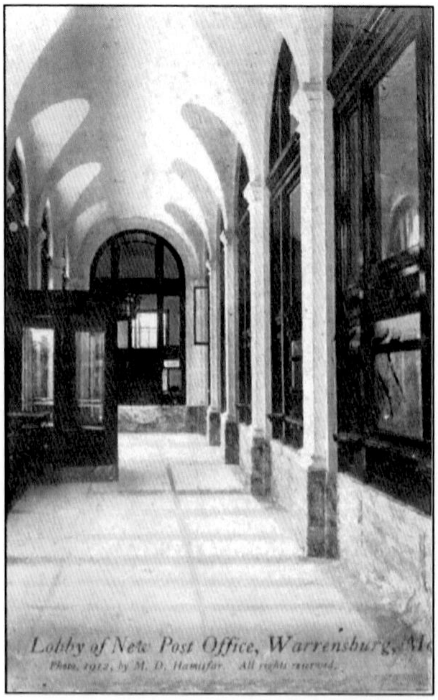

Post Office. This 1912 photo, by M.D. Hamisfar, shows off the lobby of the new post office. A massive revolving door admitted patrons.

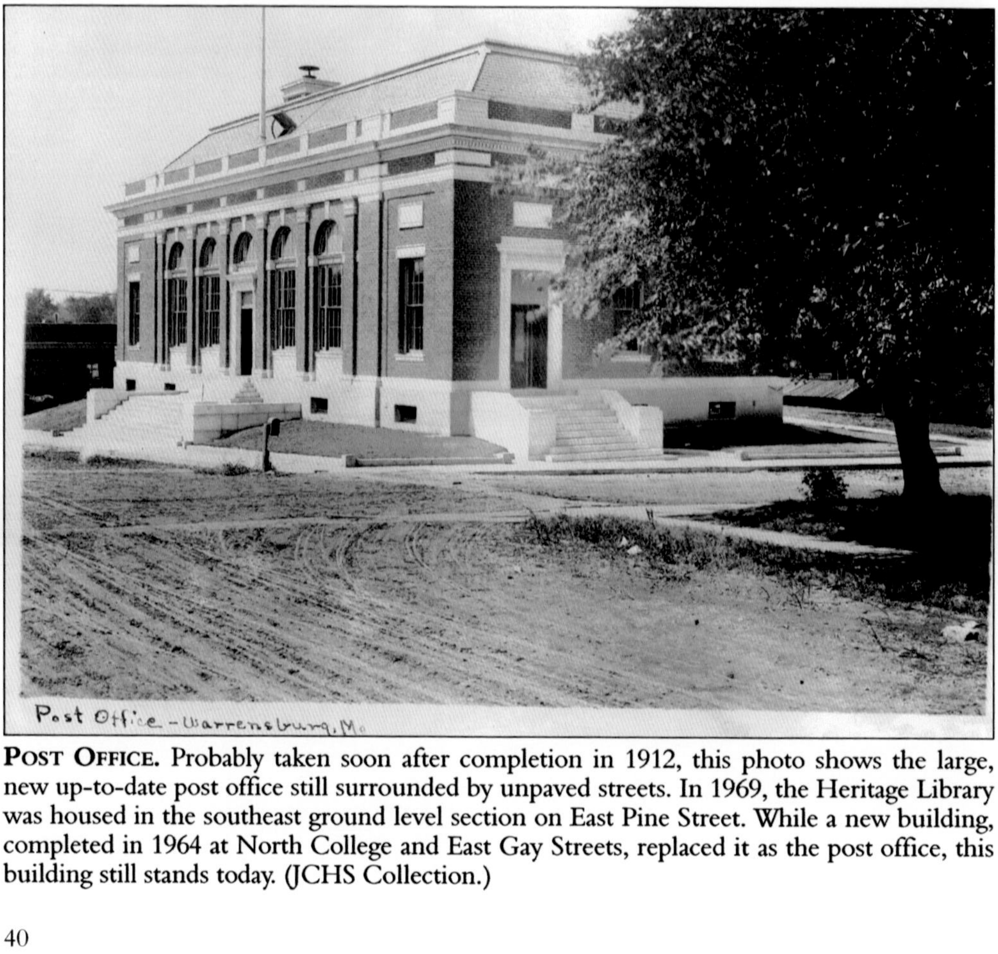

Post Office. Probably taken soon after completion in 1912, this photo shows the large, new up-to-date post office still surrounded by unpaved streets. In 1969, the Heritage Library was housed in the southeast ground level section on East Pine Street. While a new building, completed in 1964 at North College and East Gay Streets, replaced it as the post office, this building still stands today. (JCHS Collection.)

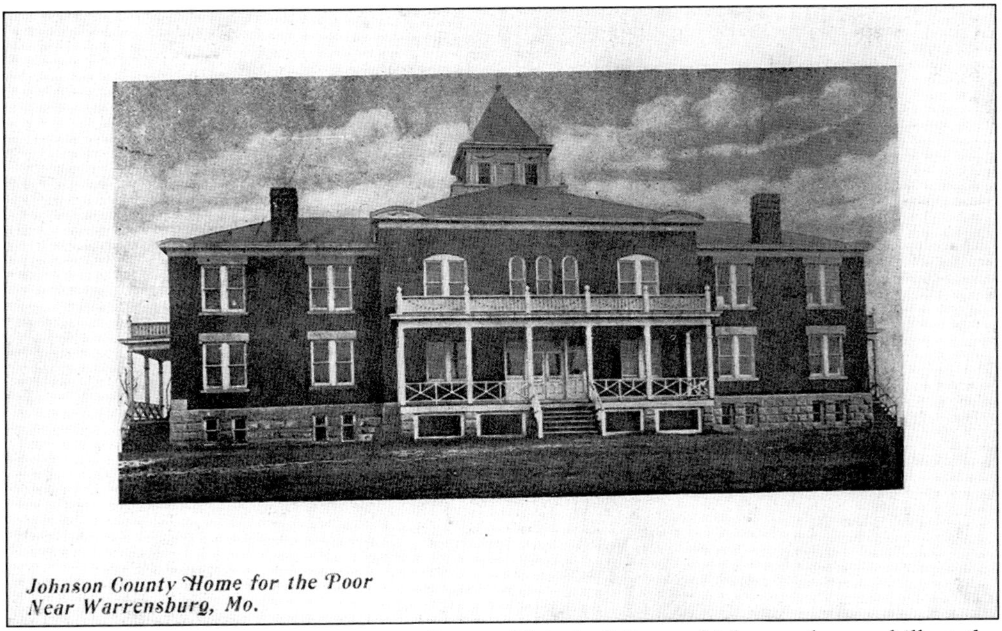

JOHNSON COUNTY HOME FOR THE POOR. This building, which stood on a hill at the northeast edge of town, had various titles, among them, County Home, Home for the Poor, and Poor Folks Home. Its intended use was to care for low-income persons. (*c.* 1910.)

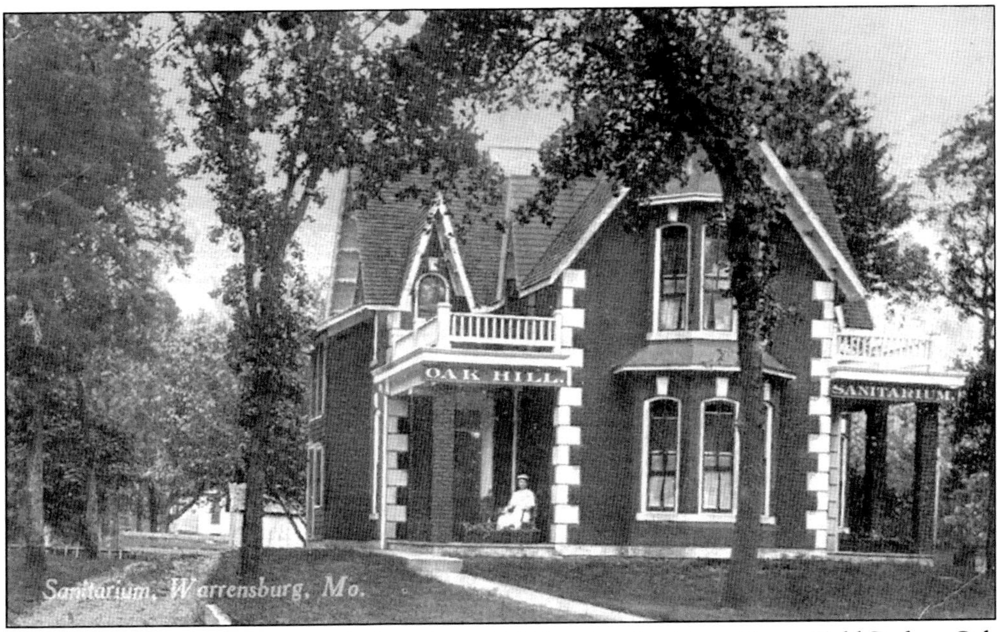

OAK HILL SANITARIUM. Founded in about 1911 by the physician, Harry Field Parker, Oak Hill served the community well for a number of years. One of the youngest graduates of Warrensburg High School, Dr. Parker at the age of 16, was both a physician and a surgeon. All doctors of Johnson County could use the sanitarium. Located at 519 South Holden Street, an area now occupied by the Student Union Building of Central Missouri State University.

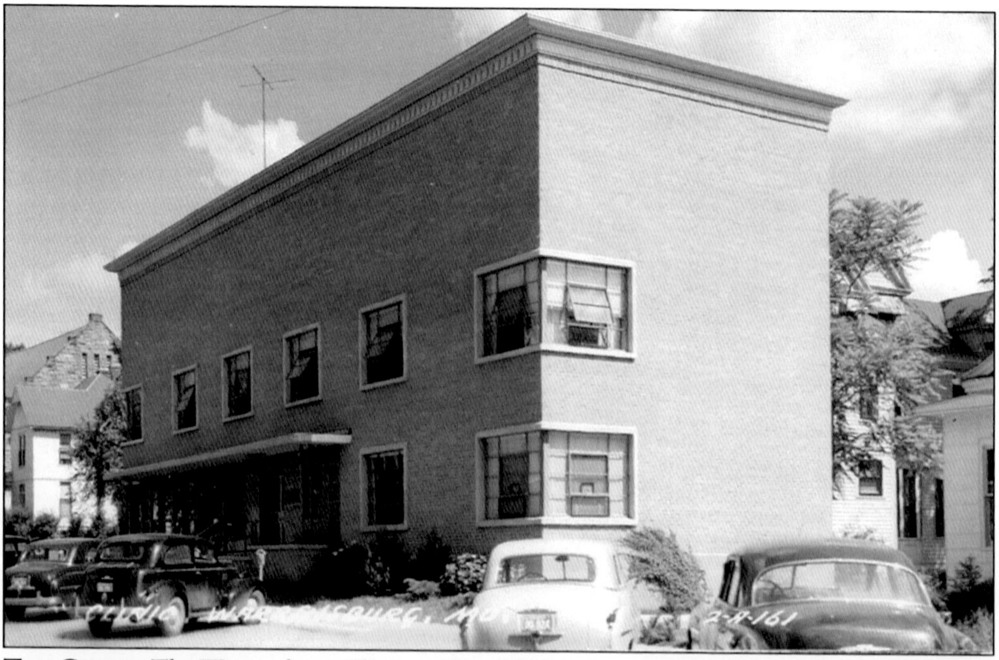

THE CLINIC. The Warrensburg Clinic on East Market Street was built *c.* 1950. The first clinic was opened in the Shanklin Gilkeson home, around 1920, to augment the services of the Oak Hill Sanitarium. Early board members were Mrs. Avis Tucker, John L. Innes, and Phillip C. Houx. The First Presbyterian Church can be seen at left in this photo.

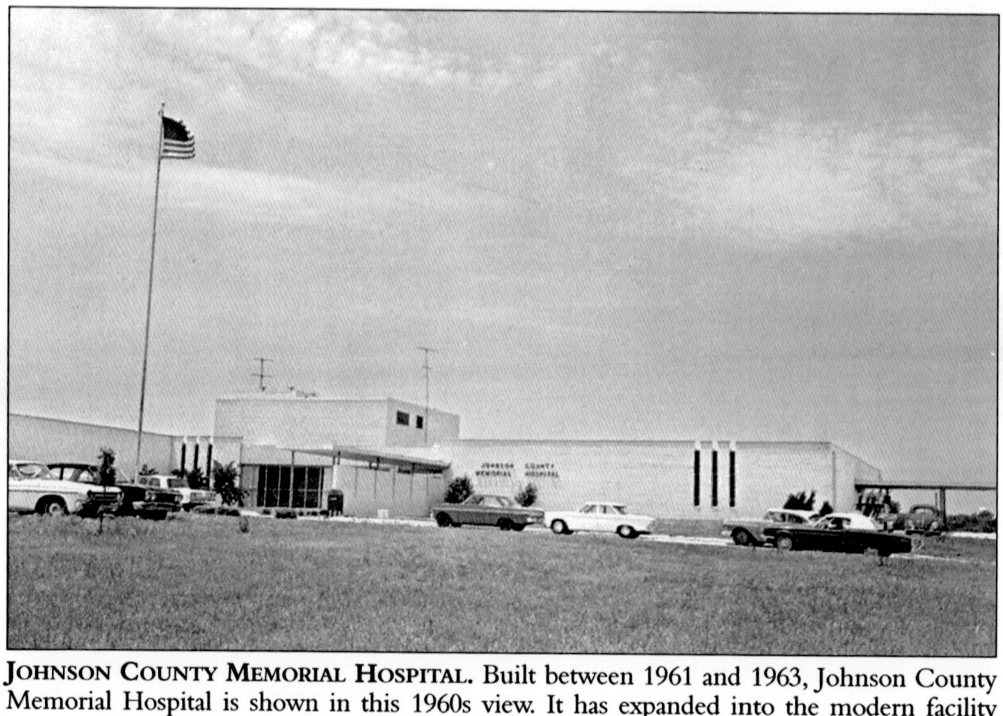

JOHNSON COUNTY MEMORIAL HOSPITAL. Built between 1961 and 1963, Johnson County Memorial Hospital is shown in this 1960s view. It has expanded into the modern facility known today as Western Missouri Medical Center.

Four

Building Minds and Tending Souls

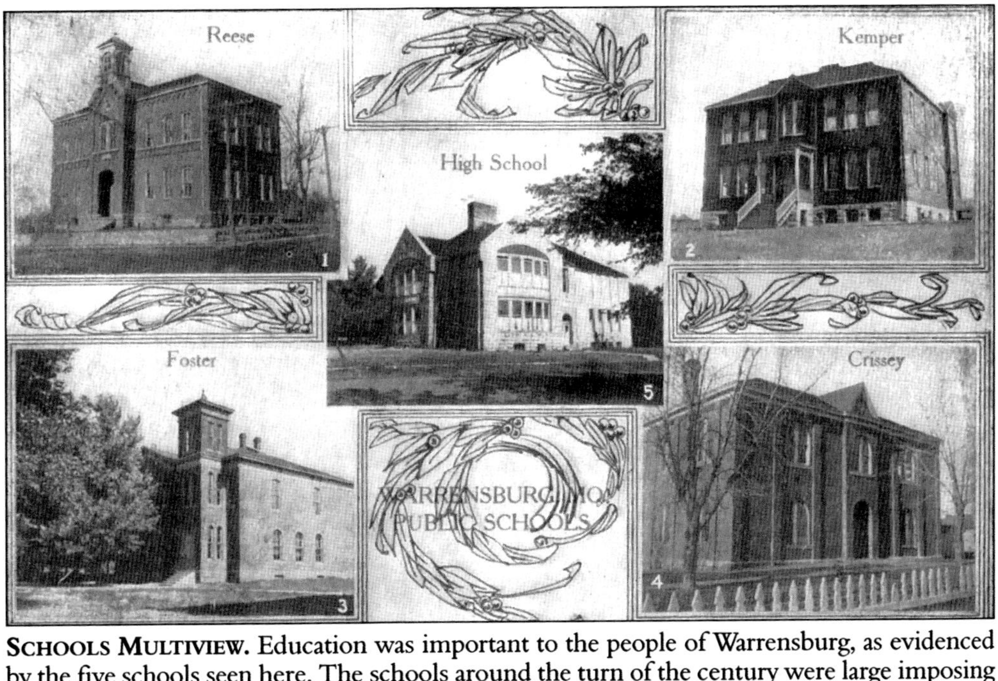

Schools Multiview. Education was important to the people of Warrensburg, as evidenced by the five schools seen here. The schools around the turn of the century were large imposing buildings, the elementary schools named for notable residents. In a simpler time, the playground was just the yard. Notably absent is the Howard School, at Culton and Mulberry Streets, where African-American children were taught separately until the mid-1960s.

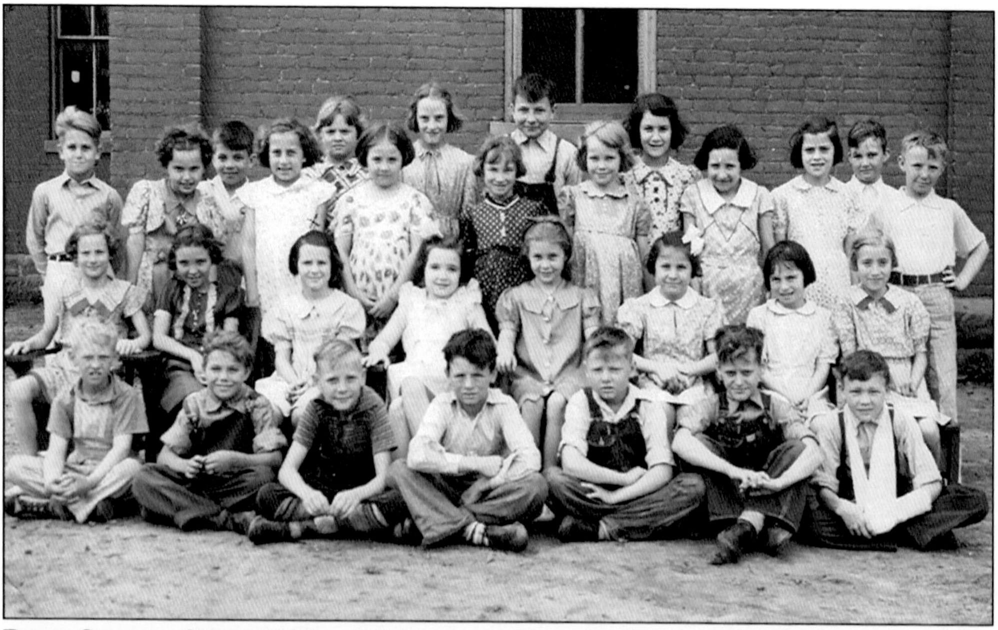

Reese School Group. This *c.* 1937 postcard shows the third and fourth grade classes. The original redbrick building was built in 1868 at a cost of $4,500 at the corner of Warren and Market Streets. It was named for Dr. A.W. Reese, then president of the board of education. Marcine Pennington, third from the left in row two, is the only student identified in this photo. The teacher (not pictured) was Miss Theiss. (Marcine Pennington Collection.)

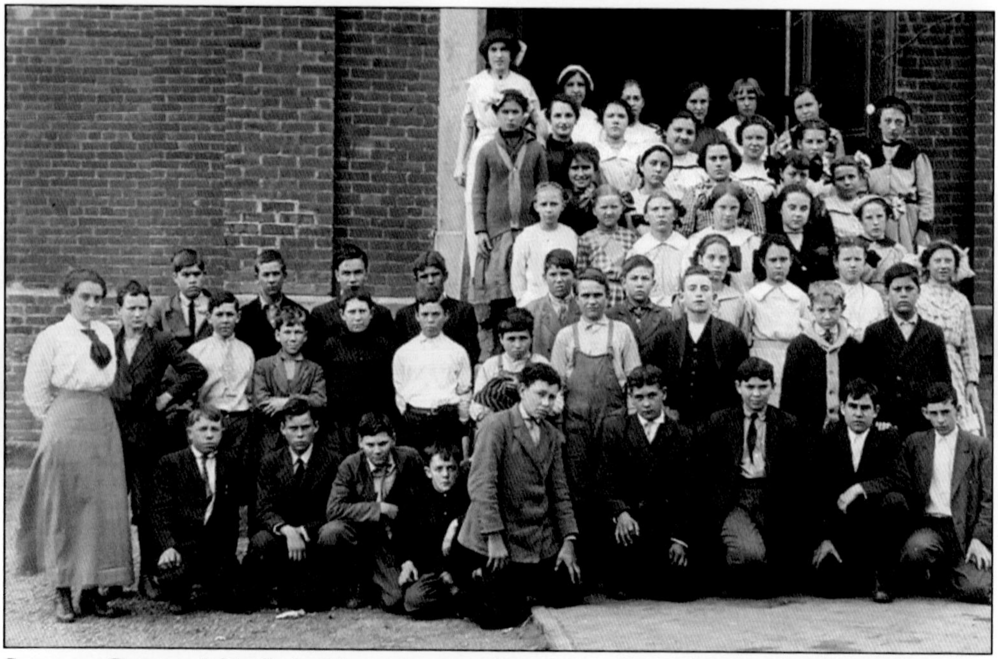

School Group. A kindly looking young teacher at one of the old elementary schools seems to have the students in hand, except perhaps for the young man in motion in the front row. (JCHS Collection.)

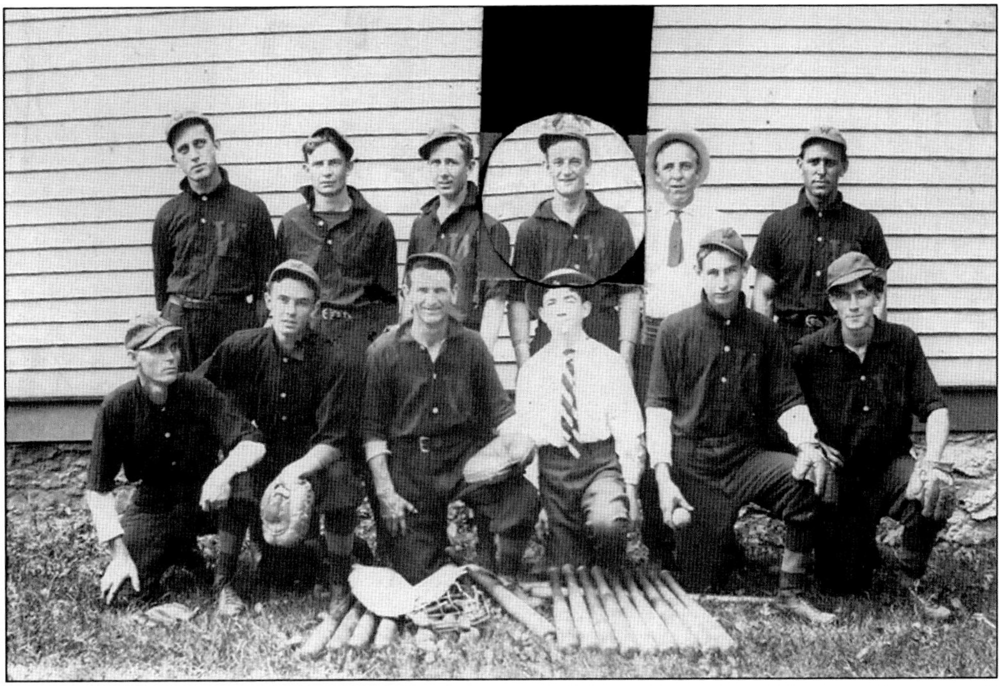

WARRENSBURG BASEBALL TEAM. This is an early Warrensburg baseball team. As you will notice, one of the young men has been removed from the image, to serve as a loving reminder in a ladies locket, and later, fortunately, carefully replaced. (Marcine Pennington Collection.)

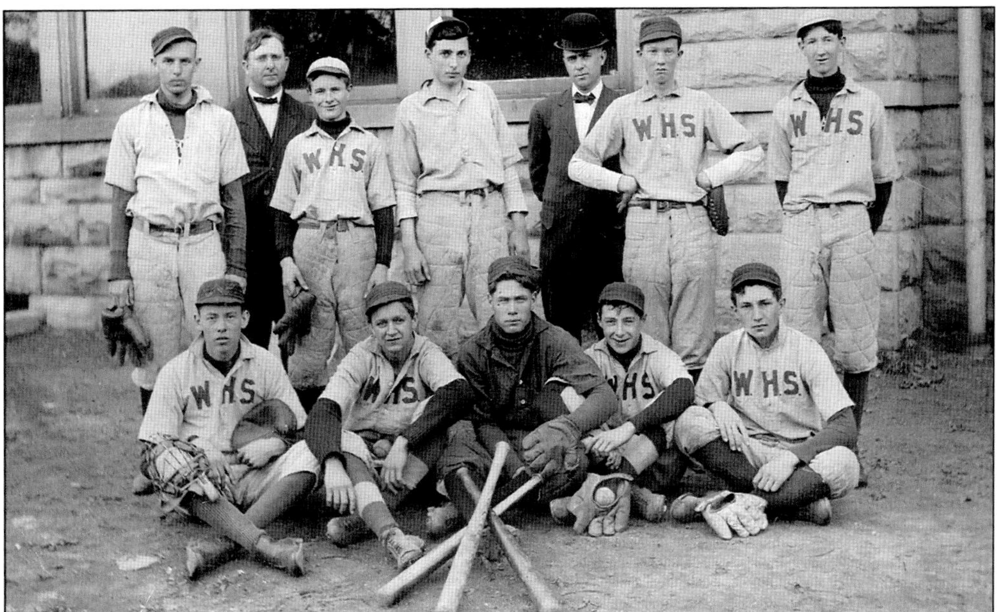

WARRENSBURG HIGH SCHOOL BASEBALL TEAM. A team of forthright and determined young men, the representatives of Warrensburg High School, gathers in front of the old building. It appears that landscaping was not a big expense for the school system at that time. (JCHS Collection.)

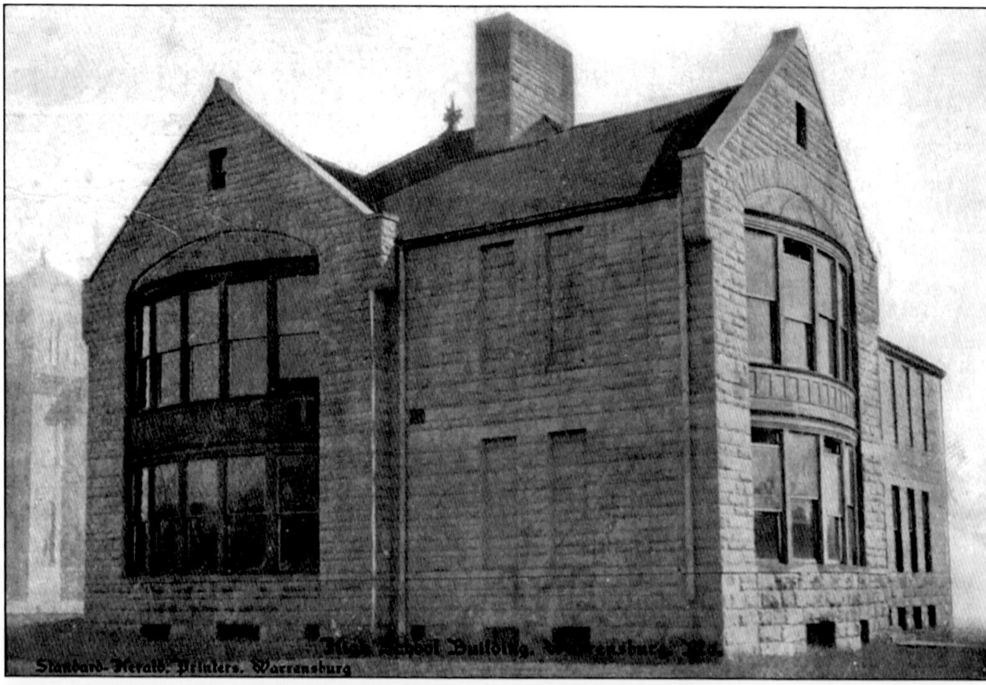

HIGH SCHOOL. The original high school was completed in 1896 and was located near the northeast corner of Maguire and Grover Streets. In this early 1900s view one can also see the Foster School in the background.

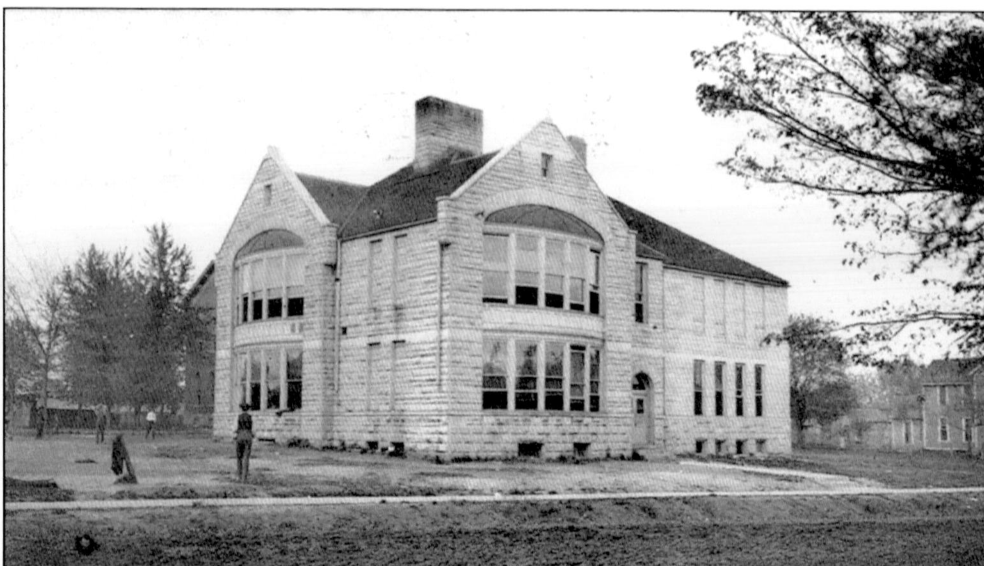

HIGH SCHOOL. Even in 1915 the original building was too small. In a town so rife with sandstone, it must have been more economical to leave glass out of some of the windows.

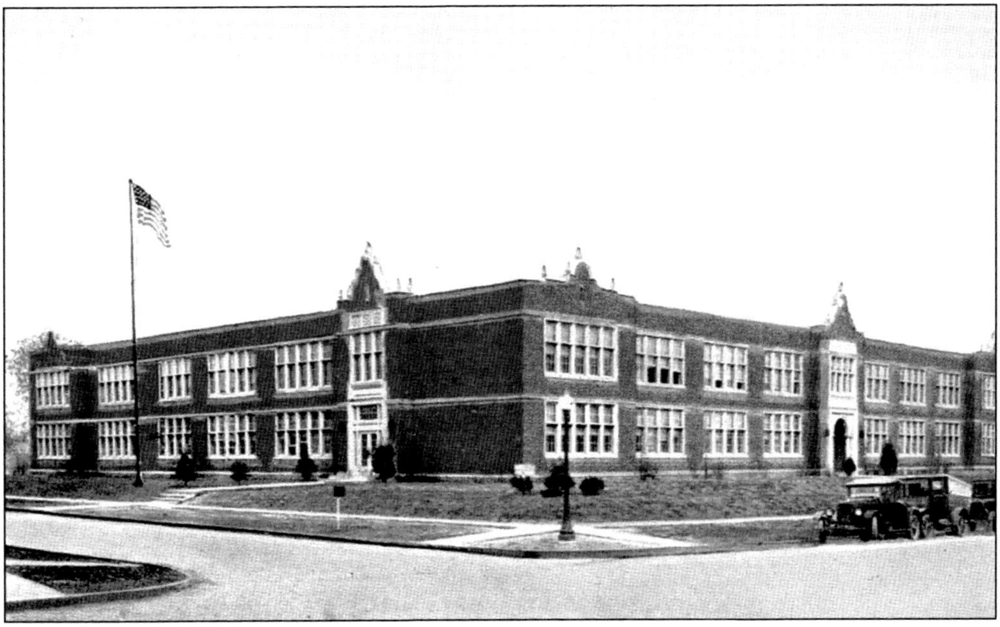

JUNIOR-SENIOR HIGH SCHOOL. A 1920s color postcard of Warrensburg Junior-Senior High School, which was built from 1923 to 1924 to replace the earlier high school and cost $200,000. Using brick was a very costly venture in those times.

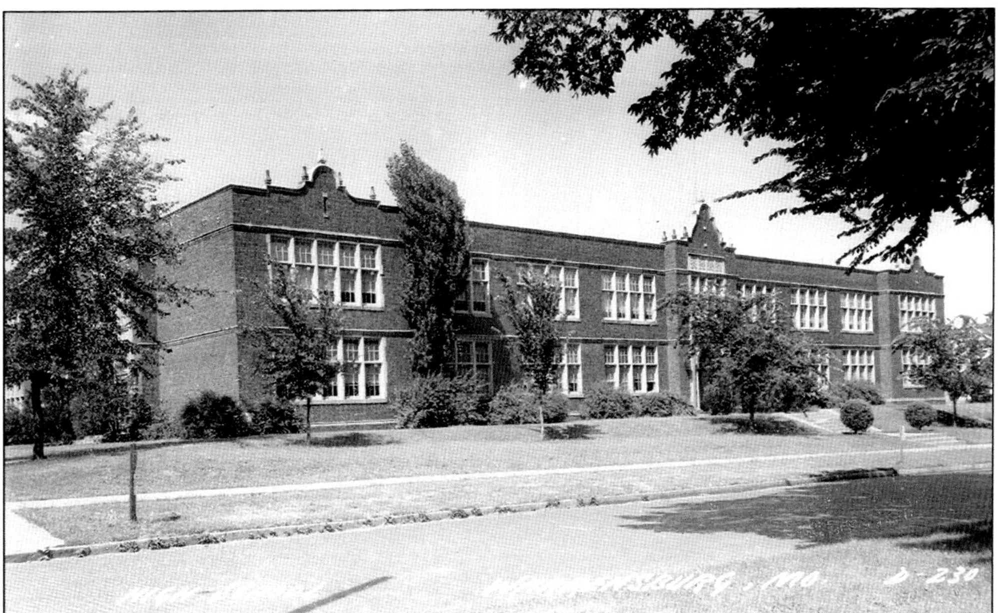

JUNIOR-SENIOR HIGH SCHOOL. The new high school, built at the corner of Grover and Highway 13, survived in that capacity until the early 1960s, becoming the Junior High at that time. In 1988, the name was changed to Martin Warren Elementary to honor the town's first resident. The enduring building still houses first, second, and third grade classes in the 21st century.

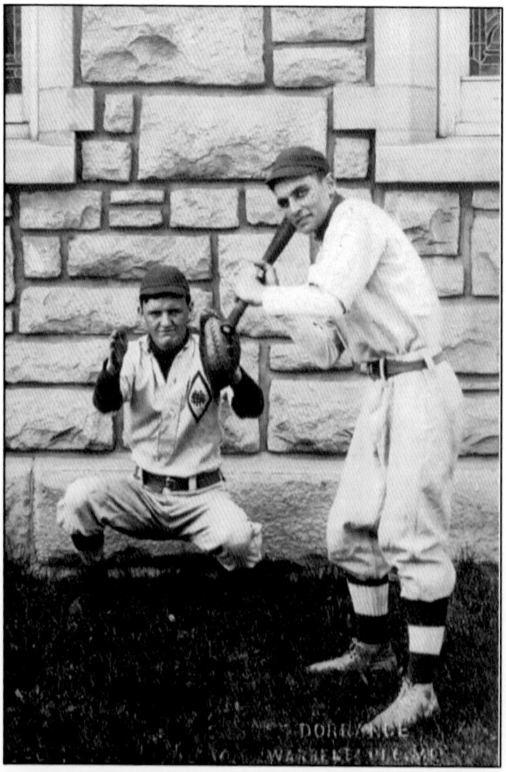

WHS Baseball Players. Batter up—ready for practice. Two players from the Warrensburg High School baseball team set up by the high school. They are George "Puny" Caldwell and Burwell "Skinflint" Moles. This is a Dorrance photo, probably taken about 1925. (Tom Christopher Collection.)

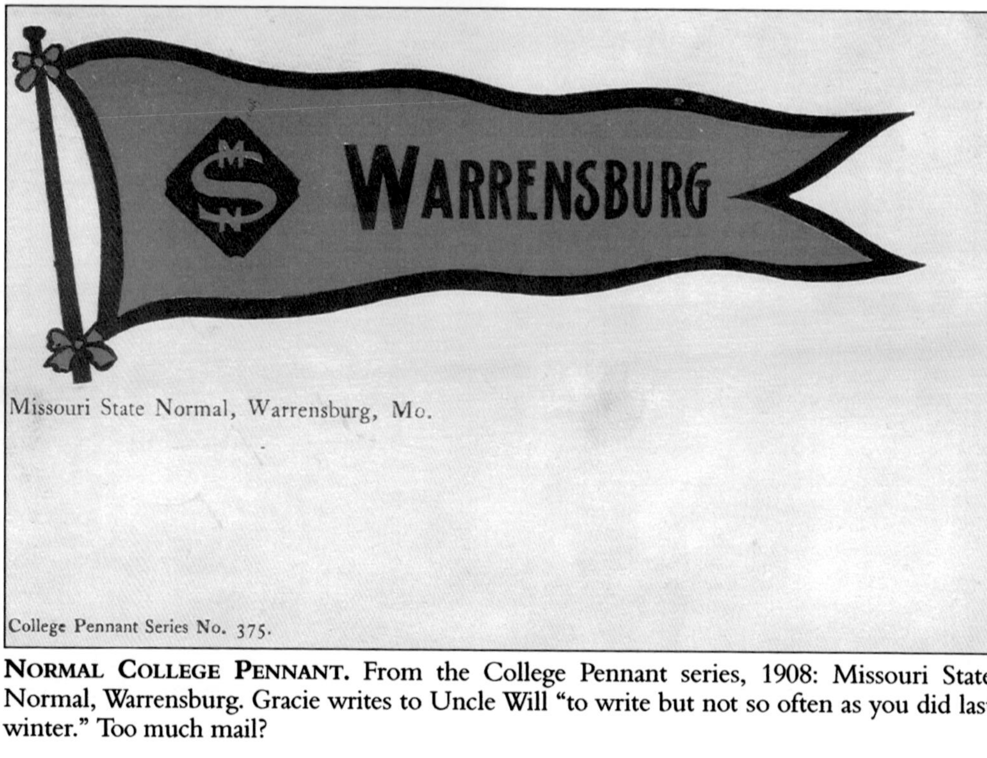

Normal College Pennant. From the College Pennant series, 1908: Missouri State Normal, Warrensburg. Gracie writes to Uncle Will "to write but not so often as you did last winter." Too much mail?

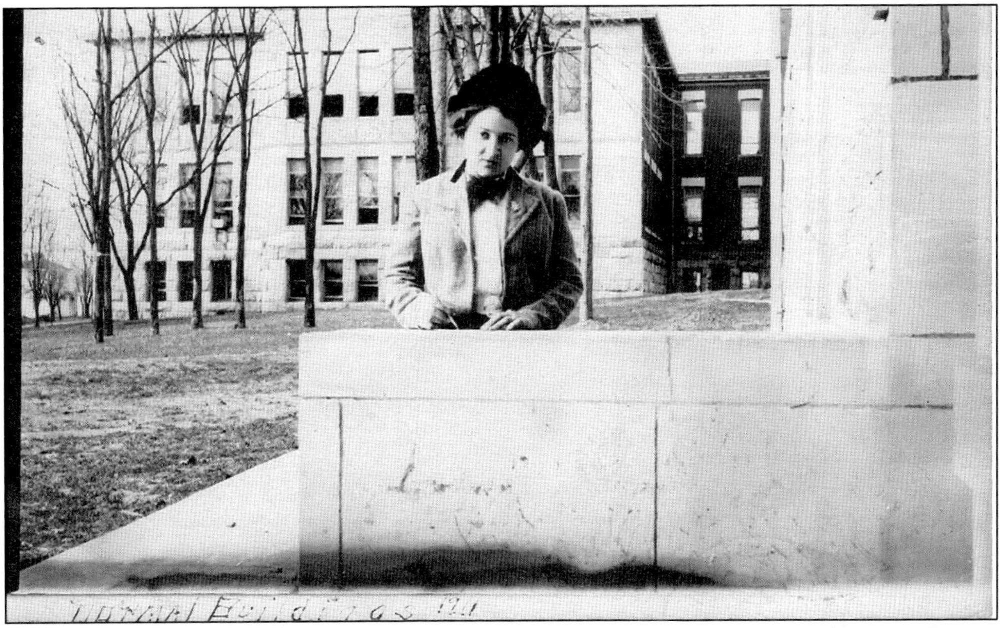

Girl with Normal Buildings. This card was sent to Mr. Earnest Winkler, Norborne, Missouri, Rural Free Delivery #3. "Hello Earn.—Guess who this is? Just a remembrance. Was afraid you would forget how I looked – Much luck. Eltah R." Writing on the front of the card indicates these are the Normal Buildings in 1911.

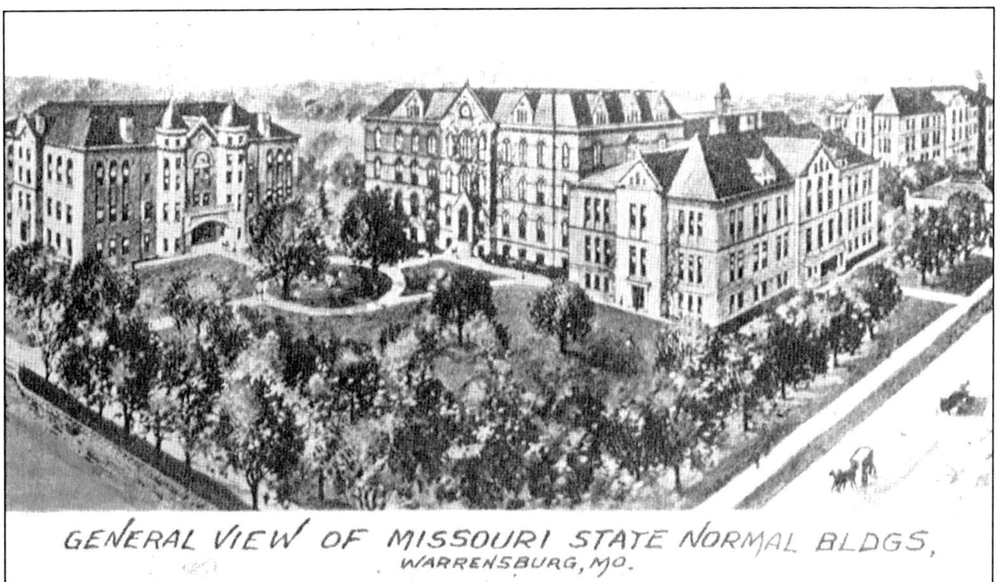

Birdseye View of Normal Campus. On April 21, 1871 the Board of Regents cleared the way for Warrensburg to be the site of Normal No. 2. The buildings shown here and their construction dates are Dockery Gymnasium in 1903, Old Main in 1872, the auditorium in 1884, Science Annex in 1895, Training School in 1906, and the powerhouse and Fine Arts Building in 1904. Running in front of the powerhouse, Normal Street (now College Street), is closed to traffic.

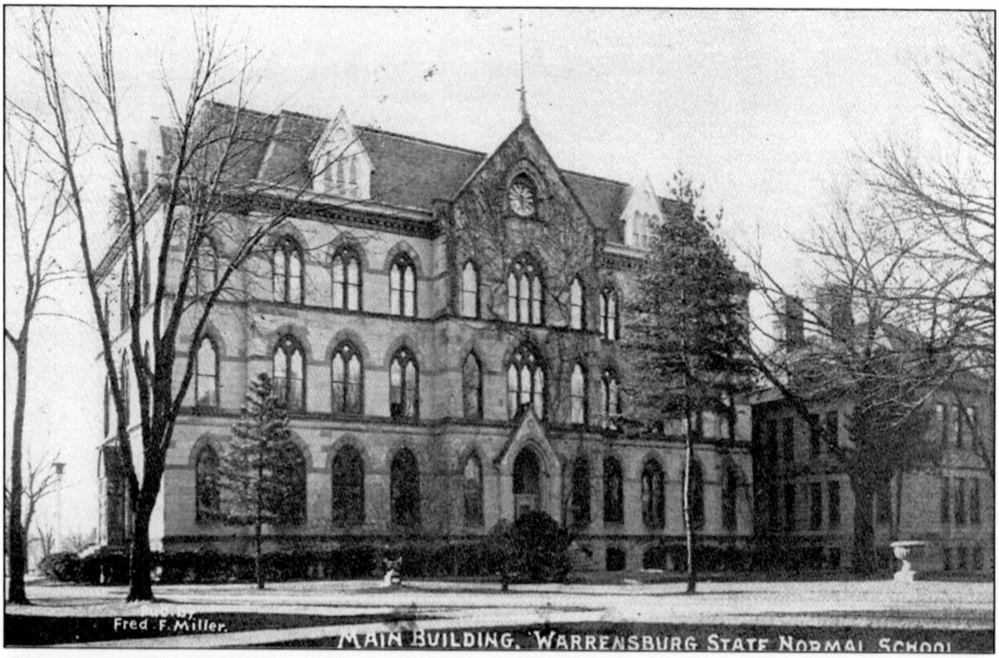

OLD MAIN. The Old Main, completed in 1872, was Normal No. 2's first building, an elegantly designed four-story building with a Mansard roof and church-like arched windows. The north side utilized native sandstone, other sides used pressed brick. The lower floor was ready in September 1872 with four rooms and an unfinished assembly hall. In 1882, the upper floors were completed. In 1893 and 1894 the building saw the installation of electric lights. (*c.* late 1800s.)

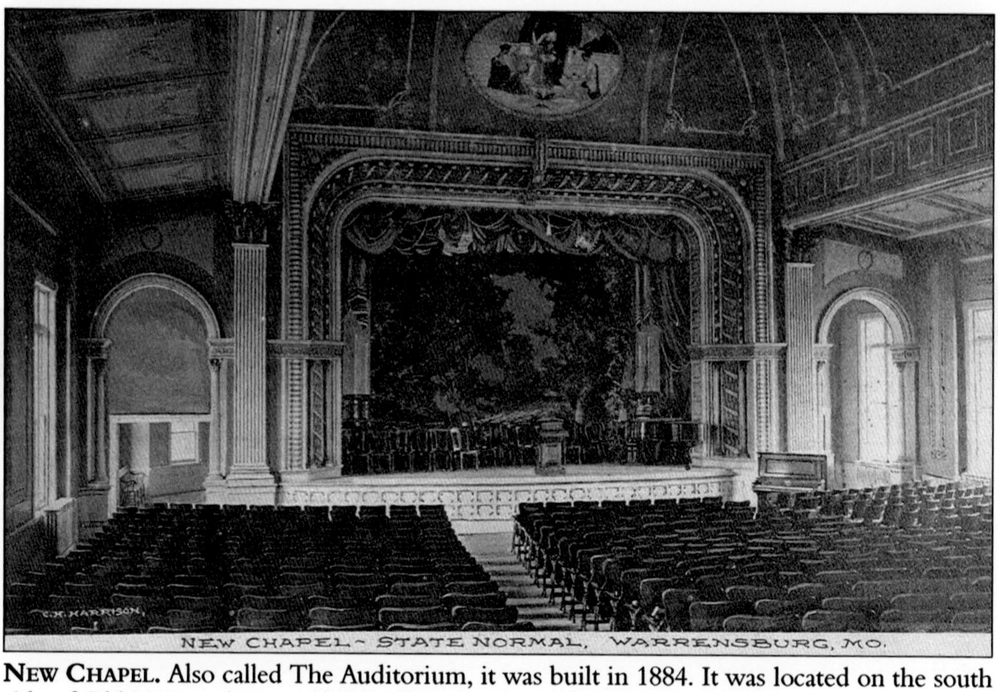

NEW CHAPEL. Also called The Auditorium, it was built in 1884. It was located on the south side of Old Main and was used for a chapel and a study hall. (*c.* late 1800s.)

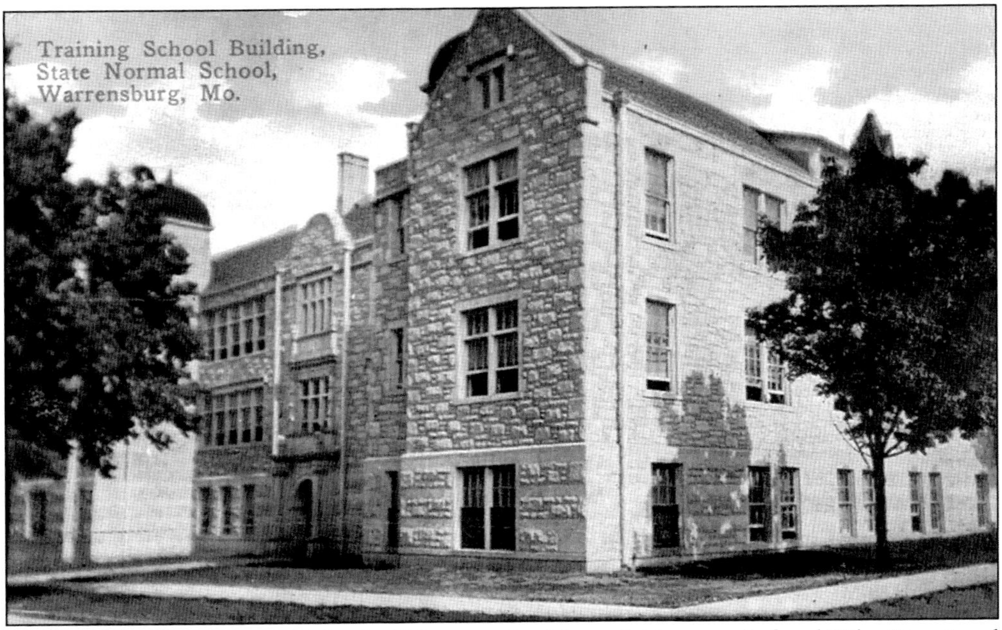

TRAINING SCHOOL. One of the buildings on the Normal Campus, it faced Tyler Street and was one of those destroyed by the 1915 fire. This less common, *c.* 1910 northwest-facing photograph illustrates further use of the local sandstone.

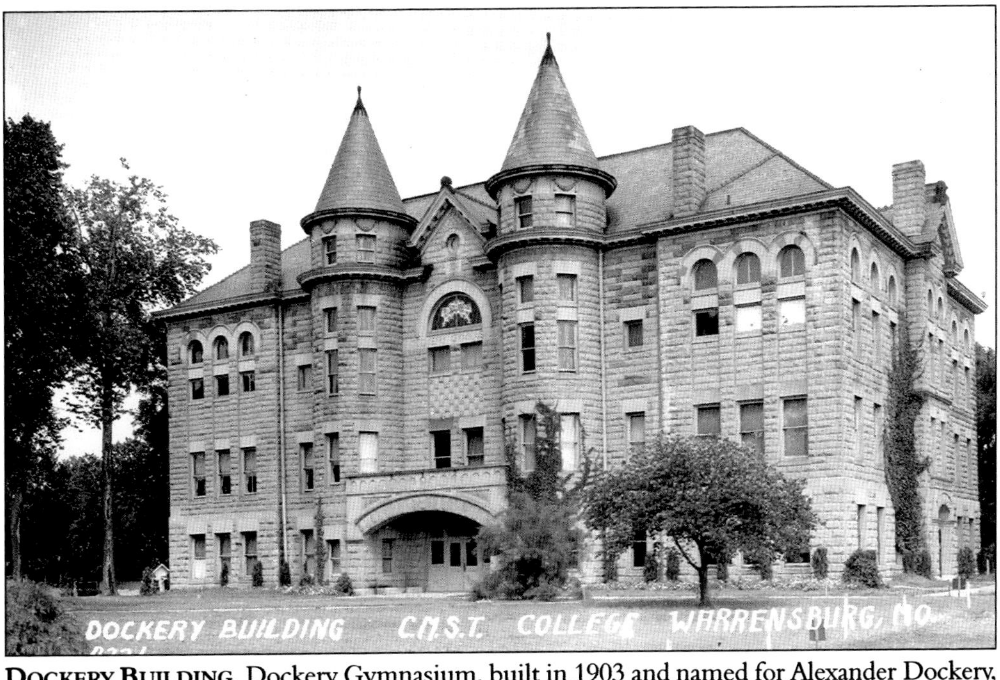

DOCKERY BUILDING. Dockery Gymnasium, built in 1903 and named for Alexander Dockery, the then governor of Missouri, is the oldest building that still exists on the CMSU campus. It survived the 1915 fire, as did West Hall. The original top floor was a basketball court with a 7 ft. wide running track 20 feet up the wall. The last basketball game held there was on Feb. 24, 1939. A 1960 renovation turned Dockery into a classroom facility with four floors.

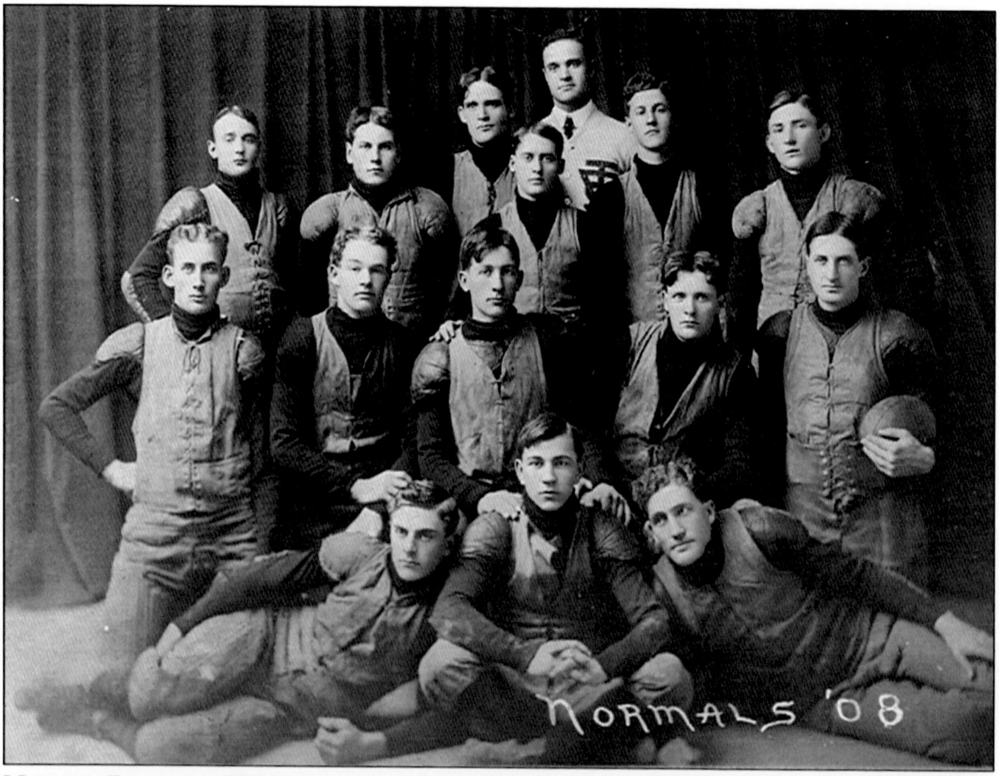

NORMAL FOOTBALL TEAM. Known as the "Normals," these players made up the 1908 football team. A.A. Mason, the man in the back row with the light colored sweater and tie, was their coach.

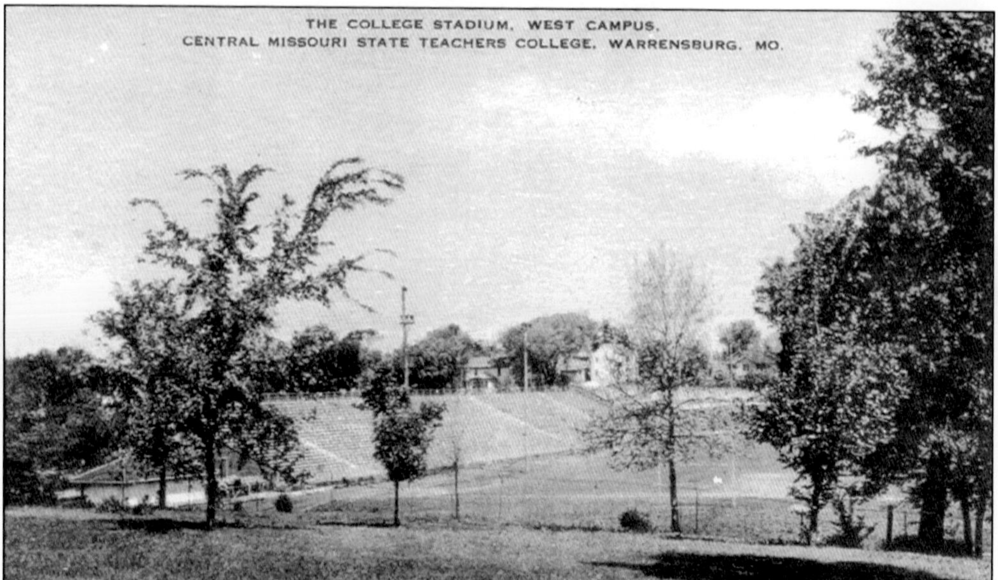

VERNON KENNEDY FIELD. Officially named in 1954 to honor the outstanding athlete, Vernon Kennedy, it shared 19 acres of land with Selmo Park, purchased in 1926. October 11, 1929 saw the first night football game played in Missouri on West Campus Field, as it was then known.

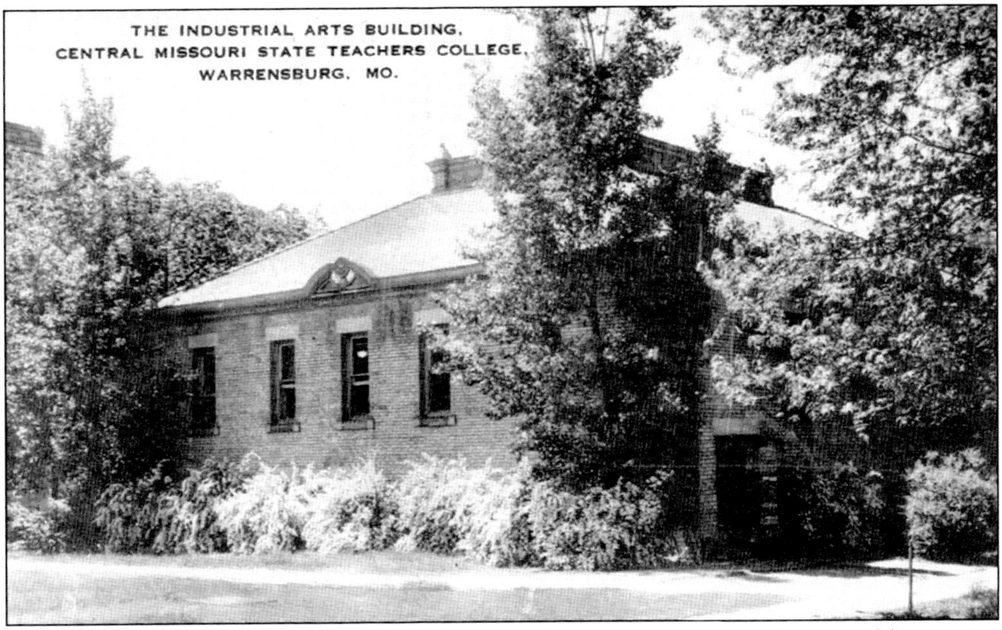

POWER HOUSE AND FINE ARTS BUILDING. Built of brick in 1904, at a cost of $40,000, it housed the heating plant in the basement. The Industrial Arts Department was on the main floor. Standing southwest of Old Main, often referred to as West Hall, it was located at the west edge of the current quadrangle. It was torn down in 1968.

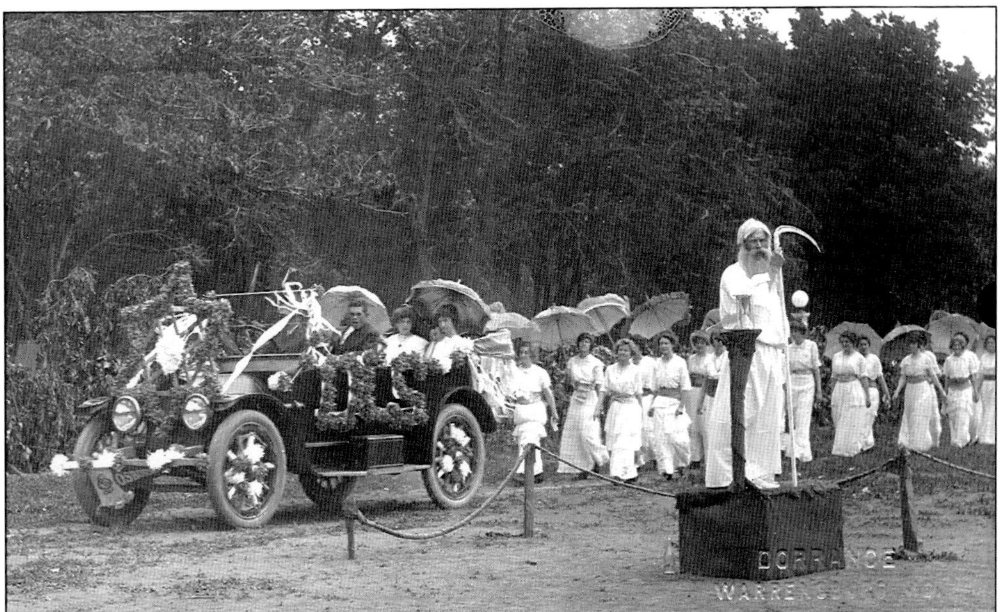

MAY FETE AT THE NORMAL. Father Time presides over a pageant at Normal No. 2, *c.* 1905. The ladies in their white dresses suggest this could have been the May Fete, a popular celebration for students at the time. Other views suggest this may have been a homecoming of sorts, with graduating classes holding up signs for the classes of 1898, 1901, and 1903. (JCHS Collection.)

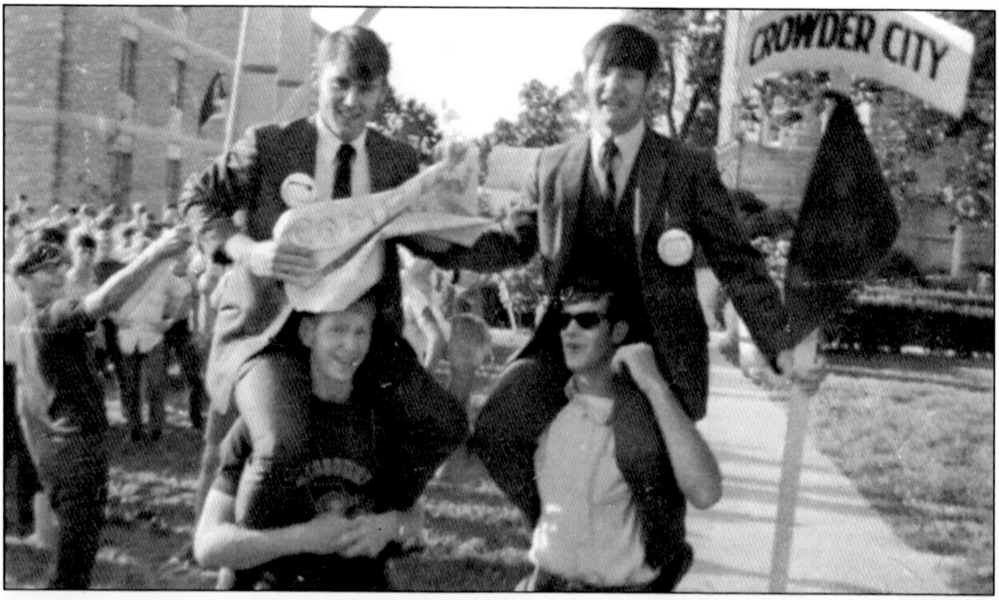

BOYS STATE GROUP. Each year outstanding juniors from all over Missouri come together to form the 51st state—"Missouri Boys State." First forming cities, then counties, they end the week by electing the governor of their new state. They also enroll in one of five schools of instruction. The American Legion has sponsored the leadership program since 1938. Past "boys staters" are very loyal to the program and comprise most of the 120 volunteers each summer.

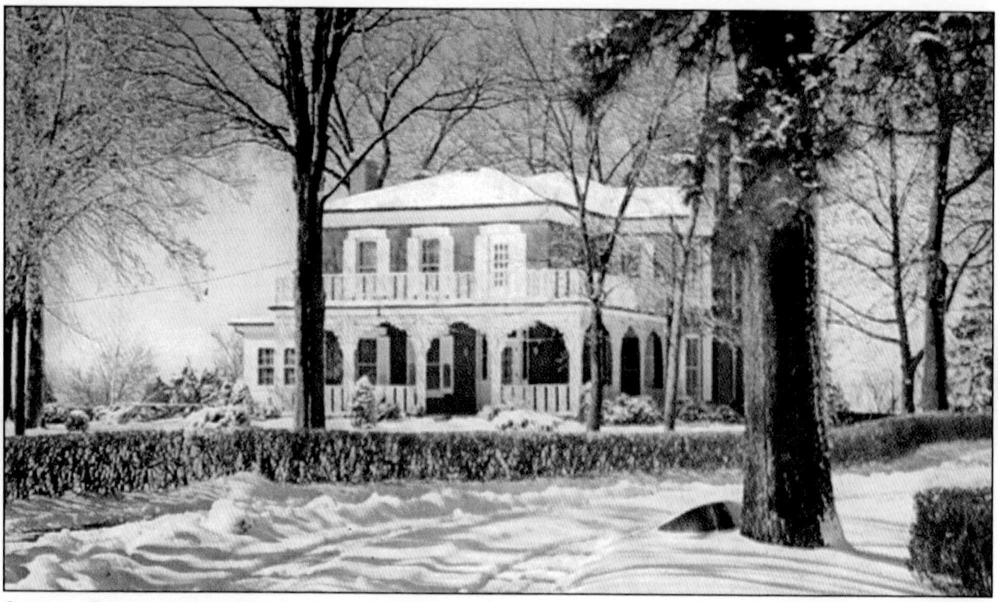

SELMO PARK. Originally the home of Major E.A. Nickerson, it became the official residence for presidents of the institution in 1926. Selmo Park, built in 1866 with 18-inch thick brick walls, was named in honor of a trusted slave who cared for the Major during the Civil War. It was partially rebuilt in 1951, adding wrought iron work, white shutters, and replacing the wood flooring of the porches with eight-and-one-half-inch square bricks from the crosswalks of the Old Normal.

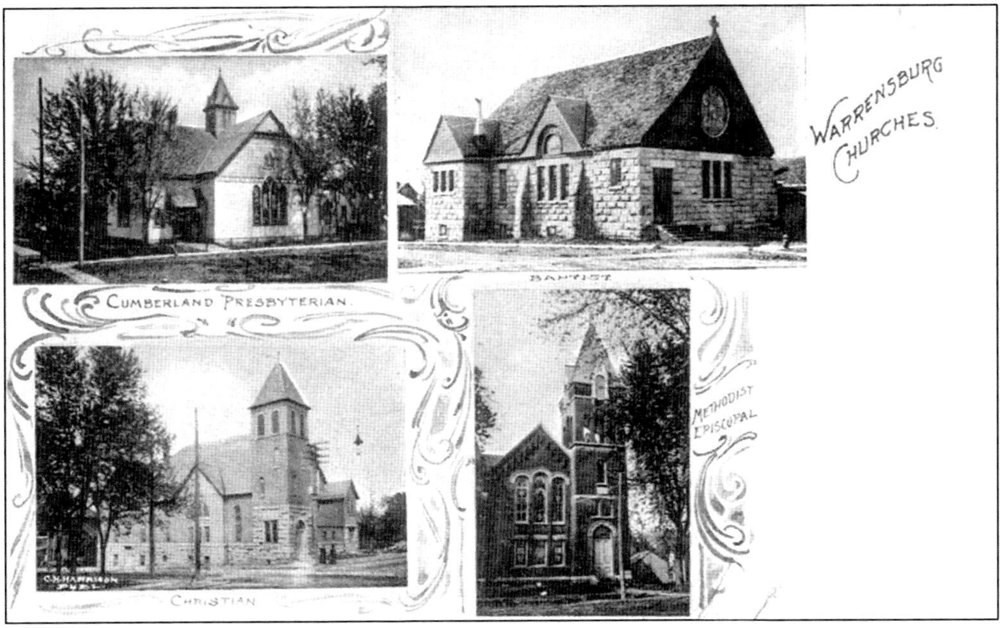

CHURCH MULTIVIEW. A composite card on a few of Warrensburg's houses of worship—Cumberland Presbyterian, Christ Episcopal (incorrectly named "Baptist"), Christian, and Methodist Episcopal.

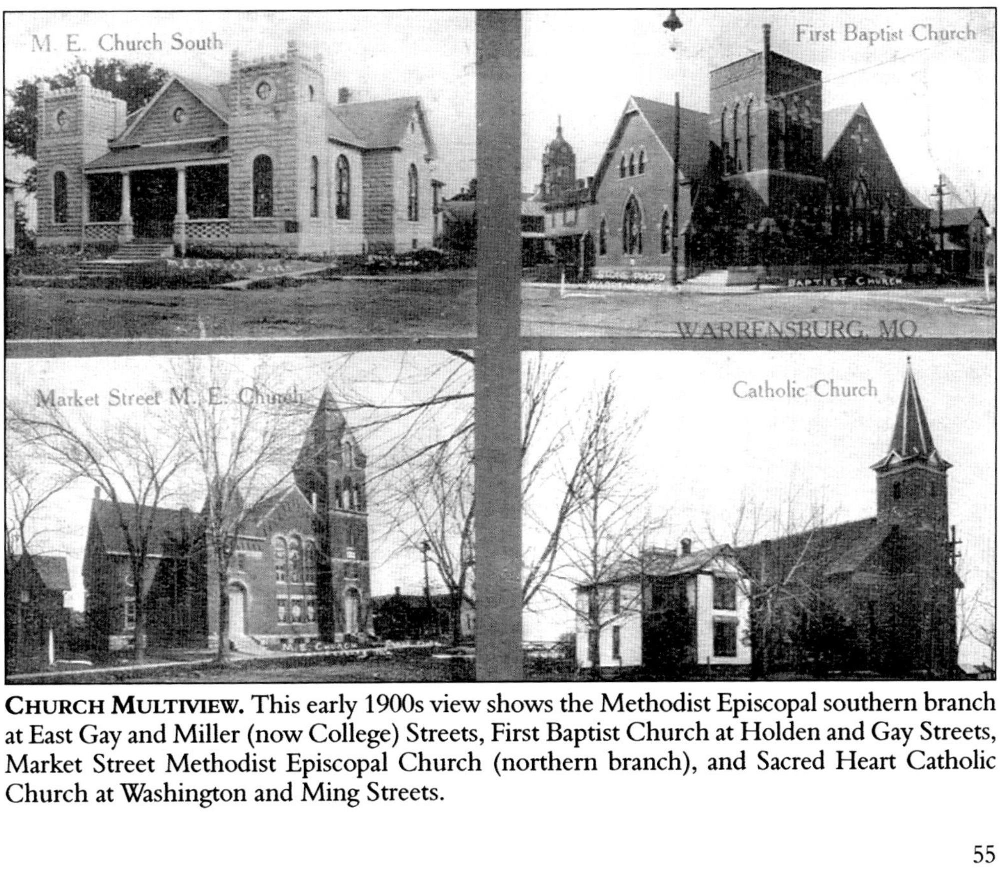

CHURCH MULTIVIEW. This early 1900s view shows the Methodist Episcopal southern branch at East Gay and Miller (now College) Streets, First Baptist Church at Holden and Gay Streets, Market Street Methodist Episcopal Church (northern branch), and Sacred Heart Catholic Church at Washington and Ming Streets.

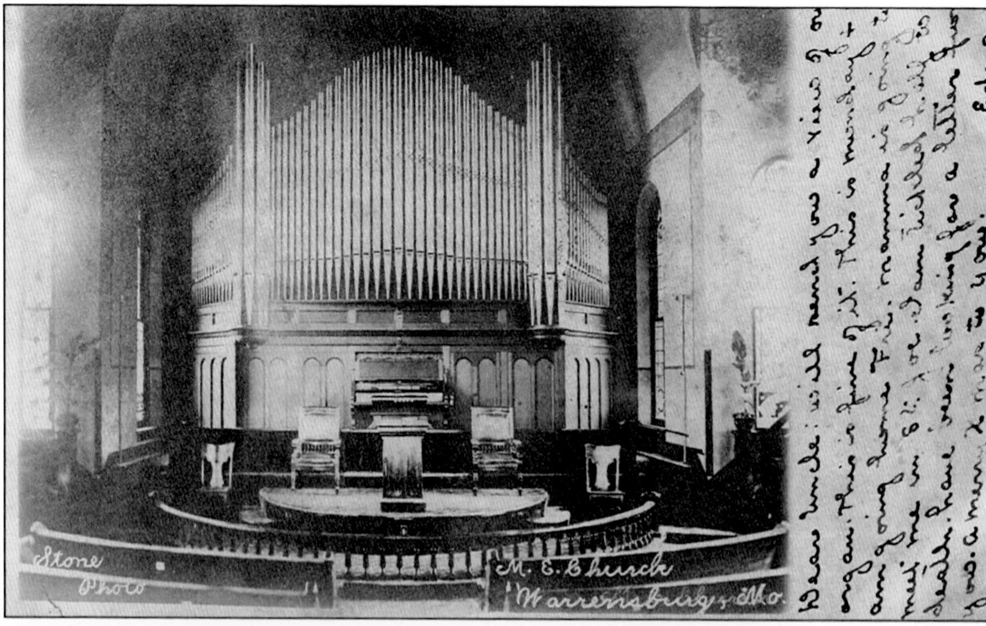

PIPE ORGAN. A Grand Sanctuary! Here we see an early 1900s interior shot of the Market Street Methodist Episcopal Church, showing the huge pipe organ. It was moved to the Methodist Episcopal South Church after being rebuilt around 1950.

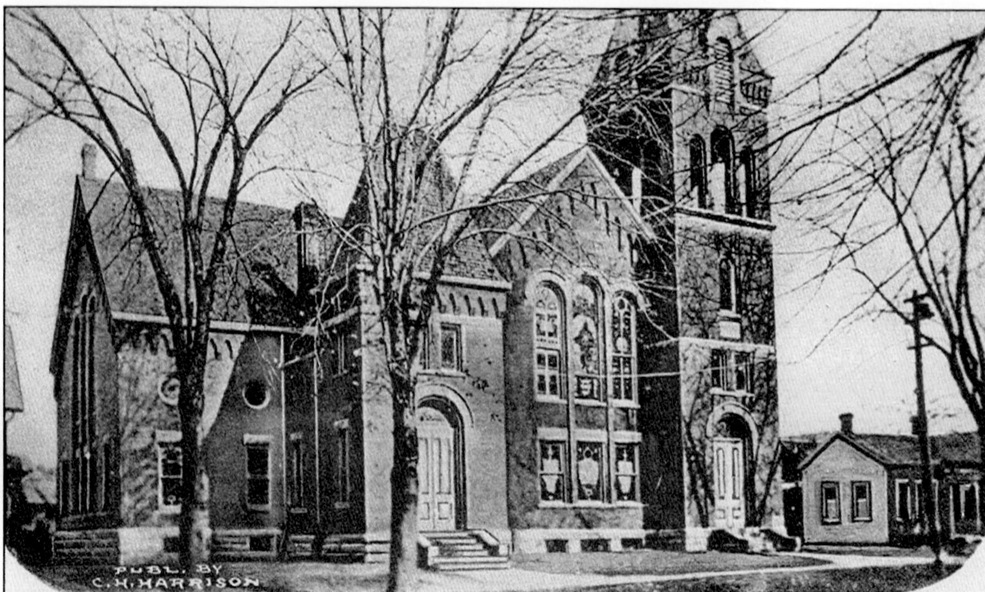

METHODIST EPISCOPAL CHURCH (NORTHERN BRANCH). This is the Market Street Church in about 1910. Union sympathizers erected the first church in approximately 1865. By 1940, the northern branch reunited with the southern to form United Methodist. The building pictured was sold to RLDS (Reorganized Church of Jesus Christ of Latter Day Saints) in about 1948. After serving its useful purpose as a house of worship it was razed in 1974, becoming a parking lot for the Sweeney-Phillips Funeral Parlor.

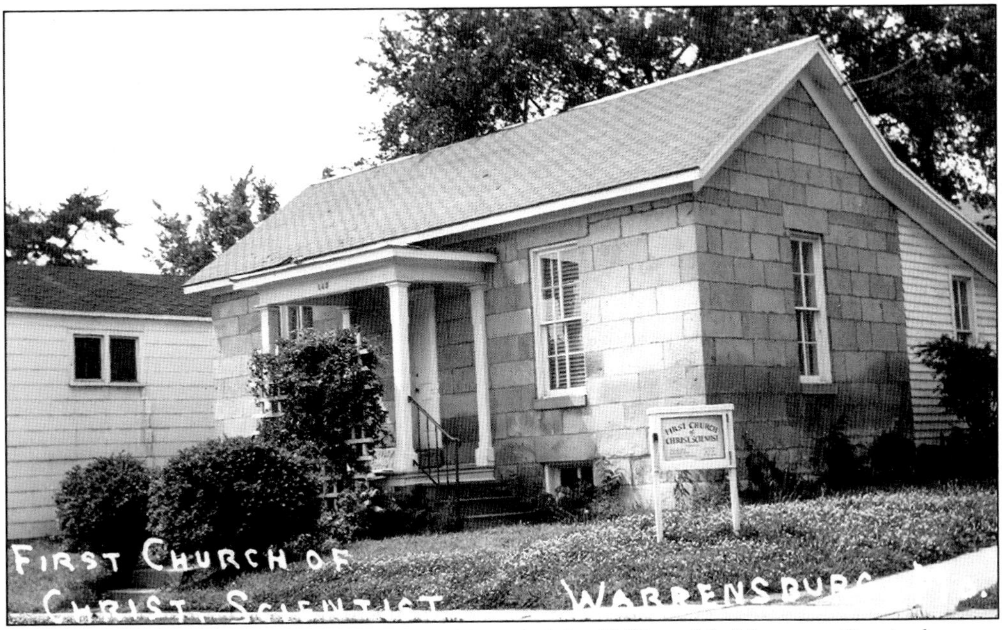

FIRST CHURCH OF CHRIST SCIENTIST. Founded in 1902 , with Margaret Cassingham as first reader, the church moved from temporary quarters to this building, purchased from the Home Telephone Co. in 1916. A new church built on the same site at College and East Culton Streets in 1957 now houses the Islamic Center.

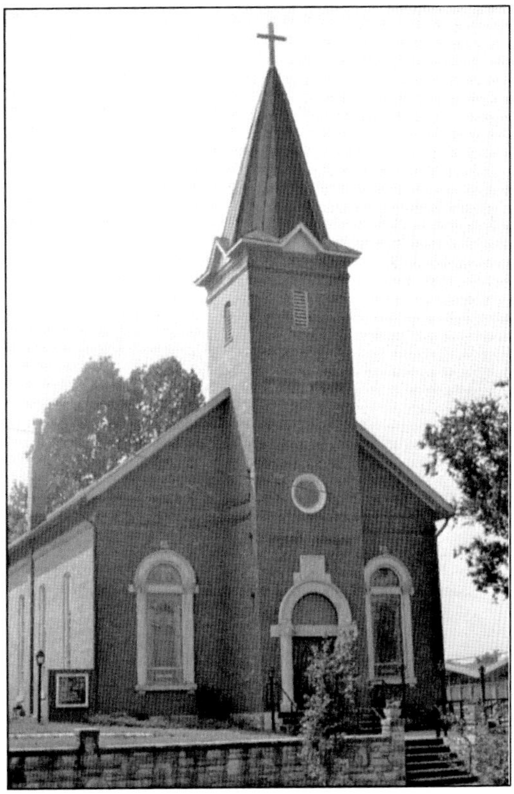

SACRED HEART CHURCH. For a time, mass was held in a hall over the Gilkeson Store. In 1885, Father William Sherry came to Warrensburg and in the fall of 1886 this brick structure was completed at 120 Ming Street, now a parking lot. In 1915, after the Normal fire, Scottish stone masons, who were rebuilding the Normal, built the Sacred Heart sandstone retaining wall in gratitude for the hospitality of the congregation. (JCHS Collection.)

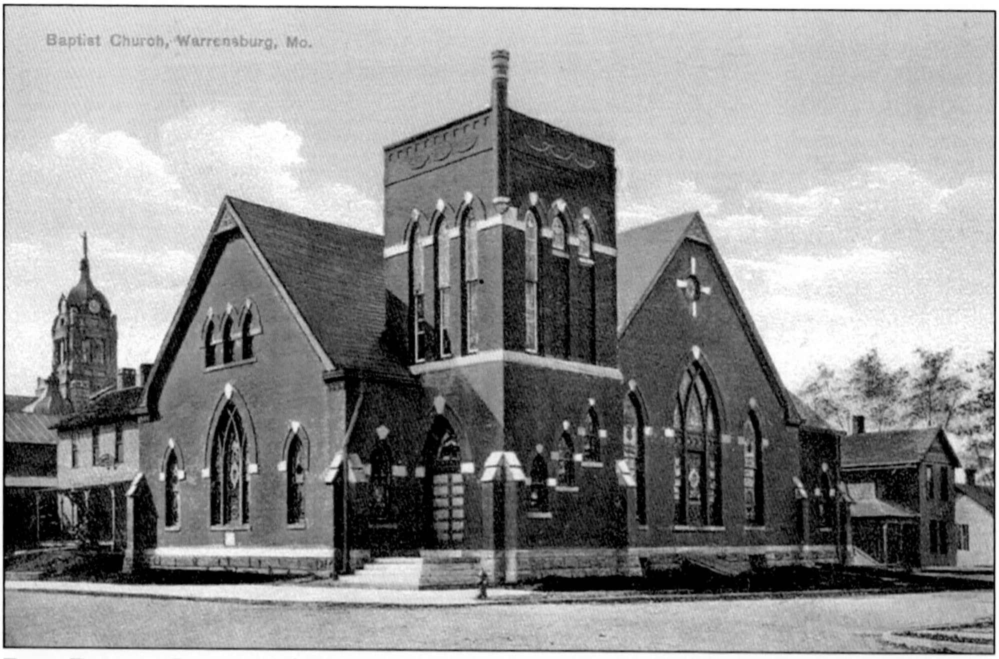

FIRST BAPTIST CHURCH. The First Baptist Church was built in 1904. This view looks southwest from the intersection of Holden and Gay Streets. Notice the courthouse in the background.

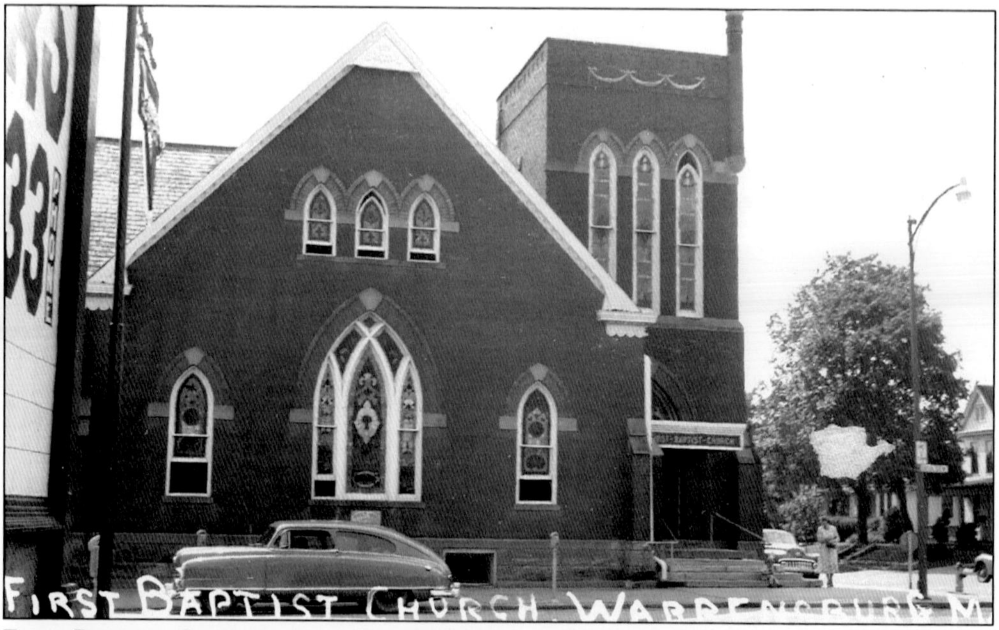

FIRST BAPTIST CHURCH. An early 1950s picture shows the east side of the Baptist Church, as viewed from the Conoco Service Station across the street.

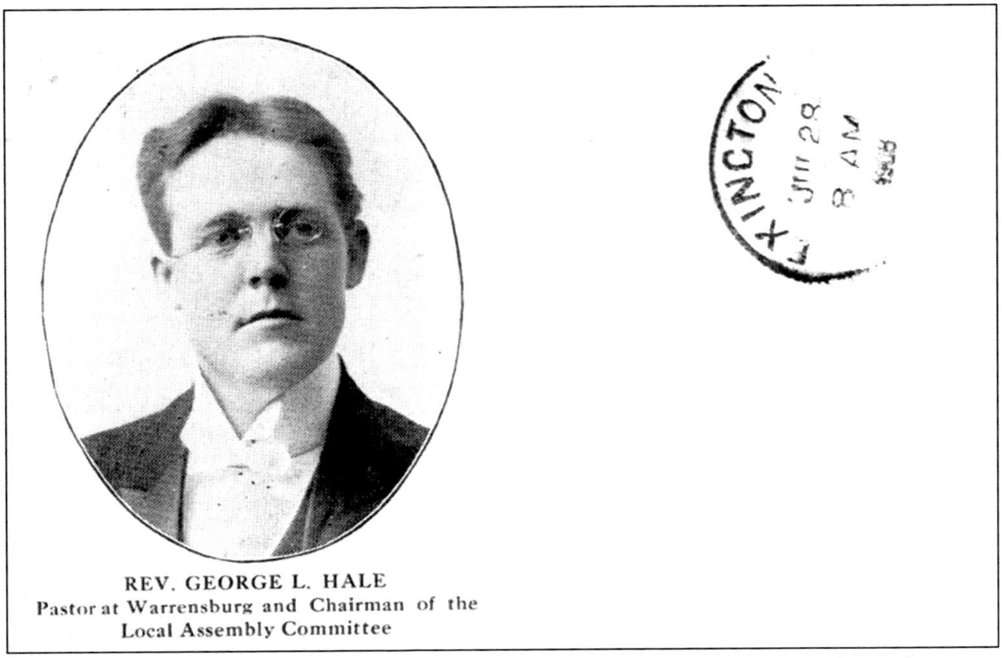

REV. GEORGE L. HALE. Hale was the pastor of the First Baptist Church in 1908. This card was part of the 1908 Assembly Post Card Series and was free by writing to Central Baptist in St. Louis.

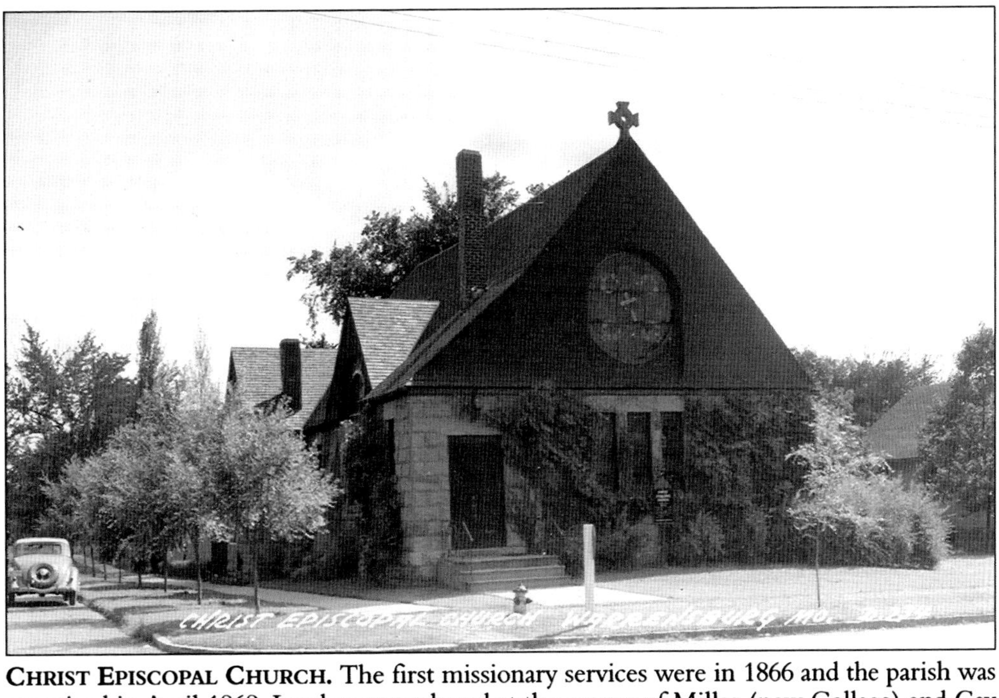

CHRIST EPISCOPAL CHURCH. The first missionary services were in 1866 and the parish was organized in April 1868. Land was purchased at the corner of Miller (now College) and Gay Streets in 1892. The small house at that location was moved west, enlarged, and became the rectory. Financial depression delayed progress on the church . Work was resumed in 1899 and the church was completed in May 1900. This is a late 1930s photo.

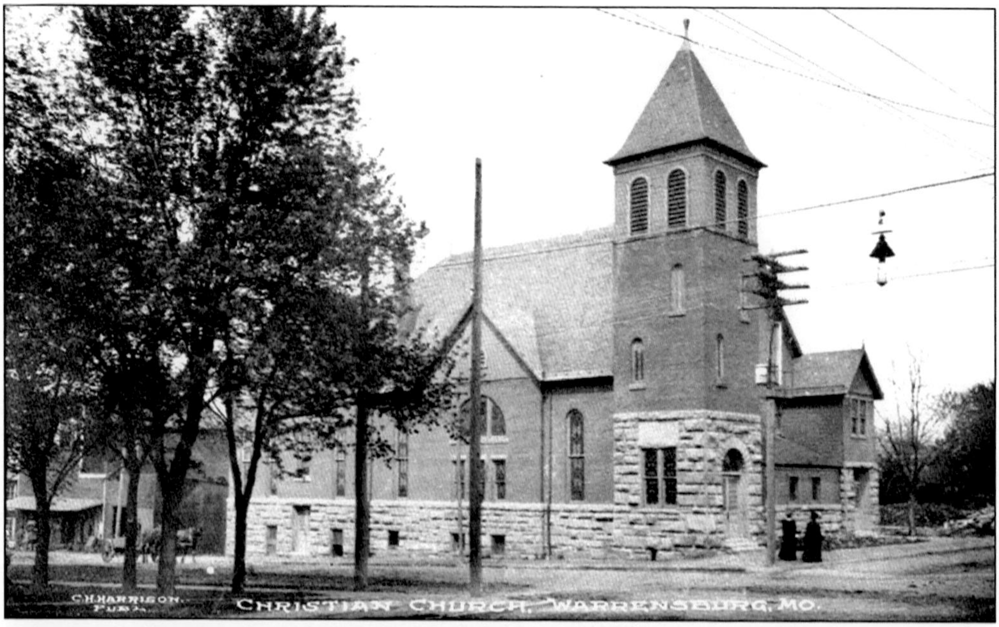

Christian Church. Seen from the intersection of Holden and Gay Streets, diagonally from the Baptist Church. To the left is a horse-drawn wagon and the building that later became the Stockton Mills. In 1888 and 1889, the church was built at the present site and dedicated in 1890. The *Weekly Standard* described the proposed church as "having native stone to the windows, brick from windows to cornice, and gables will be wood and pebble work."

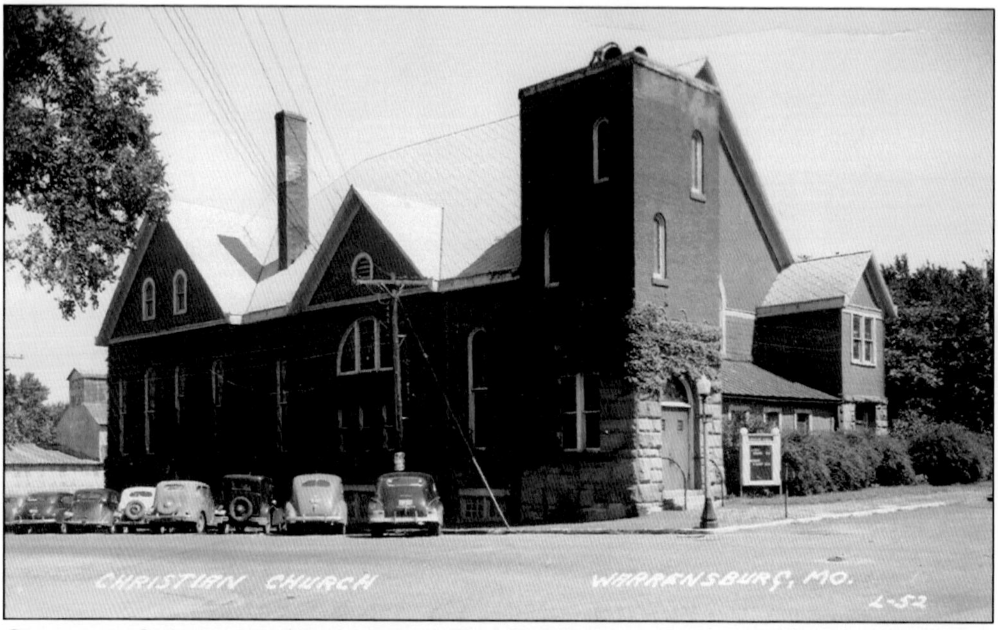

Christian Church. Looking northeast from the Holden and Gay Streets intersection, this mid-1920s picture shows that both the steeple and bell tower were missing from the church for some time but were reinstalled on September 13, 1985.

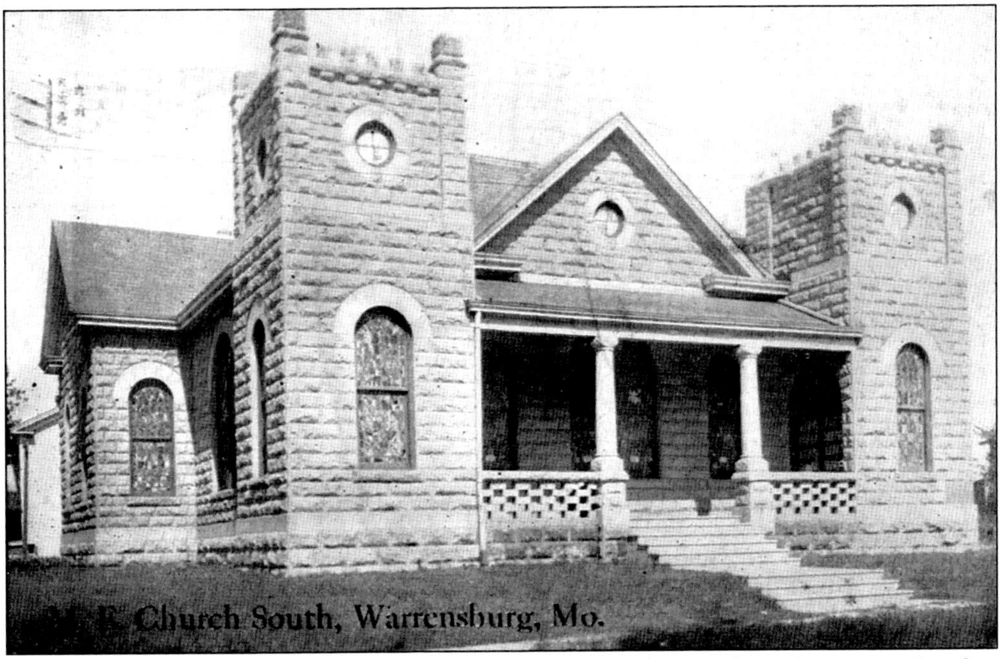

METHODIST EPISCOPAL CHURCH SOUTH. The Methodist Episcopal South congregation first held services around 1838 in an old, log building, with a puncheon floor constructed in 1837 for the clerk's office. This log structure probably served as the courthouse until 1842. The building pictured was built in approximately 1908 at Gay and College Streets. Warrensburg sandstone was used for construction at a cost of $112,321.

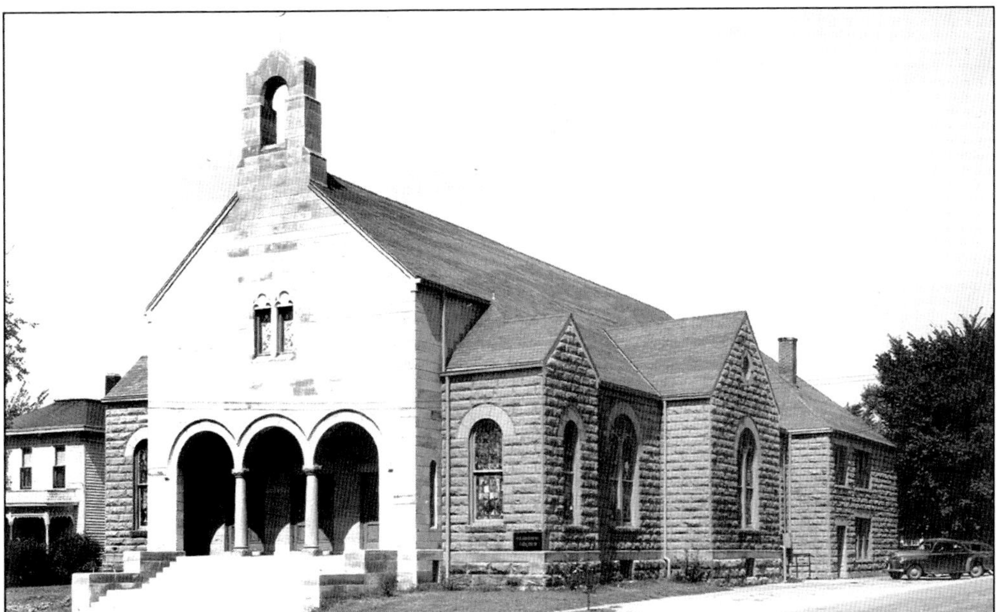

METHODIST CHURCH. The new front, built in approximately 1950, is seen in this *c.* 1950 image. To the left, note the dwelling that exists where the education wing and the church parking lot are now.

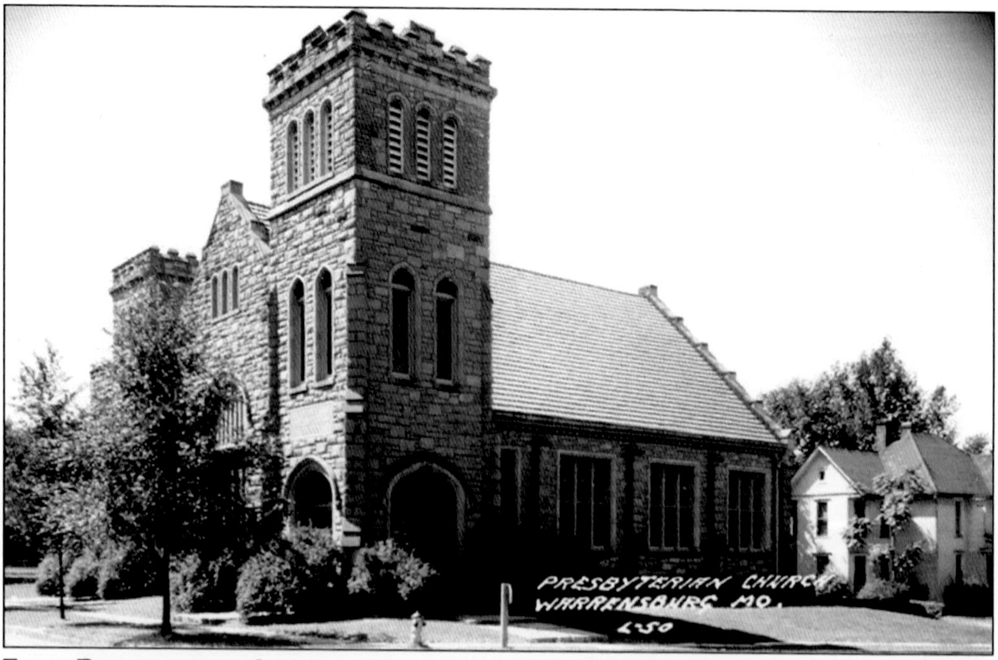

First Presbyterian Church. The First Presbyterian Church, on the corner of Market and College Streets, was the second structure at this location, which housed the faithful of that denomination. The first was brick, but later this version was constructed of Warrensburg Sandstone. The congregation celebrated its sesquicentennial in 2002, restoring a lovely pipe organ prior to that event. (JCHS Collection.)

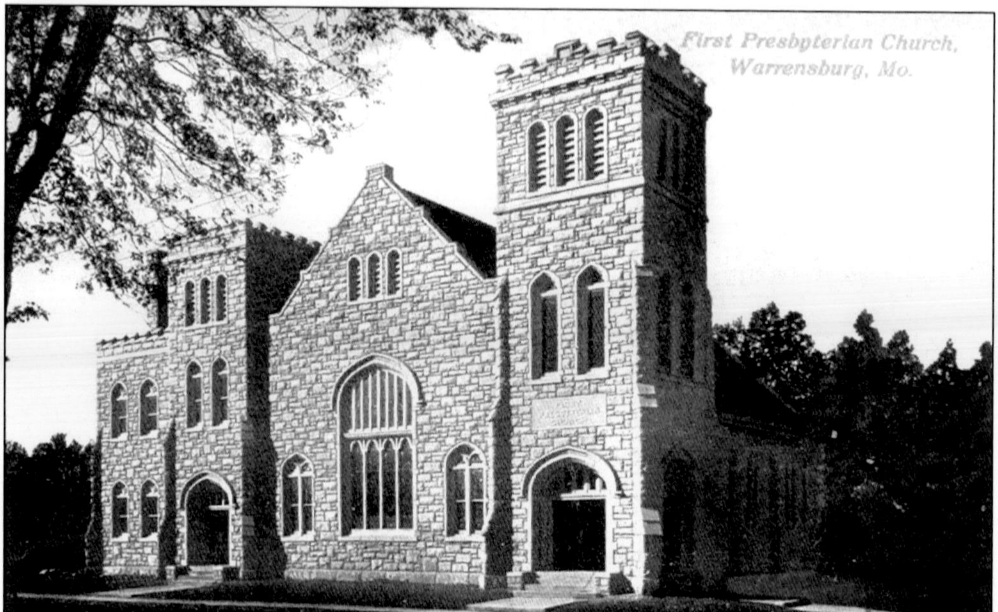

First Presbyterian Church. This view is of the east side of the church. First organized on May 30, 1852, by Reverend Schenk and Elder Green, the orignial building was located on Gay Street, near Warren Street, and was used as a hospital during the Civil War.

Five

Just Visiting

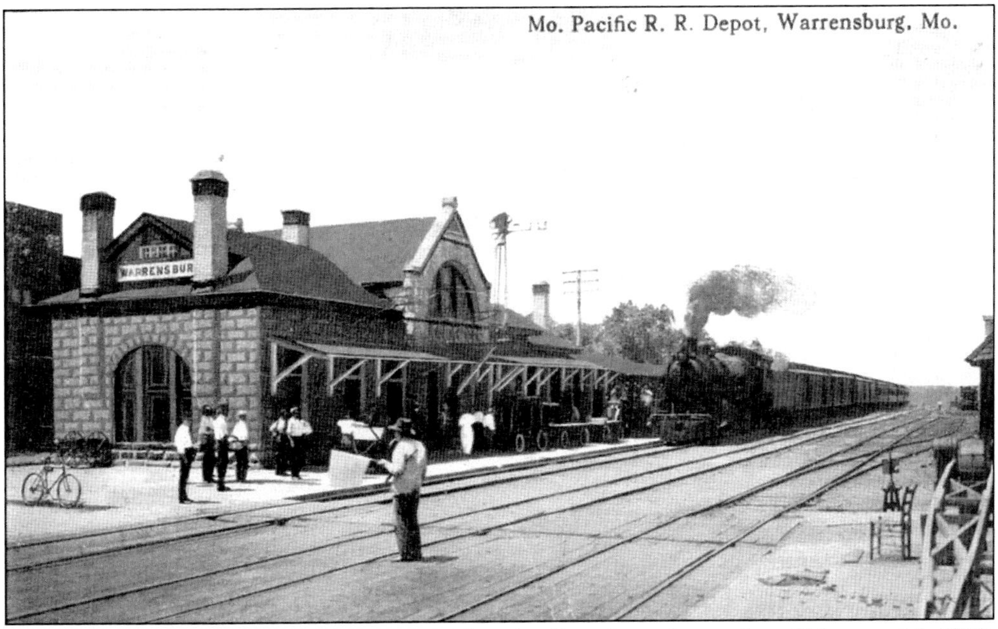

Missouri Pacific Railroad Depot. After the first depot burned on February 16, 1889, this pleasing native sandstone structure replaced it in December of that year. In the early 1900s, passengers wait to board the noon eastbound as the flagman guards the Holden Street crossing. Note the flagman's chair to the right.

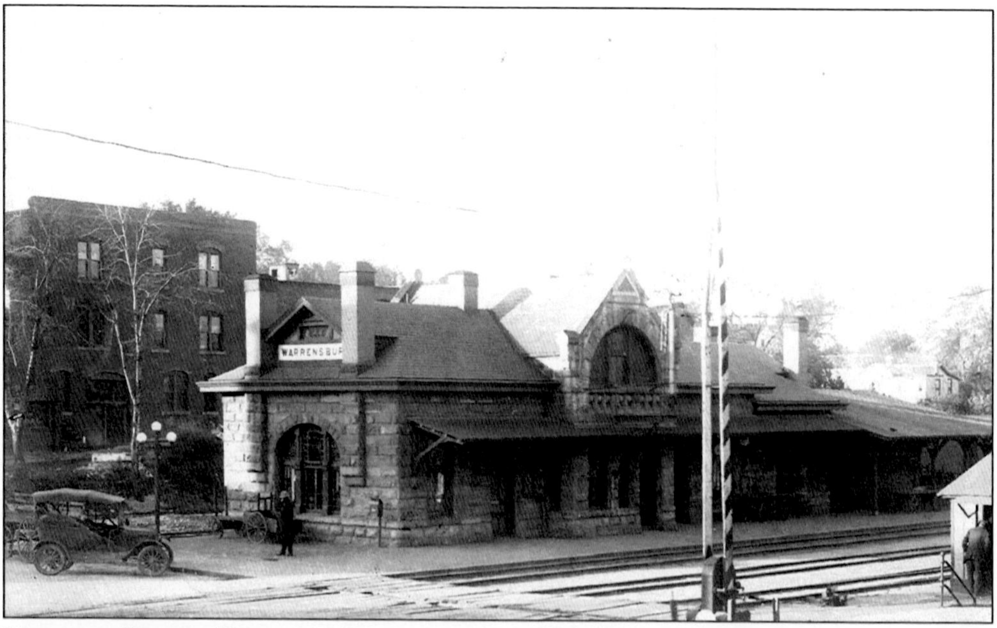

Missouri Pacific Railroad Depot. By the early 1920s, a crossing gate has replaced the flagman and his chair.

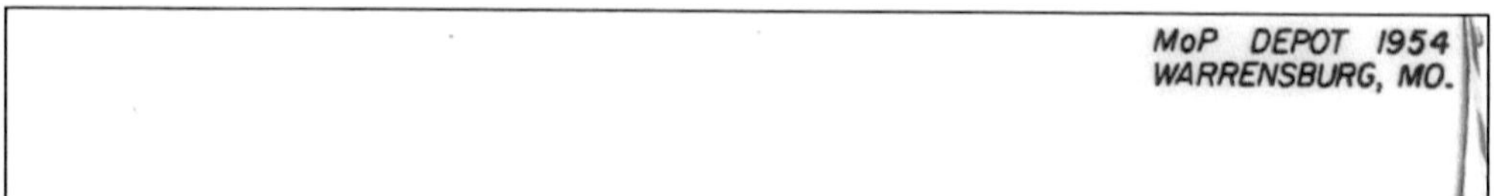

Missouri Pacific Railroad Depot. In 1954, a more up-to-date crossing gate, a newer semaphore, and a new door on the east end of the building are evident. It ceased operation as a depot in 1972, but reopened as a passenger waiting room in 1992. The depot has housed the chamber of commerce for a number of years. Restoration continues in 2004 with the help of the Depot Renovation Group.

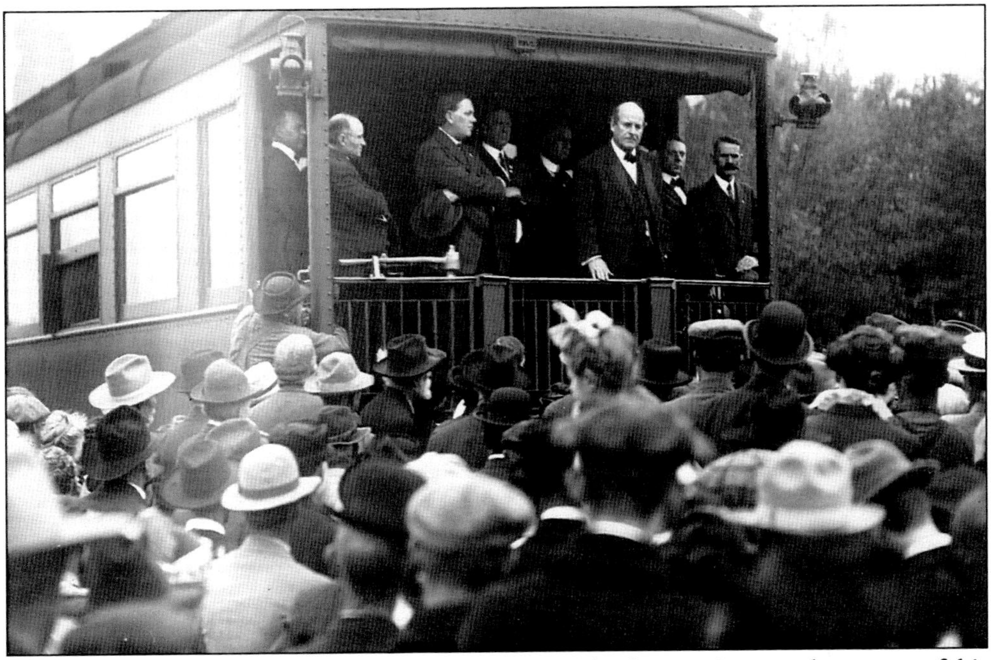

WHISTLE STOP. "Whistle Stop—Warrensburg *c.* 1920s" has been written on the reverse of this image. The volunteers at the Johnson County Historical Society would love to identify this politician, who looks very familiar. (JCHS Collection.)

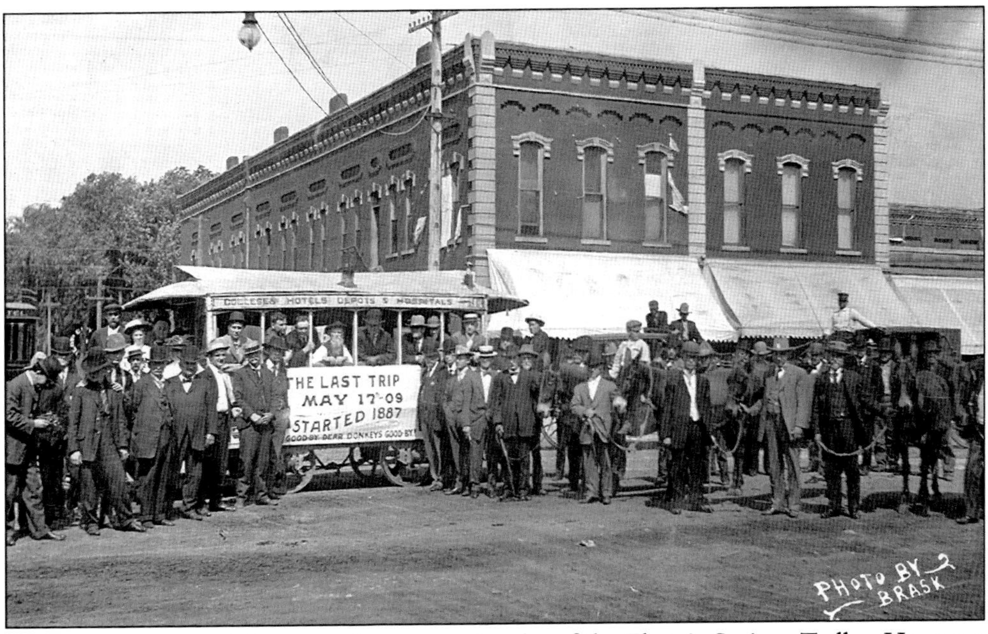

ELECTRIC SPRINGS. This photo is purported to be of the Electric Springs Trolley. However, the authors cannot find the pictured buildings in Warrensburg now, nor in any photographs of Warrensburg. Electric Springs recreational area provided mineral springs, a bowling alley, the large Oakes Hotel (burned in 1906), and a 40-tub bathhouse. By 1887, transportation between the springs and town was by one of four two-mule-team street cars. (JCHS Collection.)

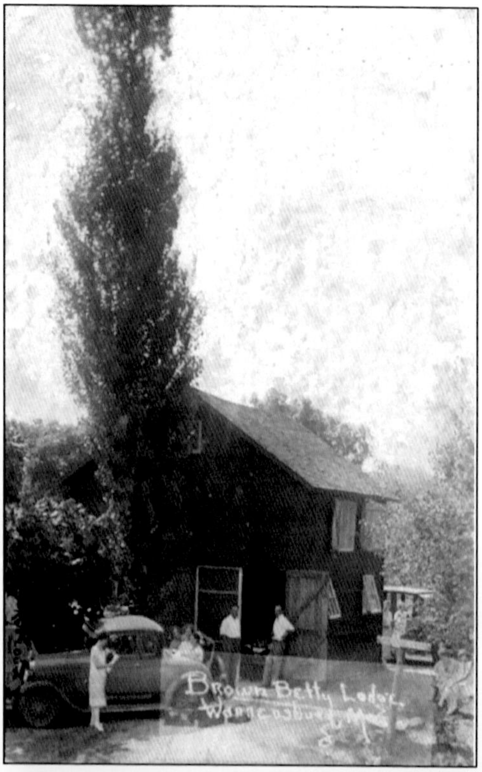

THE BROWN BETTY LODGE. The Brown Betty Lodge offered a room for the night and breakfast at the Intersection of U.S. 50 and Highway 13 (now Holden Street and Business 50). The charming cottage of A. Lee and Mary Miller Smiser had room for overnight guests, a modern bath, and a small tearoom. Notice the girls in the rumble seat. (JCHS Collection.)

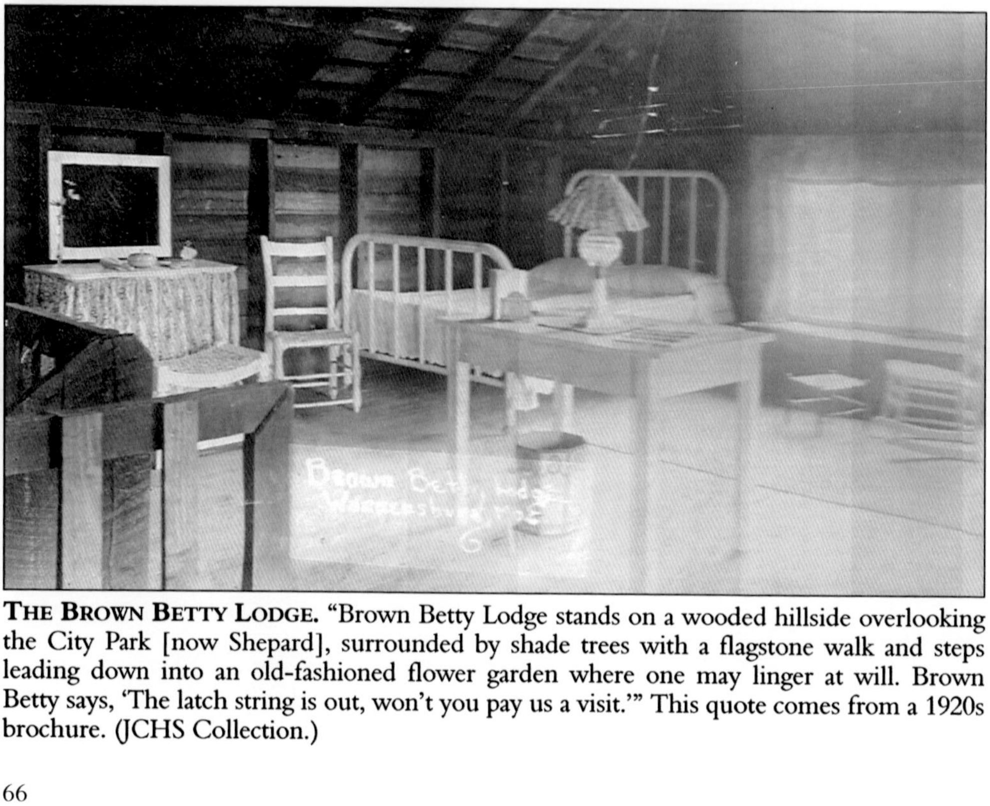

THE BROWN BETTY LODGE. "Brown Betty Lodge stands on a wooded hillside overlooking the City Park [now Shepard], surrounded by shade trees with a flagstone walk and steps leading down into an old-fashioned flower garden where one may linger at will. Brown Betty says, 'The latch string is out, won't you pay us a visit.'" This quote comes from a 1920s brochure. (JCHS Collection.)

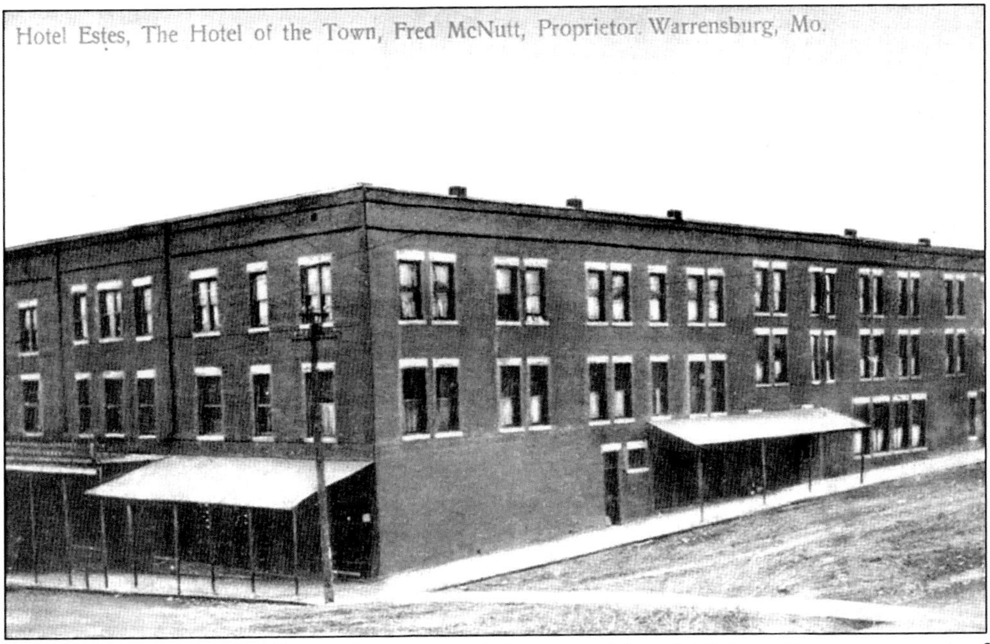

HOTEL ESTES. Built *c.* 1905 at the corner of Grover and South Holden Streets, at a cost of $40,000, it became the gateway to Col. J.H. Christopher's grand resort. Named for owner William Estes, it offered "the only respectable service there for years." A three-story brick building, it had 90 rooms, 65 of which were sleeping rooms with hot and cold running water and steam heat, many with private baths. It was destroyed by fire on July 9, 1997.

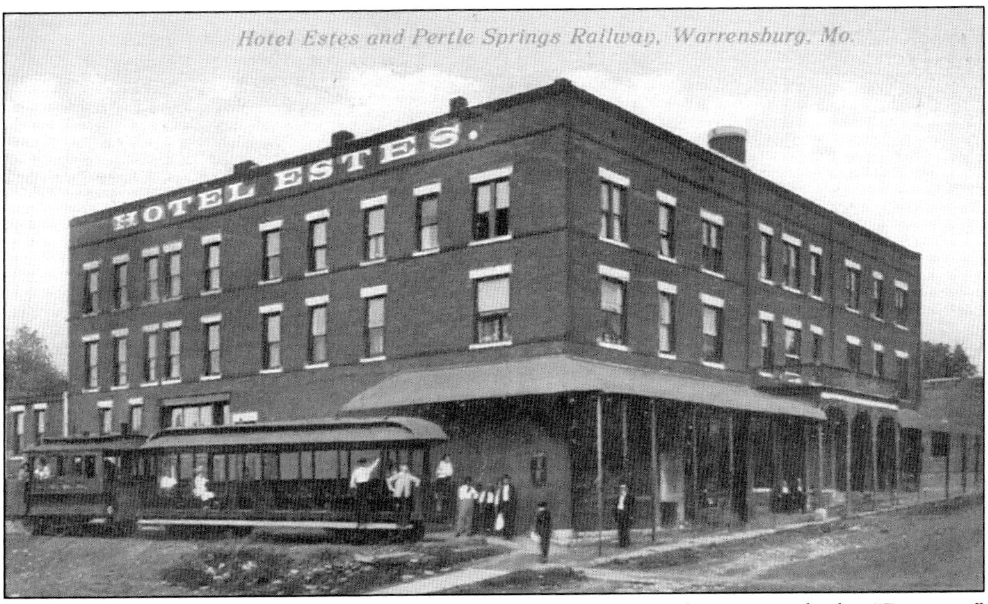

HOTEL ESTES. The place to stay if you wanted to be first in line to catch the "Dummy" to Pertle Springs, this hostelry featured a steam laundry, maid service, coffee shop, and meeting rooms. The Missouri Pacific Depot was less than a block away, making the Estes easily accessible to out-of-town visitors. The hotel used both the European plan (board paid separately from room) and the American plan (room and board all paid together).

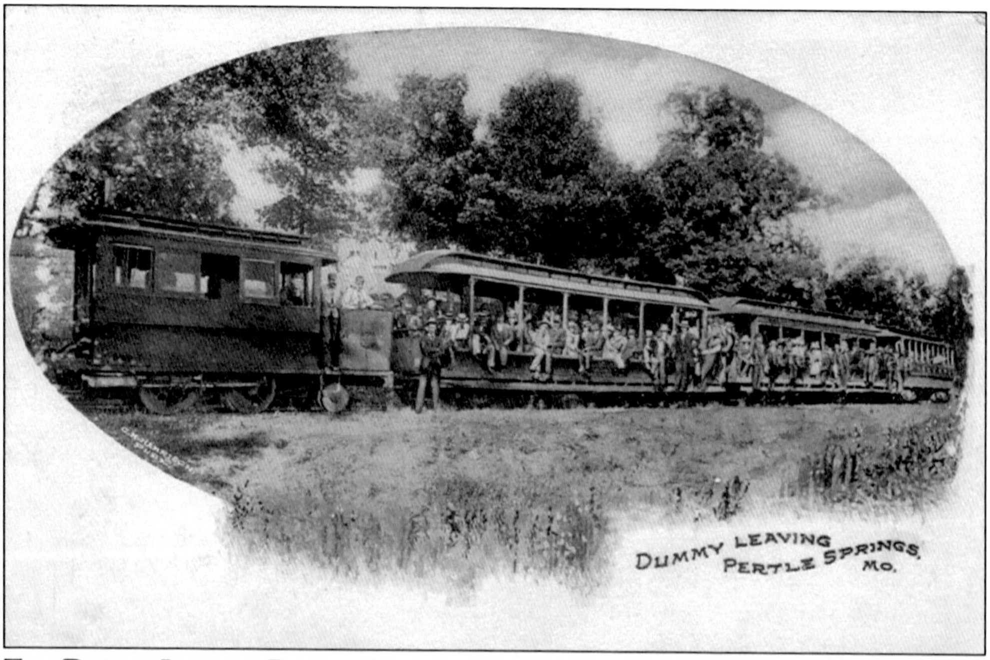

THE DUMMY LEAVING PERTLE SPRINGS. The Dummy Line got its name from the three specially silenced engines that were used to take visitors between the Estes Hotel and Pertle Springs, south of town. Operation of the line started in 1889. The train, painted orange and trimmed in black and aluminum, was three cars long, each car holding as many as 70 people, and made eight to twenty trips daily.

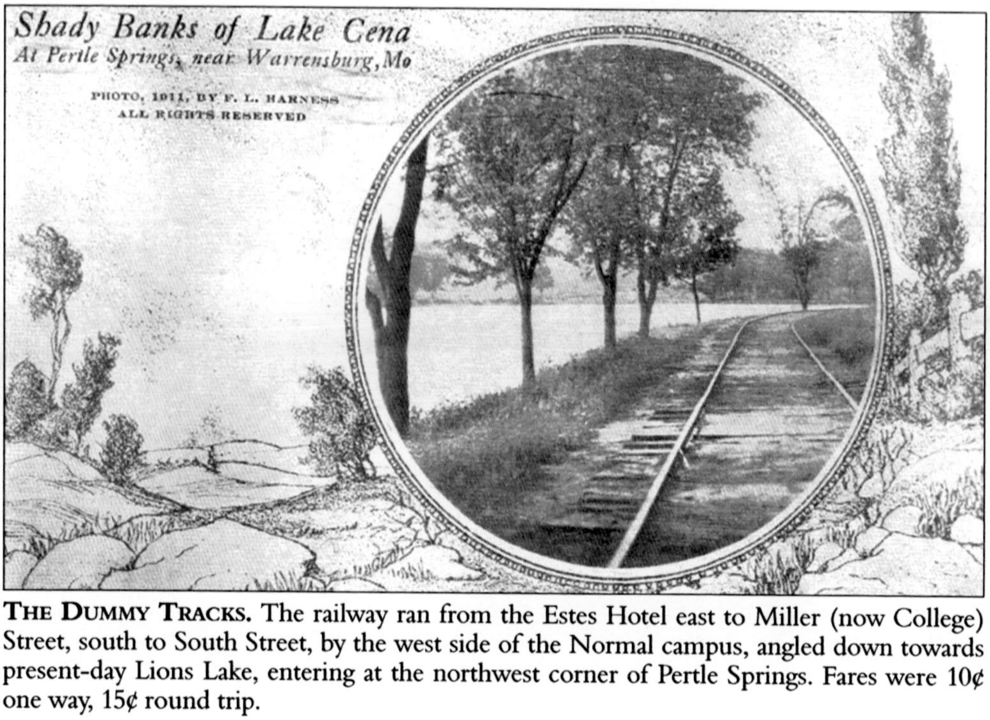

THE DUMMY TRACKS. The railway ran from the Estes Hotel east to Miller (now College) Street, south to South Street, by the west side of the Normal campus, angled down towards present-day Lions Lake, entering at the northwest corner of Pertle Springs. Fares were 10¢ one way, 15¢ round trip.

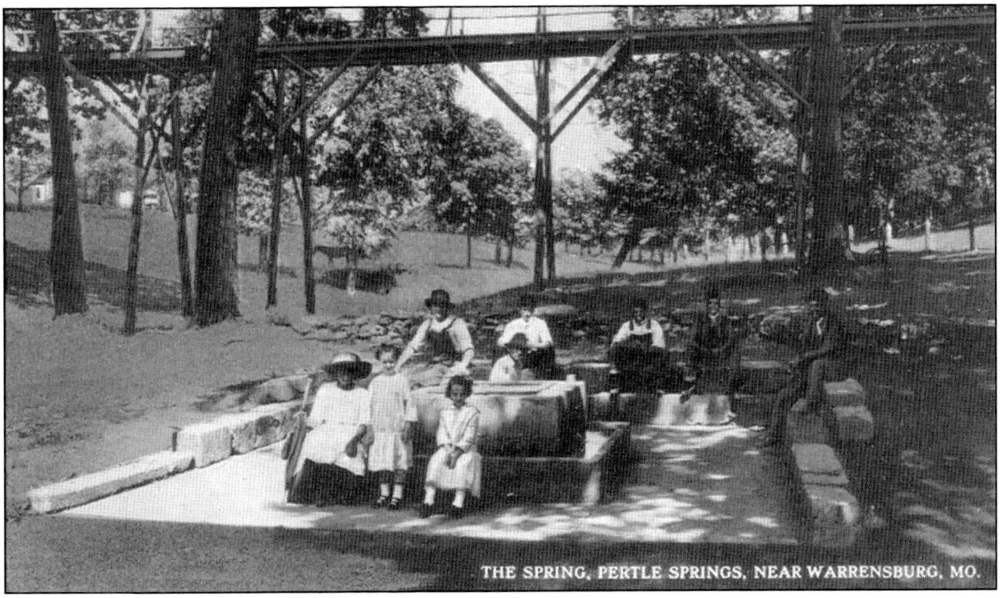

PEOPLE BY THE SPRING HOUSE. Two of the most attractive features of the springs were the healing waters and the cool shade. This card was tinted so that the green shady spot near the drinking spring was highlighted. An 1888 letter reports, "grandma that water down to the springs tastes peculiar and has made some terrible sick, but it is all one has to drink. The coffee and tea and lemonade are made with it too." Others found the water refreshing and healthful.

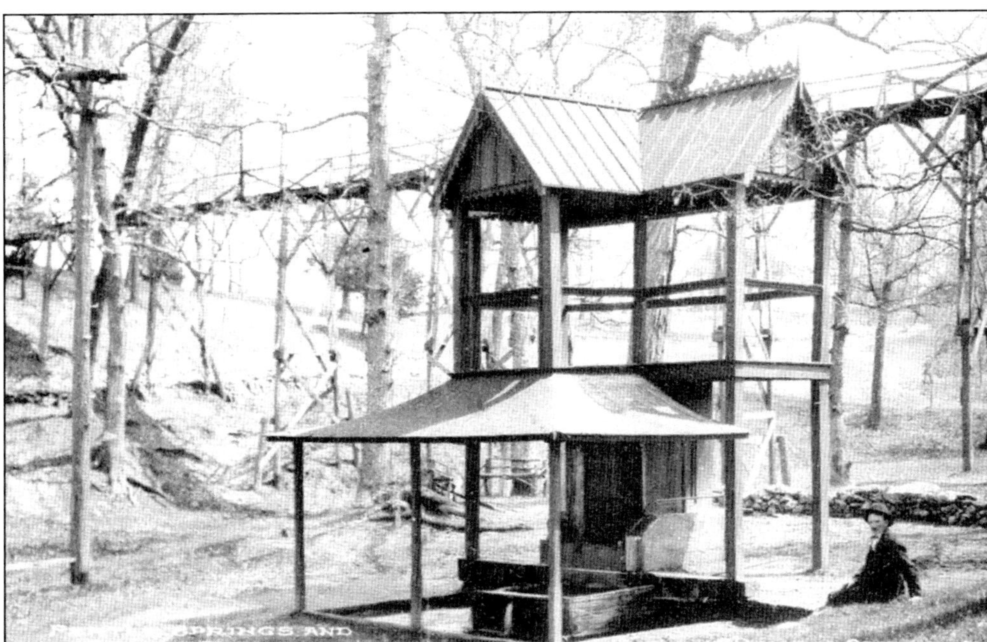

SPRING HOUSE AND BANDSTAND. One photograph of Pertle shows a different spring house, but a bandstand was eventually built over the spring, protecting the water from falling leaves and such.

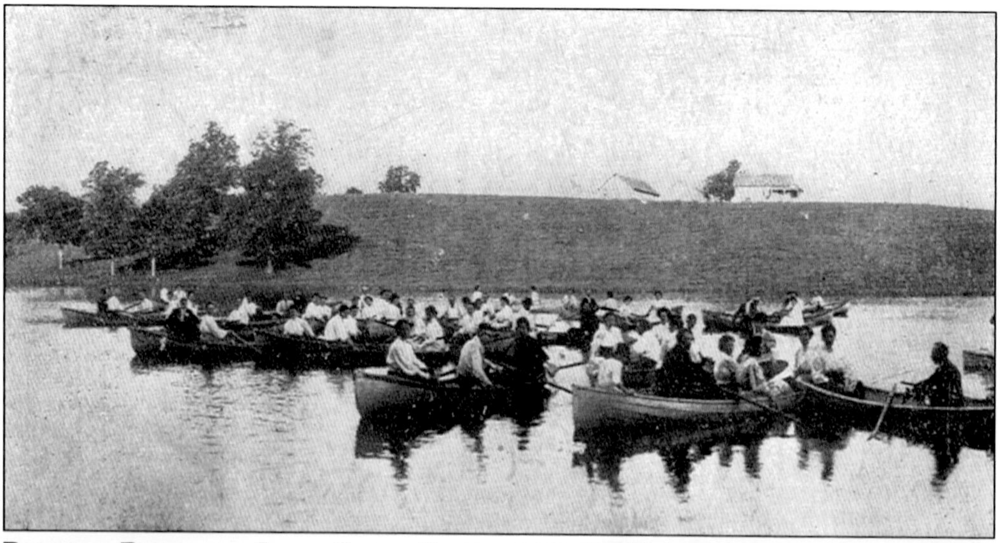

Boating Party on Lake Cena. Resort guests could participate in many different entertainments during their stay. Boating was popular, with guests lining up for their canoes at a boat house and concession area. Since only men were allowed to swim, this got the fairer sex out on the water. An aerial railway, a two-handled wheel on a wire (not shown), allowed gals to cross the lake without getting wet.

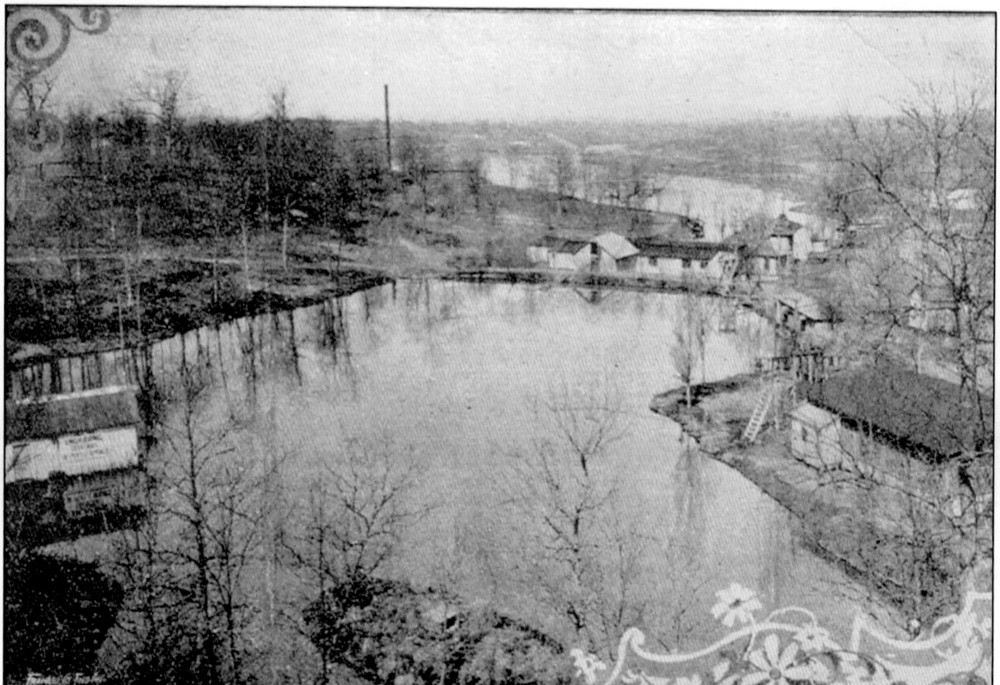

Lake Cena. This shows Lake Cena, possibly from the foot bridge. The lake was named for J.H. Christopher's wife, Miss Cena Jackson of Cass County. Their granddaughter, Cena Christopher Draper, also carried on the name, as does one of her granddaughters. Note the embellished edges on this print.

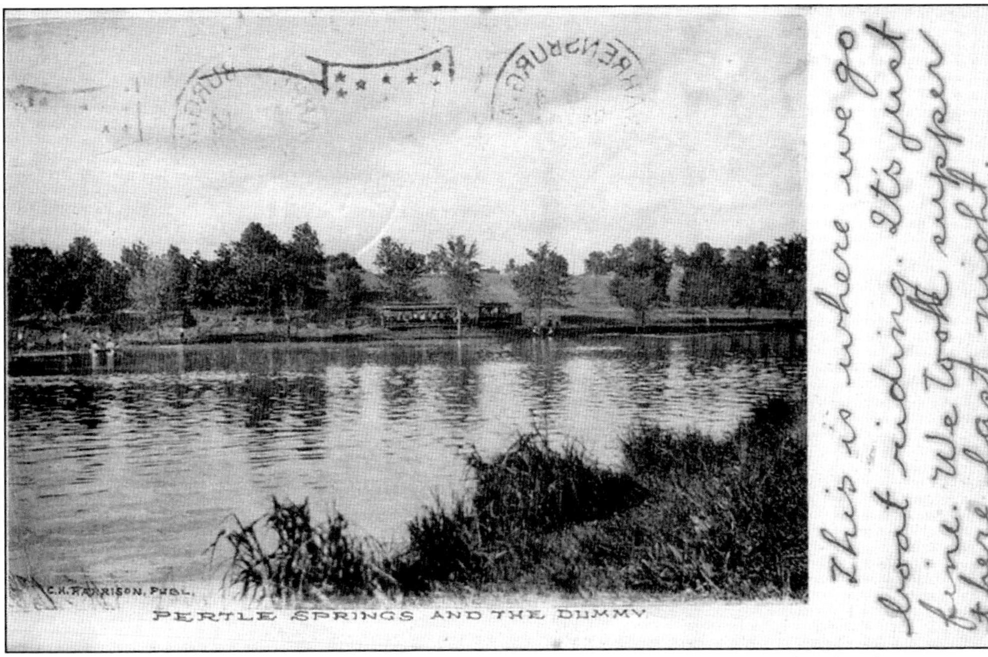

LAKE CENA AND THE DUMMY LINE. Although the steam engine ran silently, the Dummy Line made its presence known. There were ringing bells and steam whistles, which blew loudly at the turns. If there was trouble, five loud blasts from the whistle indicated an engine was off the track.

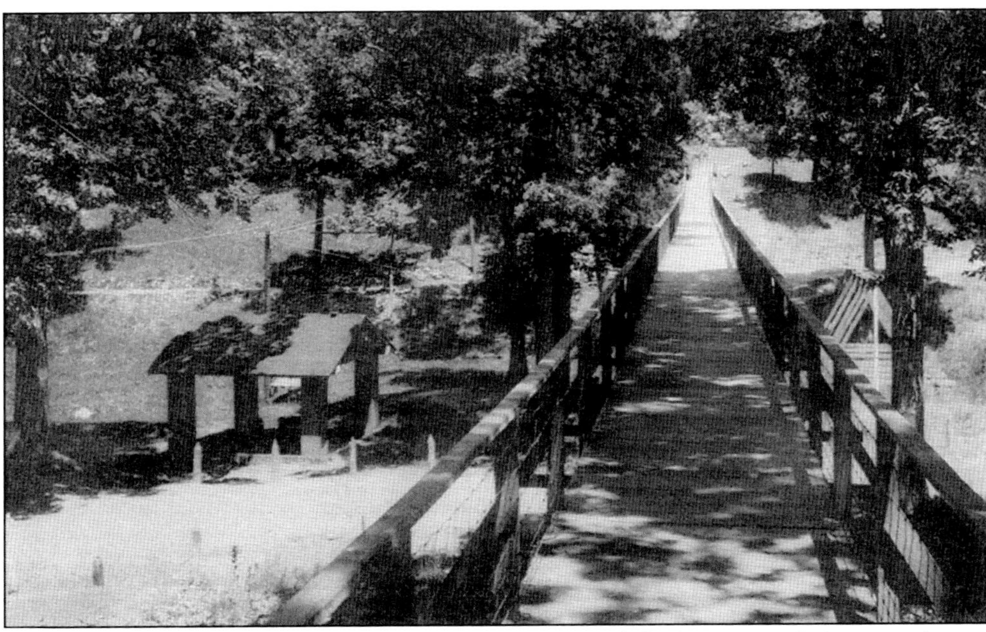

FOOT BRIDGE AT PERTLE SPRINGS. During evenings, while the sun made its westerly way, crowds of guests flocked across the long expanse of the foot bridge to the Tabernacle for worship and entertainment. The programs were varied and included music, theatre from a resident troupe, and intellectually inspiring lectures. (JCHS Collection.)

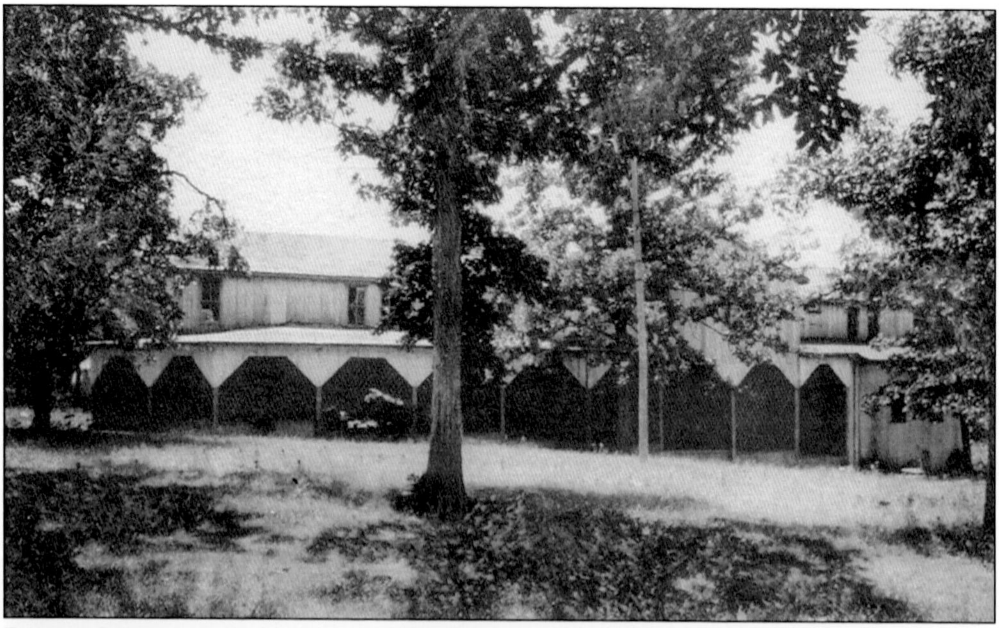

Pertle Springs Auditorium. By 1886, the Assembly Hall, capable of seating 3,000 people, had been added across the ravine from the hotel, near Stewart Cottage. Many performers trod the boards out at Pertle Springs. Travelling Chautauqua groups featured music, theater, comedy, and intellectual orators. The acoustics in this building, sometimes called the Tabernacle, were exemplary.

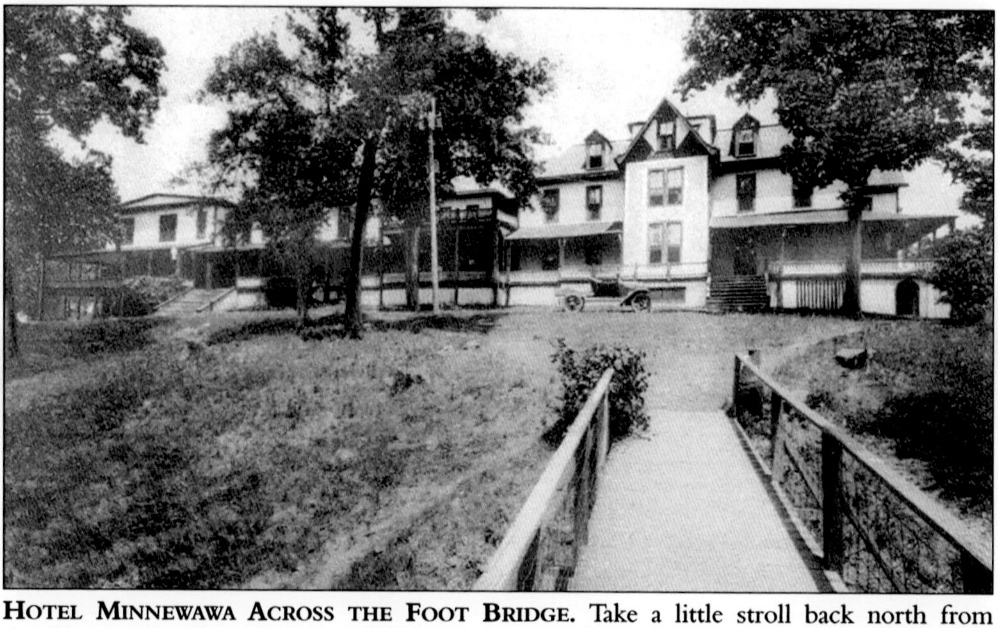

Hotel Minnewawa Across the Foot Bridge. Take a little stroll back north from the Tabernacle, across the long bridge and arrive at the immense Minnewawa hotel. The Minnewawa was an expansive rambling structure. During conventions and the high season there were no vacancies, but tents could be had and there were rooming houses back in town—a short Dummy ride away. (JCHS Collection.)

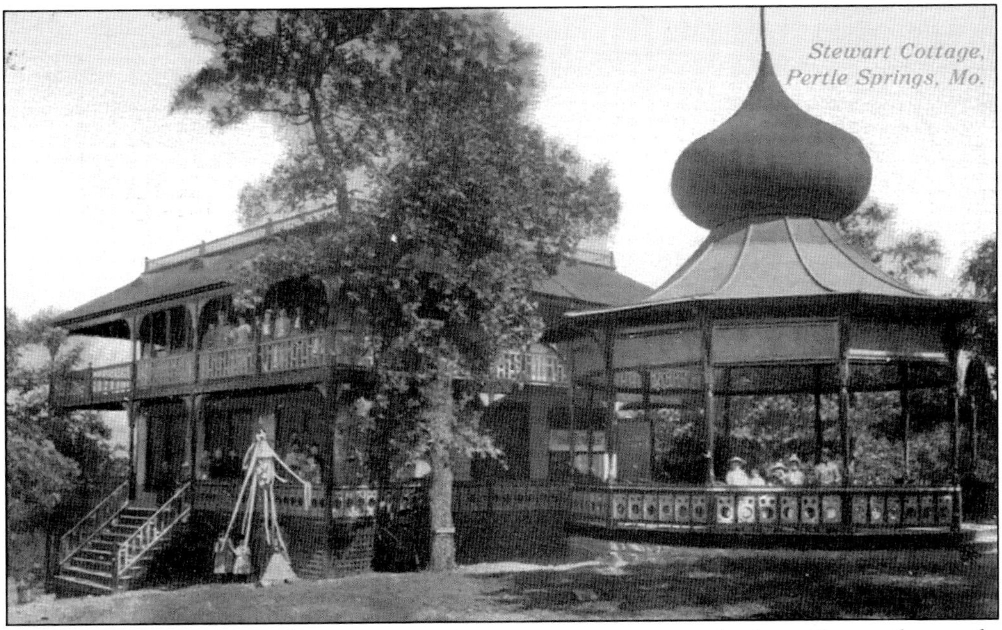

STEWART COTTAGE. There were private cottages scattered throughout the park, accommodating up to 500 people. Cena Christopher Draper described the oft-photographed Stewart Cottage, "with its golden domed roof, its picture gallery of brightly colored religious scenes, its encircling porches, its ornate hand railings." Notice the children dancing around the Maypole, as many guests watched from the magnificent porches and gazebo.

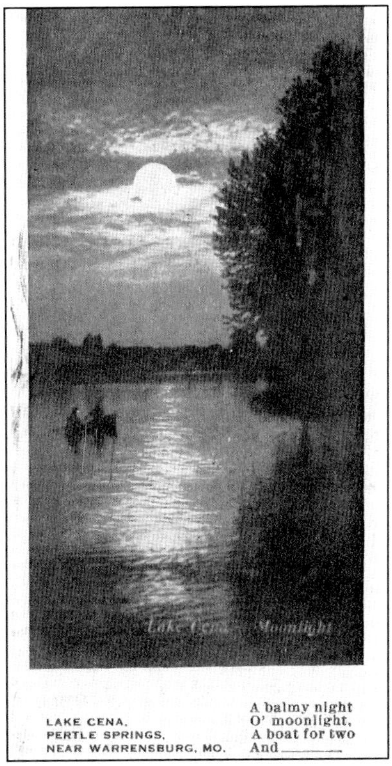

LAKE CENA BY MOONLIGHT. Good clean fun was available all day at the springs. There was a cave, a menagerie, a bowling alley, and sometimes fireworks were available. In fact, the Fourth of July celebrations were legendary. "The Eagle Screams," shouts an ad. The verse at the bottom right holds forth the promise of romance on a quiet, little boat for two.

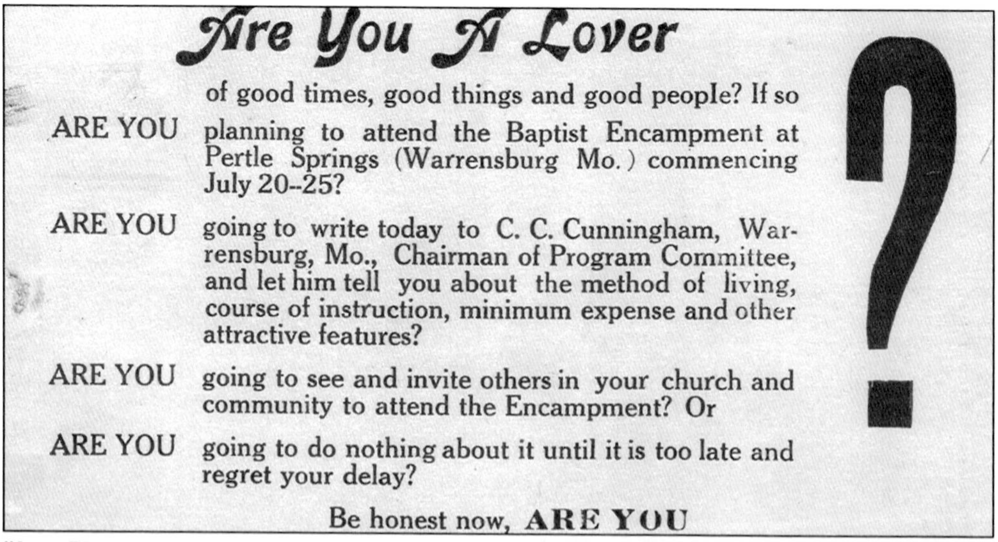

"Are You a Lover?" Huge conventions of all kinds were held at Pertle. The Baptist Encampment was one. The Dunkard convention was so large that it inspired the addition of the small railway. There were political rallies, the Missouri Pharmaceutical Convention, the State Teacher's Meeting, and more. An 1880s letter, recently found on the web, seeks to attract a religious meeting away, suggesting Hot Springs, Arkansas as an alternative.

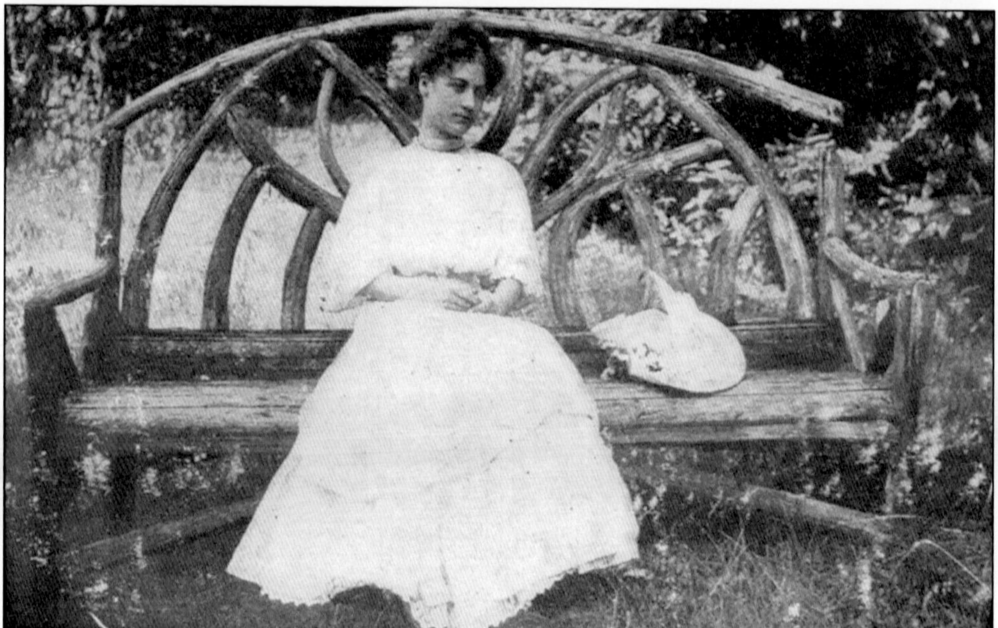

"Room For You." This young lady on a rustic bench would like some company. A gazebo matching the bench was also built and is visible in some views. J.H. Christopher built this fantastic resort, developed a water system, and promoted the electrification of town, but it was not to survive for long. A pity, looking at these scenes makes one wish for a quiet, simple outing to the south end of Holden Street.

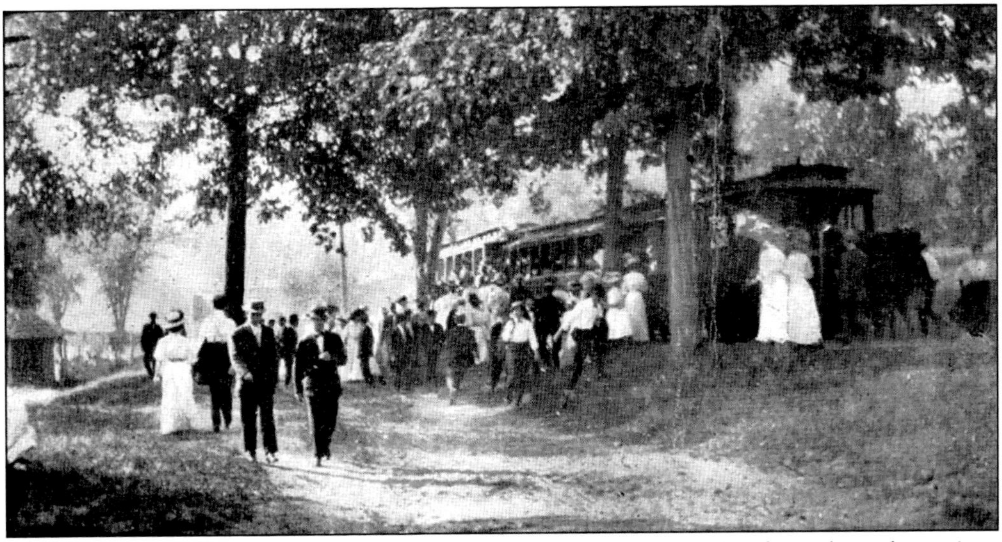

Catching the Dummy. At the end of the day there were crowds of people at the springs "depot" waiting to catch the last run to the Estes Hotel on South Holden Street downtown. Often filled to capacity, people would be standing in the aisles and on the running boards, returning from their outings of boating, fishing, bathing (for men only), entertainment, and partaking of healthful mineral water.

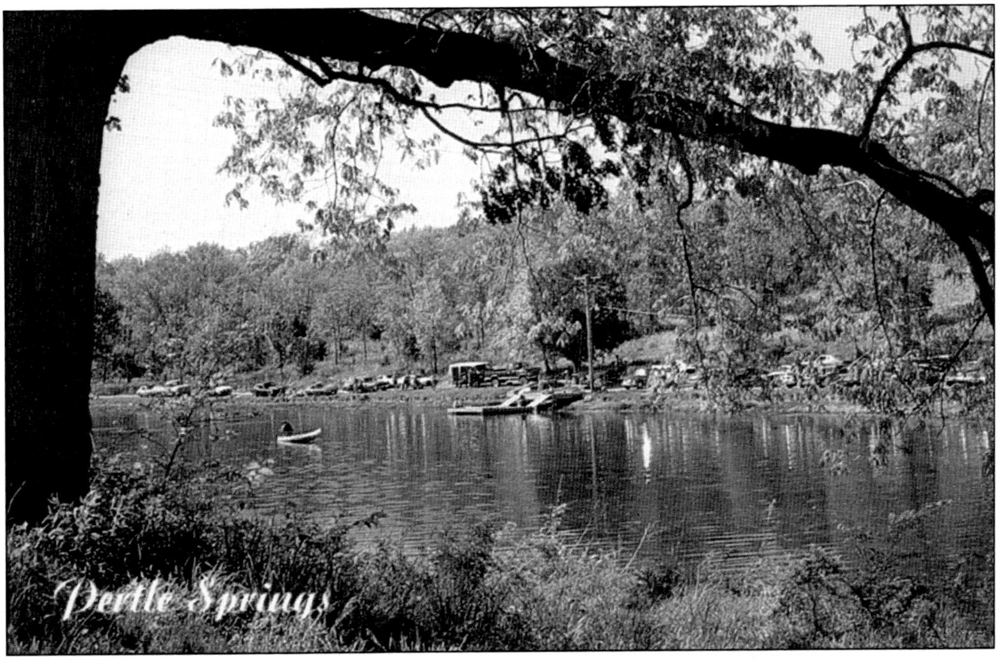

Pertle Springs Today. CMSU acquired Pertle Springs in 1959. The 300 acres now serve as a recreation spot, as well as for biological and historical research. One can still visit the area, even the spring house. By looking at old foundations and the lay of the land, one may glimpse what it might have been like to hear the little train chugging around the bend, and to hear the splashing in the water and the laughter across the lakes.

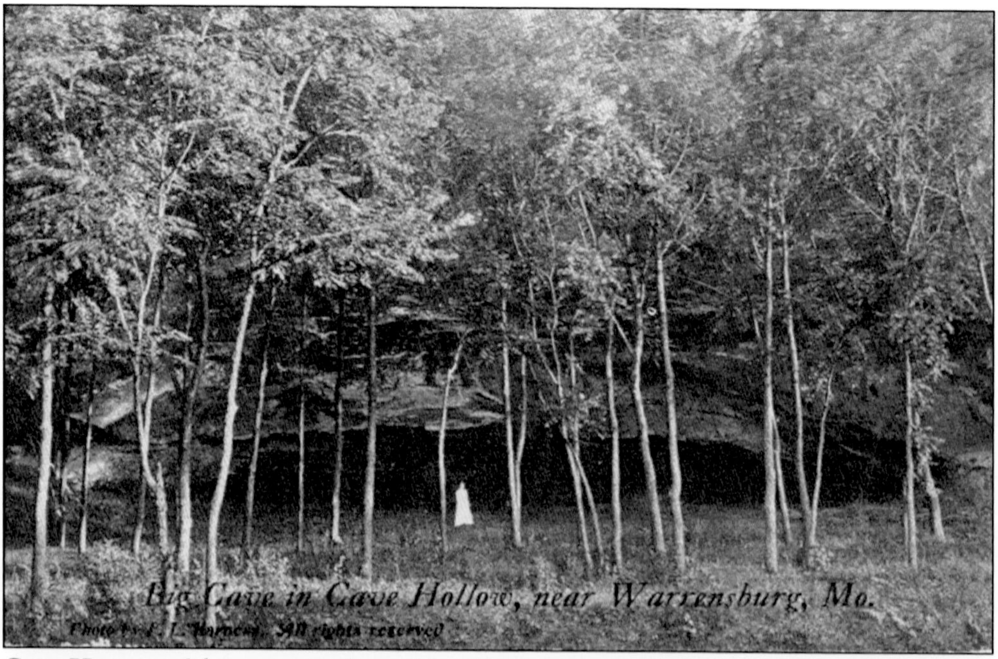

CAVE HOLLOW. A lone woman dressed in white contrasts with the large dark cave entrance at Cave Hollow. The cave, 40 ft. high, had a spring bubbling up inside. A popular site with many flowers and plants, Cave Hollow is again open at the west end of Gay Street. After serving as the city dump, the land was reclaimed for ball fields, woodland paths, and an ice skating pond. F.L. Harness, local photographer, took this *c.* 1910 photo.

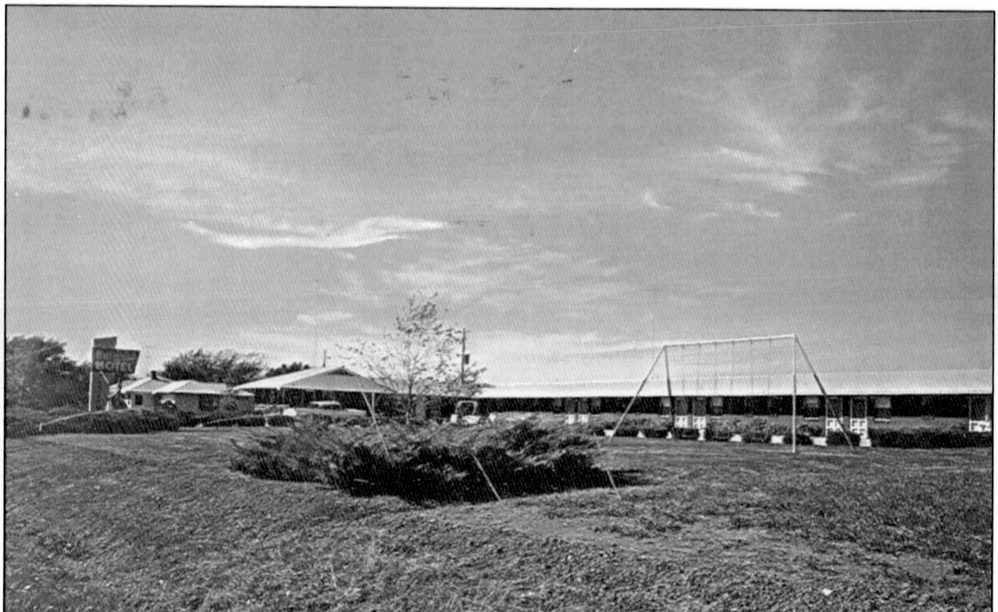

BELMONT MOTEL. The back of the card proclaims, "Steam heat, T.V., Air Conditioned," and is postmarked 1962. It is located on East Business U.S. 50.

Six

Portraits from the Past

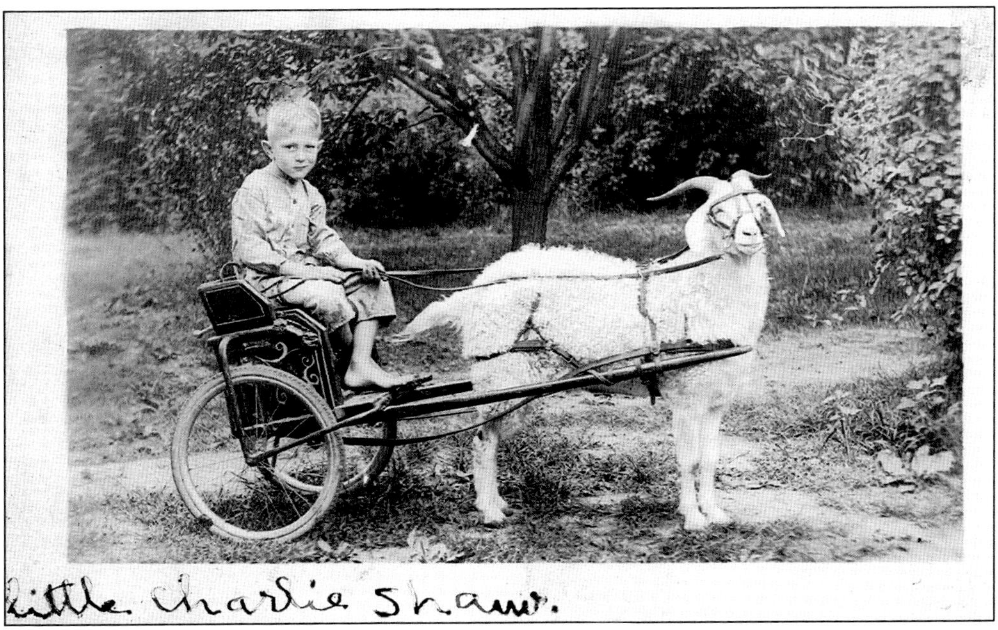

Boy and Goat Cart. Little Charlie Shaw in a wonderful goat cart. The both of them look so calm and at home, they certainly must have a working relationship, but this is not known. (Marcine Pennington Collection.)

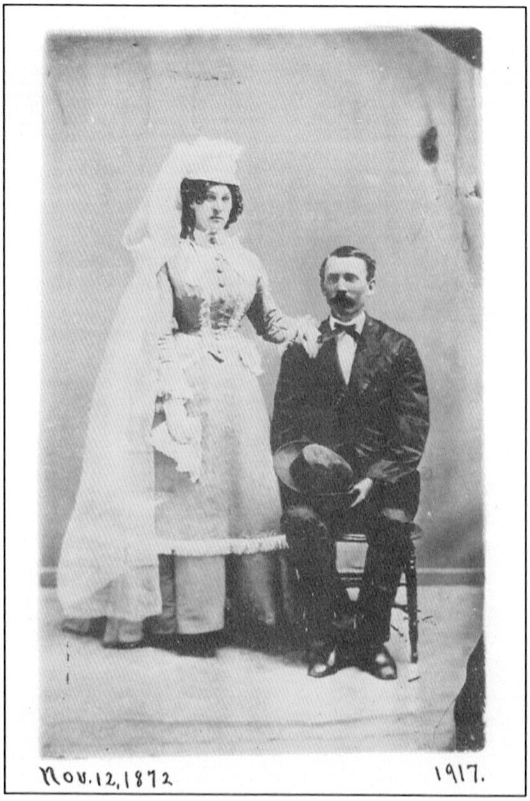

MAYES WEDDING PHOTO. Photographers reprinted old photogravures, tintypes, and daguerreotypes for special occasions. This couple, Anna Josephine Princess Lee and William James Mayes, married on November 12, 1872. Note the formal pose and different style of dress, compared to most of the postcards that are of scenes contemporary to their publication. (JCHS Collection.)

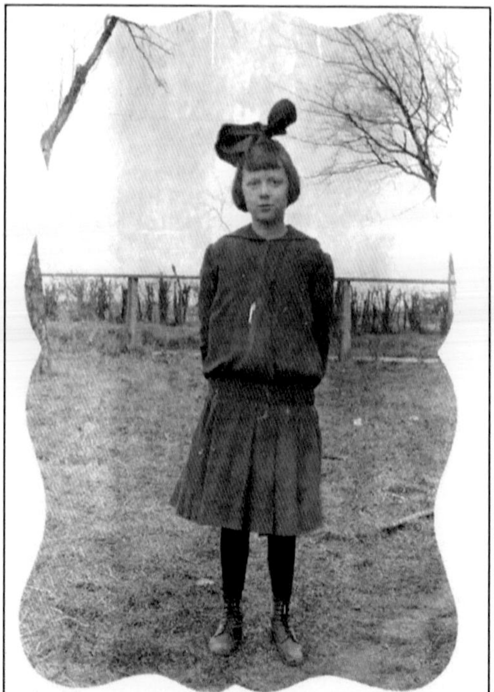

MARY ELLEN DALY. Born on December 4, 1898, Miss Daly lived at 113 Ming Street. The daughter of an early pioneer, she graduated from Central Missouri State Teachers College and was a school teacher for 50 years. The family ran the Ambrose Daly Bakery at 117 West Pine Street. She always brought birthday cake to the newspaper office. Miss Daly never married and died January 16, 1980. (JCHS Collection.)

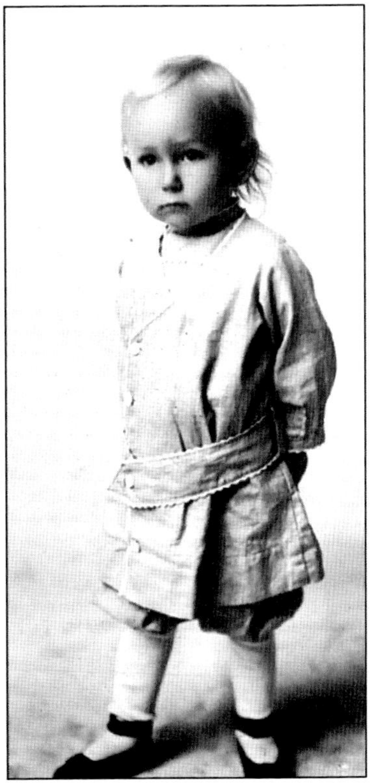

FLOYD IRLE, C. 1915. The son of Frank and Lela Irle, Centerview, appears in this dapper outfit trimmed with rickrack. Postcards announced births, deaths, and news of the weather. On another card addressed to his nephew, Mr. 'Evert' Lanning of Barnard, Missouri, and mailed January 30, 1909, George Lanning writes, "this has been a bad old day here—a blizzard. We have a new girl. She came here the 16 of this month." Both came from a postcard album prepared for Lela Lanning Irle by T.E. Lanning.

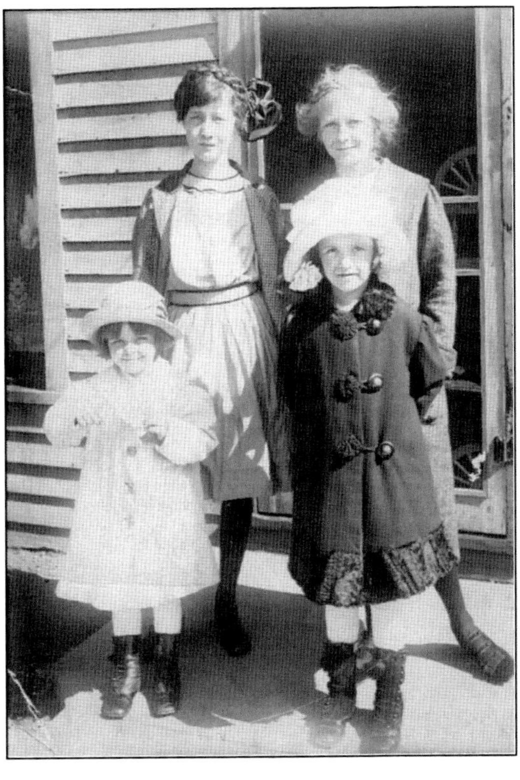

FOUR GIRLS STANDING. First names are all that are known on this card, and at one time one of the two older girls pictured gave this card to the other. She wrote, "Dear Pauline, I thought you would enjoy seeing how neat you looked & what a mess I was when we were younger. Myrt." (JCHS Collection.)

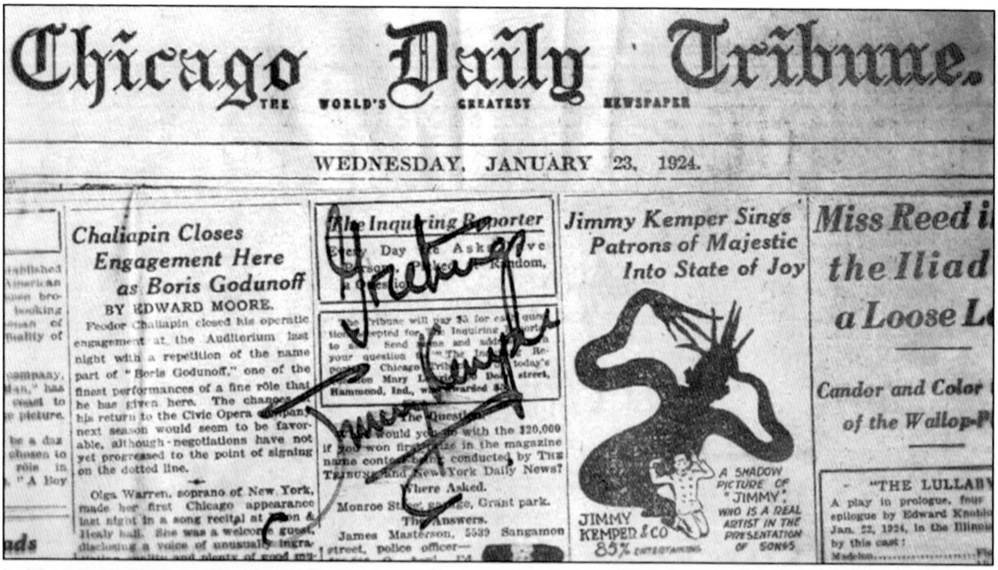

Chicago Daily Tribune.
THE WORLD'S GREATEST NEWSPAPER

WEDNESDAY, JANUARY 23, 1924.

Chaliapin Closes Engagement Here as Boris Godunoff

BY EDWARD MOORE.

Feodor Chaliapin closed his operatic engagement at the Auditorium last night with a repetition of the name part of "Boris Godunoff," one of the finest performances of a fine rôle that he has given here. The chances ... his return to the Civic Opera company next season would seem to be favorable, although negotiations have not yet progressed to the point of signing on the dotted line.

Olga Warren, soprano of New York, made her first Chicago appearance last night in a song recital at ... & Healy hall. She was a welcome guest, disclosing a voice of unusually ingra...

The Inquiring Reporter

Every Day He Asks Five Persons, Picked at Random, a Question.

The Tribune will pay $5 for each question accepted for The Inquiring Reporter ... Send name and address ... your question ... Chicago Tribune ... today's ... Mary L... Hammond, Ind., was awarded $5.

The Question.

What would you do with the $20,000 if you won first prize in the magazine name contest being conducted by THE TRIBUNE and New York Daily News?

Where Asked.

Monroe Street garage, Grant park.

The Answers.

James Masterson, 5539 Sangamon street, police officer—

Jimmy Kemper Sings Patrons of Majestic Into State of Joy

A SHADOW PICTURE OF "JIMMY" WHO IS A REAL ARTIST IN THE PRESENTATION OF SONGS

JIMMY KEMPER & CO

Miss Reed i... the Iliad a Loose L...

Candor and Color ... of the Wallop-P...

"THE LULLABY" A play in prologue, four ... epilogue by Edward Knobl... Jan. 22, 1924, in the Illinois ... by this cast:

J. KEMPER. Jimmy Kemper, the attorney's son, moved to Chicago and by 1932 was the star of a weekly broadcast, *Beautiful Thoughts*, on NBC Radio. Residents of the 'burg could tune in to listen on WREN, Lawrence, Kansas. In 1934, he was on the radio with Helen Hayes, George M. Cohan, and the Marx Brothers. He entertained the Christian Church ladies at the Vernaz home in his youth, considering this his first public performance. (JCHS Collection.)

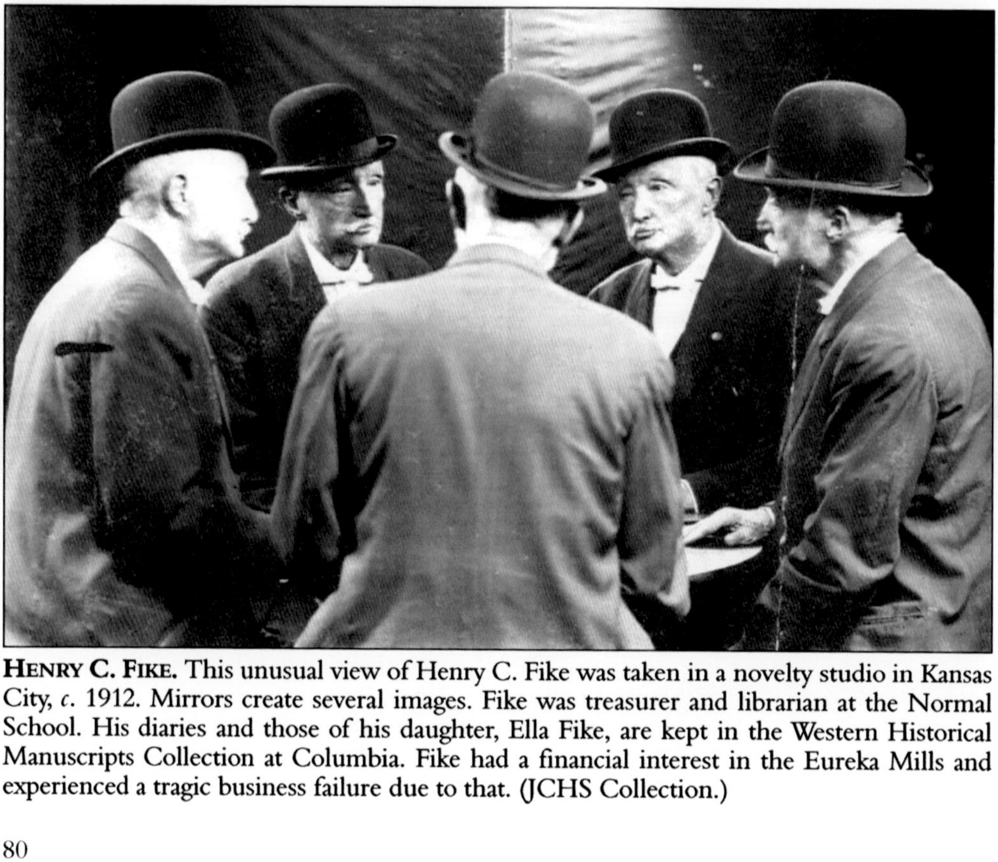

HENRY C. FIKE. This unusual view of Henry C. Fike was taken in a novelty studio in Kansas City, *c.* 1912. Mirrors create several images. Fike was treasurer and librarian at the Normal School. His diaries and those of his daughter, Ella Fike, are kept in the Western Historical Manuscripts Collection at Columbia. Fike had a financial interest in the Eureka Mills and experienced a tragic business failure due to that. (JCHS Collection.)

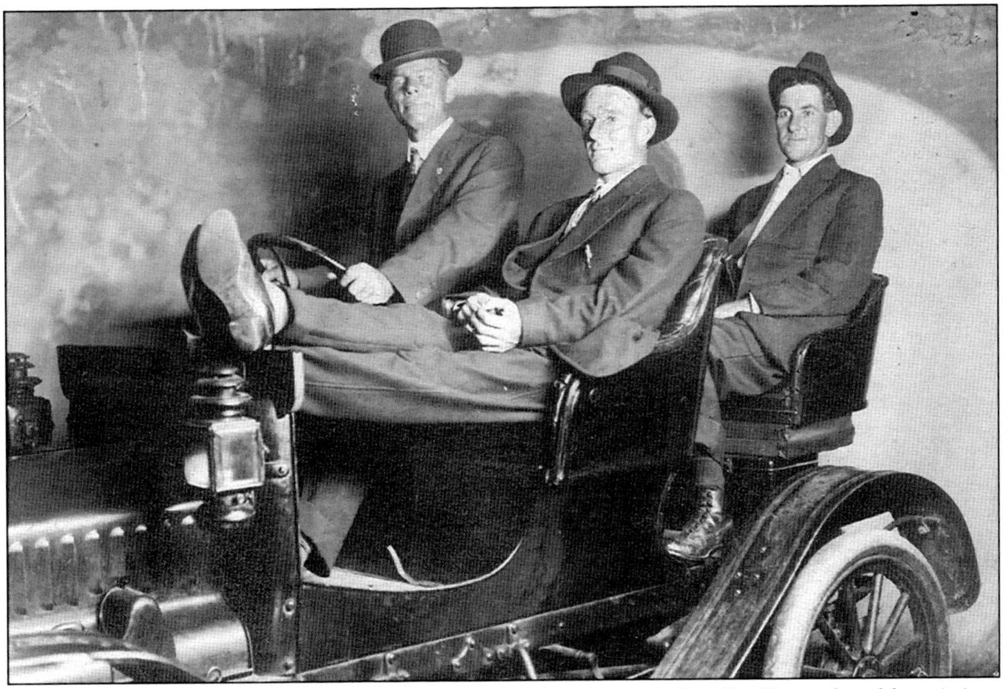

THREE MEN RELAXING IN CAR. "Dad," Hugh Rittman, and Charlie Shaw, the elder, sit in a studio photographer's prop and are photographed for all posterity—suave, men about town at their leisure. (Marcine Pennington Collection.)

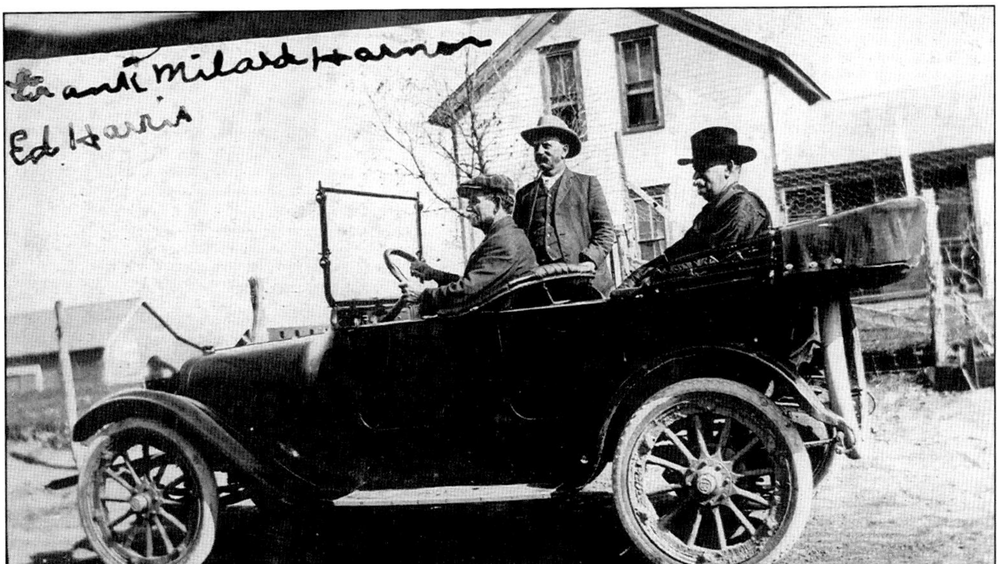

THREE MEN IN A CAR. Frank Milard Harmon and Ed Harris are two of the men identified in this view that may have been taken at the Harmon's place on Blackwater. (Marcine Pennington Collection.)

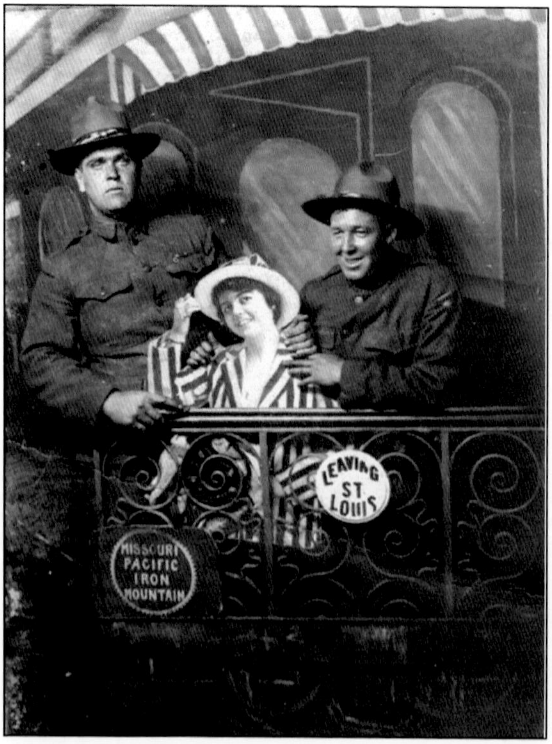

MISSOURI PACIFIC IRON MOUNTAIN. Young men, one may hope on the way home to Warrensburg from a tour of duty, pass through St. Louis and bring home this whimsical reminder of their stop. This is likely a photographer's set, the young lady a cardboard cutout. The Missouri Pacific Iron Mountain Railroad ran from Cape Girardeau to St. Louis. (Marcine Pennington Collection.)

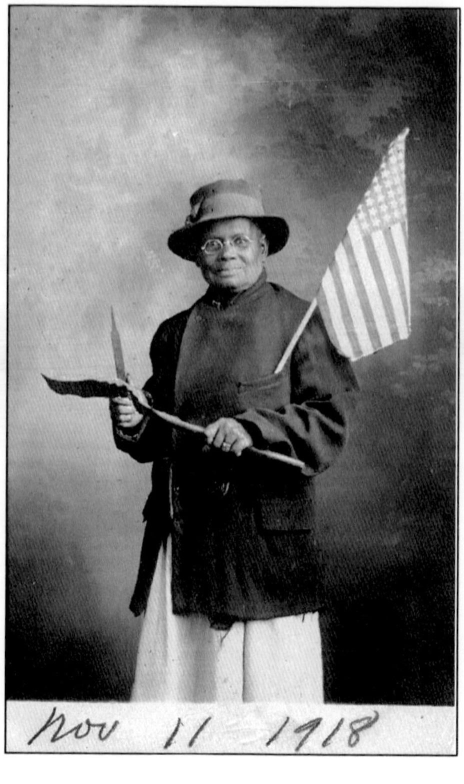

PATRIOTIC LADY. This noble lady holding a file, shovel, and flag may carry a subtle message. She was found in the scrapbook of S.R. Sweeney, the undertaker who worked both in Chilhowee and Warrensburg. The date is for Armistice Day. Her identity is unknown, as is the location. (JCHS Collection.)

MOTHER AND DAUGHTER, PERHAPS. Unidentified people, like those depicted on these cards, are captured in a moment. All that is known is that the images were collected by residents of the county. They may even have been sent to relatives and friends by far flung acquaintances. We make no claims about locale. (JCHS Collection.)

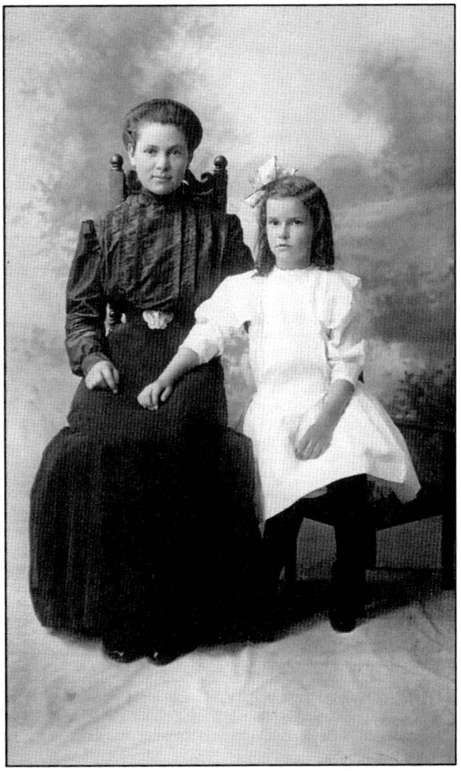

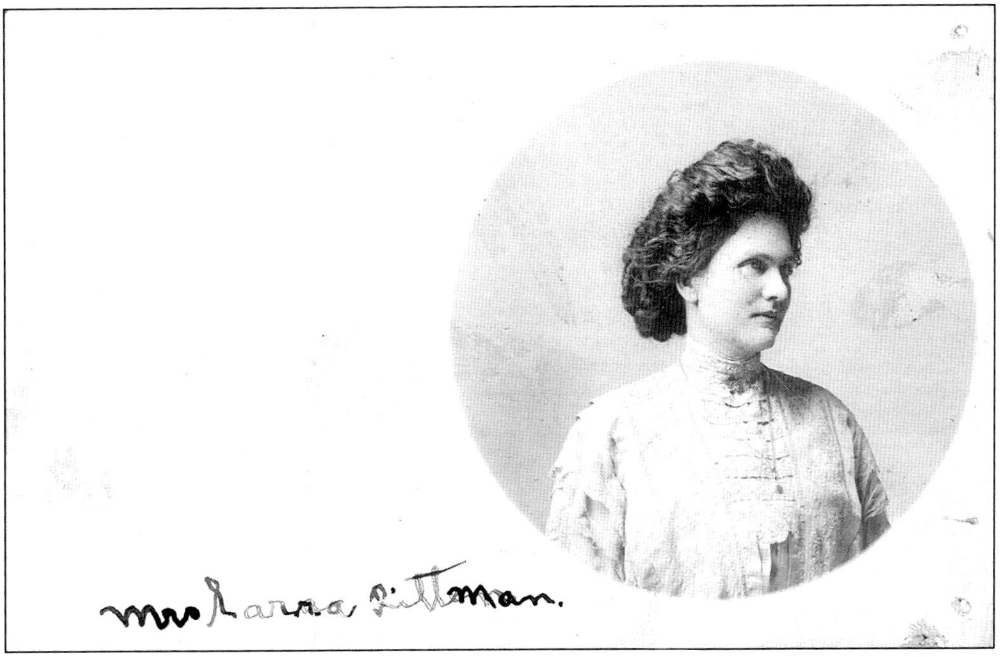

LONE LADY. She is Mrs. Larra (or Laura) Rittman, who later married James N. Wilkerson in 1909. Sometimes, even if people are identified, it is difficult to find out much about them. (Marcine Pennington Collection.)

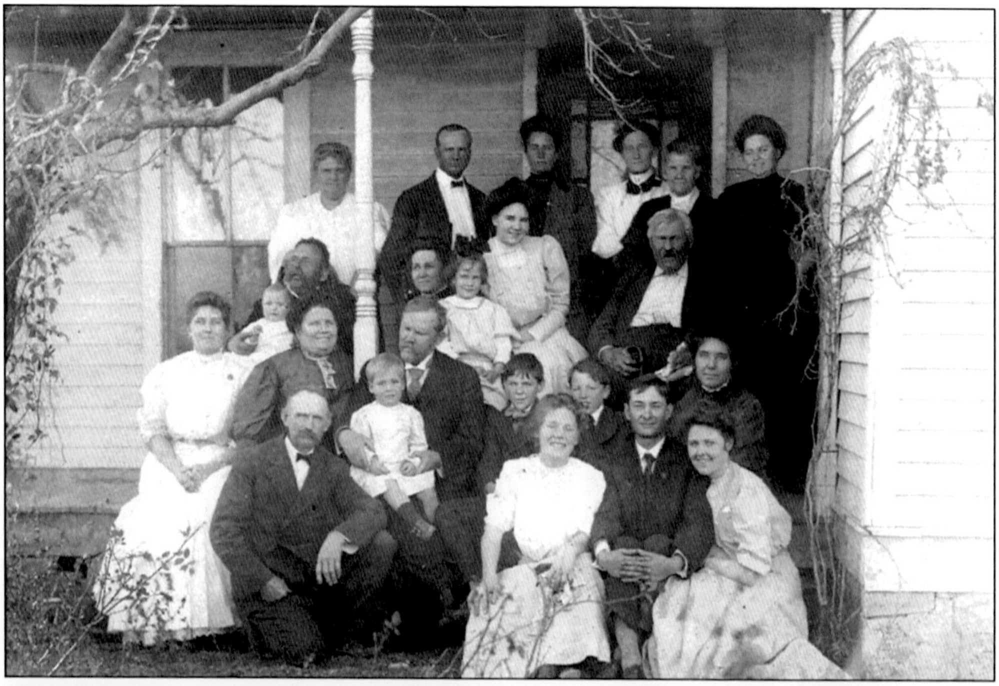

Vard Cockrell Family. On the porch of Uncle Vard Cockrell's home (perhaps in Cockrell, Missouri) the family stops for a moment, apparently in good spirits, to record their gathering. Jeremiah Vardeman Cockrell, believed to be Senator Francis Marion Cockrell's brother, is the rather imposing gentleman at right center. (JCHS Collection.)

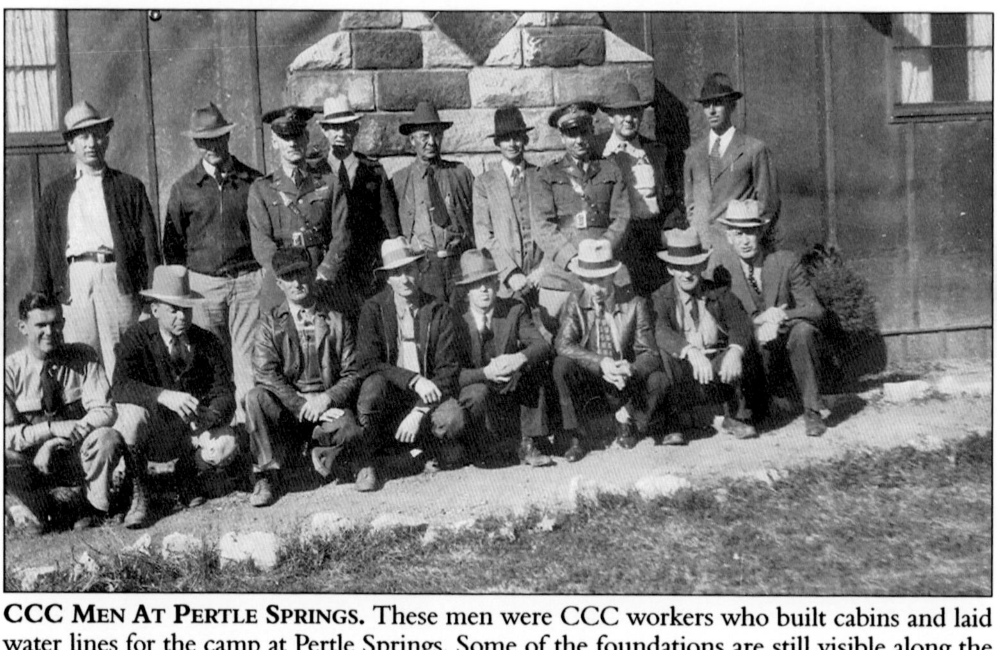

CCC Men At Pertle Springs. These men were CCC workers who built cabins and laid water lines for the camp at Pertle Springs. Some of the foundations are still visible along the trails. This photo was taken in 1936. (JCHS Collection.)

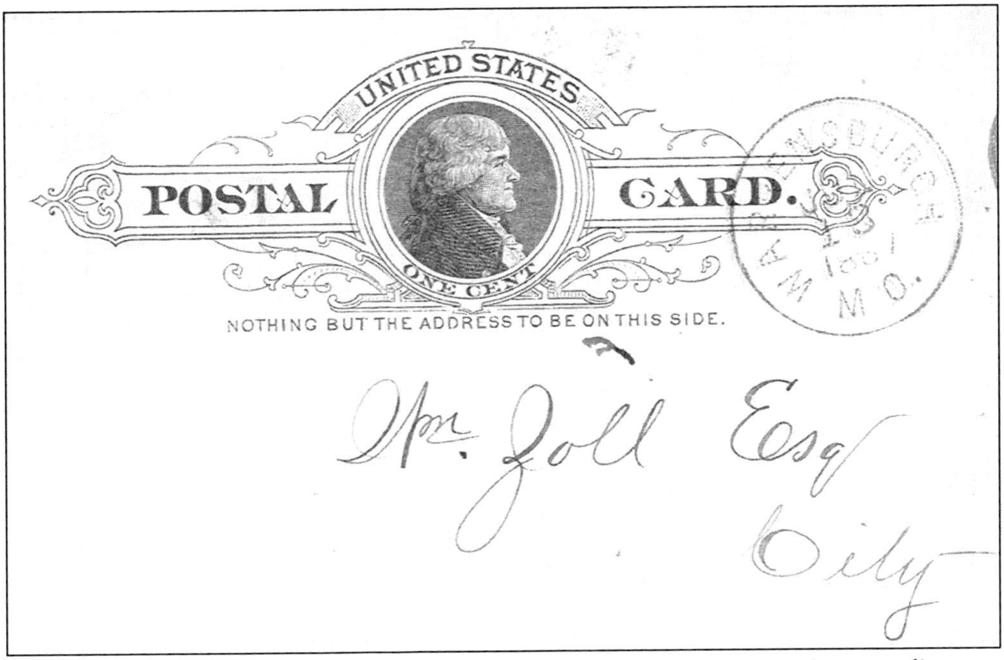

PERSONAL. Zoll was in the real estate business, according to a Missouri Gazeteer directory from 1860. Note the spelling of "Warrensburgh" on the postmark of this postal card dated August 13, 1887. It was often spelled this way in the late 1800s (*see reverse of this card, below*).

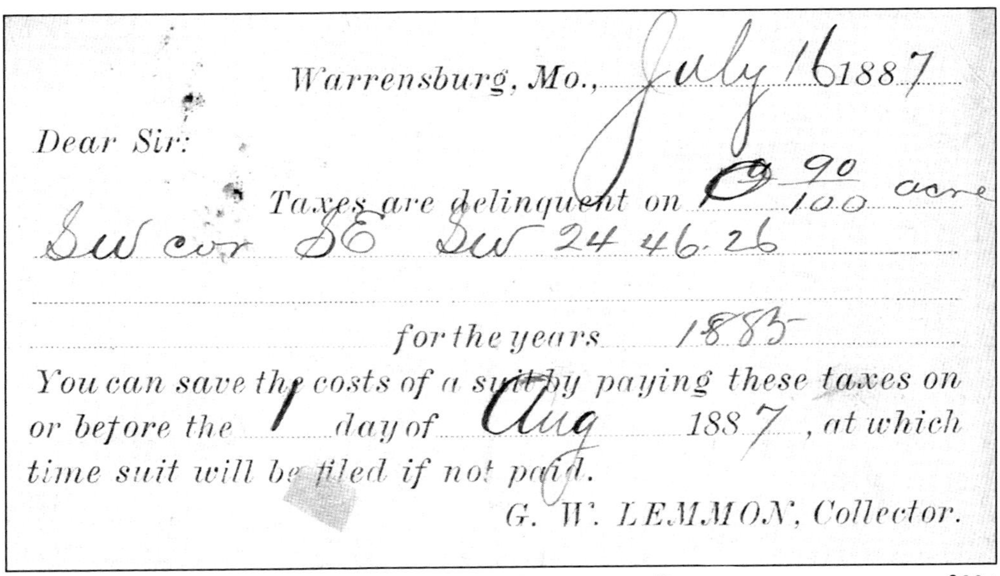

Warrensburg, Mo., July 16 1887

Dear Sir:

Taxes are delinquent on 90/100 acre SW cor SE SW 24 46 26

for the years 1885

You can save the costs of a suit by paying these taxes on or before the 1 day of Aug 1887, at which time suit will be filed if not paid.

G. W. LEMMON, Collector.

PERSONAL. Mailed to William Zoll Esq., G.W. Lemmon, collector, requests payment of 90¢ in delinquent property taxes for 1885 under the threat of a law suit. "Warrensburg" is the spelling on this side.

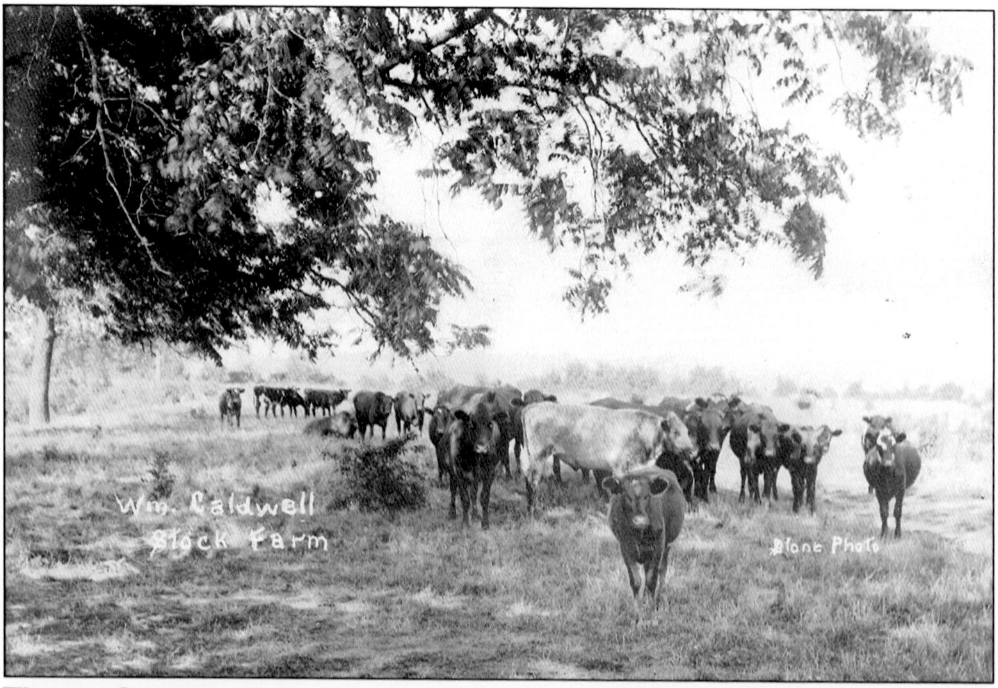

WILLIAM CALDWELL FARM. A summer scene on the William Caldwell Farm, this nice mixed herd of healthy cattle is showing great interest in Mr. Stone, the photographer. (Tom Christopher Collection.)

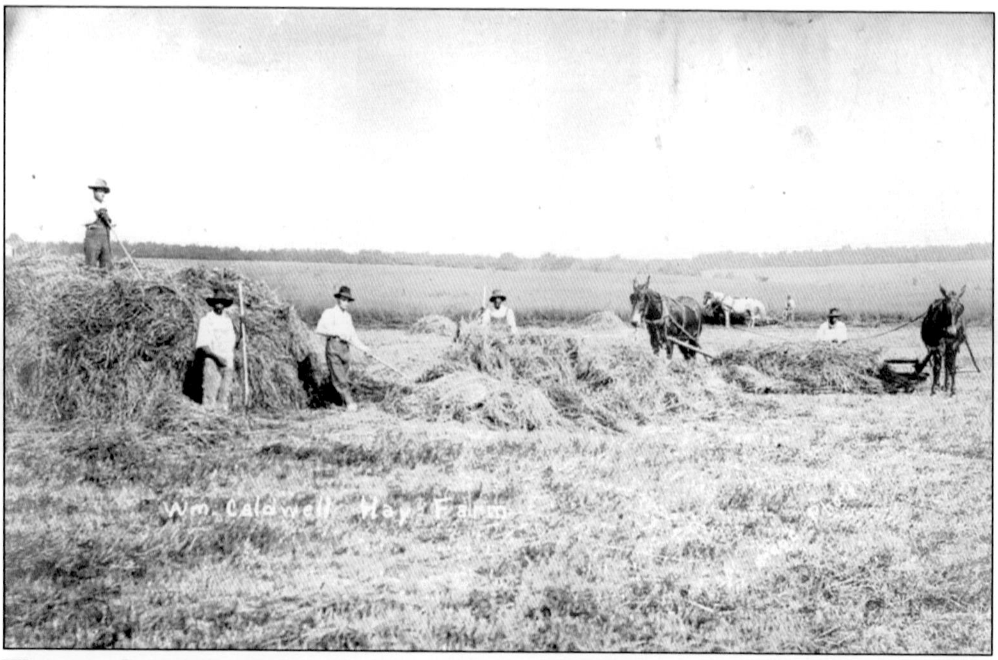

WILLIAM CALDWELL FARM. Harvesting hay on the William Caldwell Farm, two miles northwest of town. Note the dark mule team pulling the bull rake to gather the new mown hay into manageable stacks. (Tom Christopher Collection.)

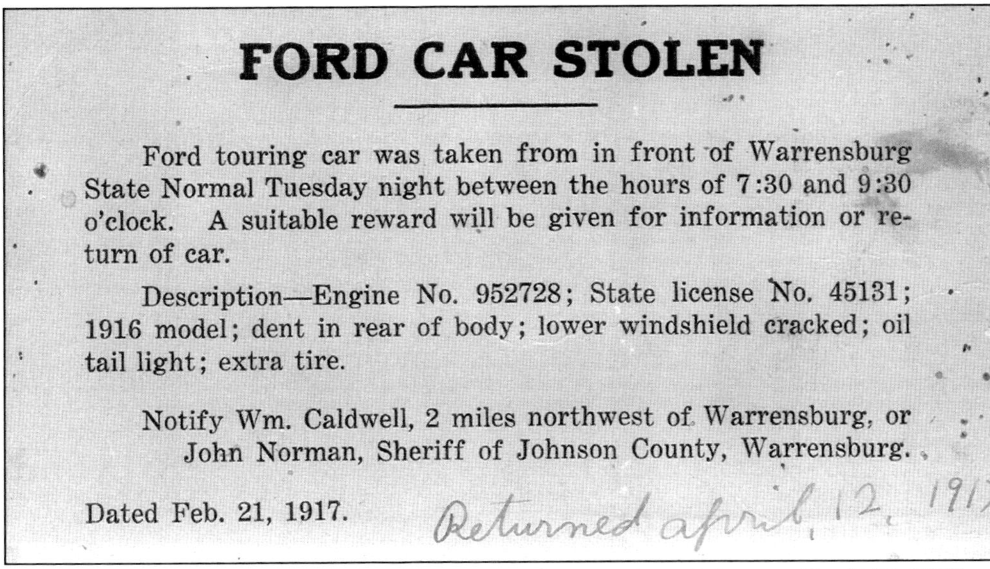

FORD CAR STOLEN

Ford touring car was taken from in front of Warrensburg State Normal Tuesday night between the hours of 7:30 and 9:30 o'clock. A suitable reward will be given for information or return of car.

Description—Engine No. 952728; State license No. 45131; 1916 model; dent in rear of body; lower windshield cracked; oil tail light; extra tire.

Notify Wm. Caldwell, 2 miles northwest of Warrensburg, or John Norman, Sheriff of Johnson County, Warrensburg.

Dated Feb. 21, 1917. Returned april 12, 1917

WILLIAM CALDWELL AUTO THEFT. On Tuesday evening, February 20, 1917, William Caldwell parked his car near the north entrance of the Normal campus, while he and his family attended a basketball game. It was stolen, but later returned on April 12. The thieves originally tried to take a different car, but when unsuccessful in getting it started chose Caldwell's vehicle instead. (Tom Christopher Collection.)

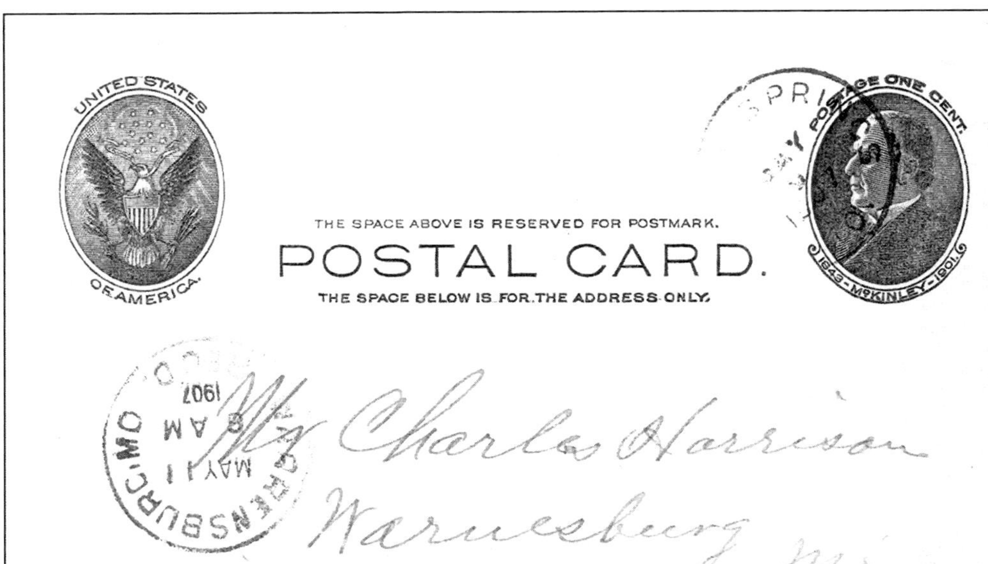

CHARLES H. HARRISON. C.H. Harrison, "the book man," owned a book store on Holden Street, in close proximity to the railroad station. He was a publisher of postcards, which he sold from his store. One interesting feature of collecting postcards is that most were sent out of the area. You never know where Warrensburg might turn up. (JCHS Collection.)

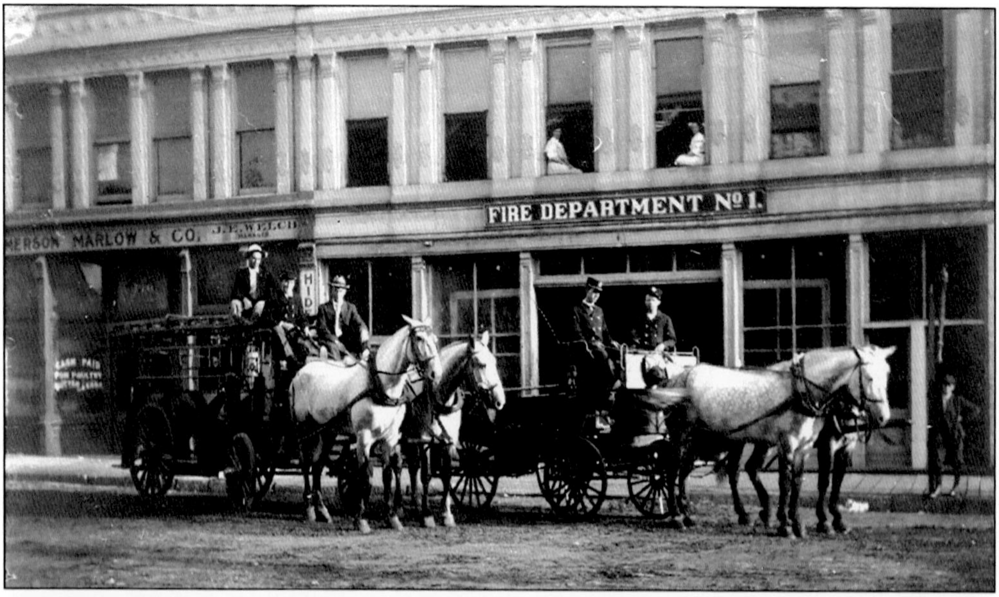

Fire Department. Some ladies are perched in the windows and wooden sidewalks with sandstone curbs line the streets. In September of 1892, the first fire equipment was purchased for $890, including a hose cart, fire engine, and a hook and ladder wagon. The first location of the fire department was on West Pine Street, between the present day Fan Club Restaurant and Those Were the Days antiques and collectables. (JCHS Collection.)

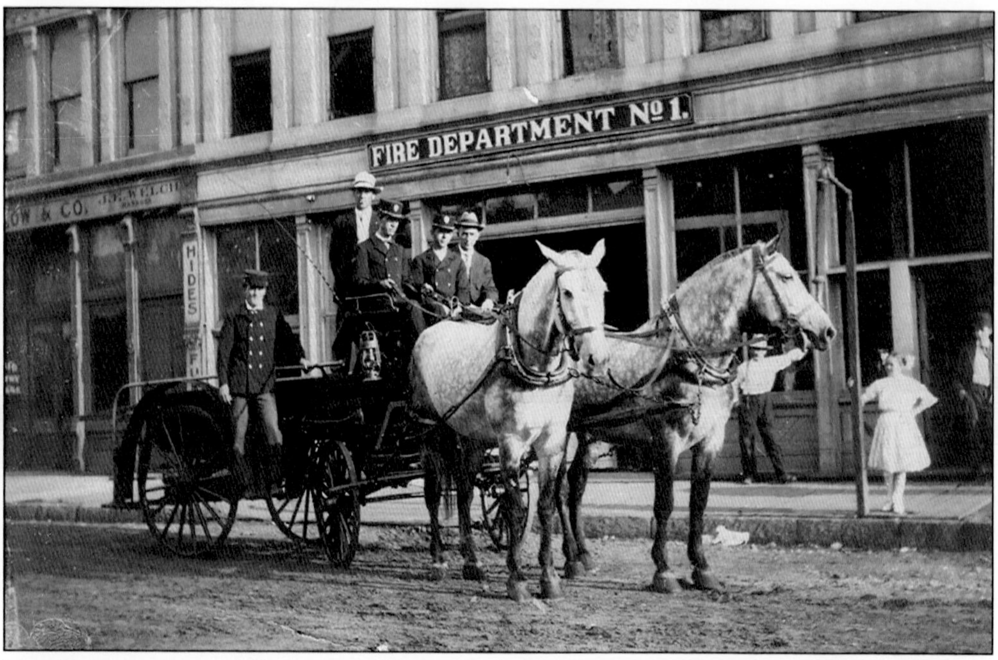

Fire Department. A fine team of horses pull this wagon for the safety of Warrensburg. A little girl and two gentlemen look on. Emerson Marlow & Co., and J.J. Welch do business right next door to Fire Department No. 1 on West Pine Street. Hides and Furs are a part of their trade. (JCHS Collection.)

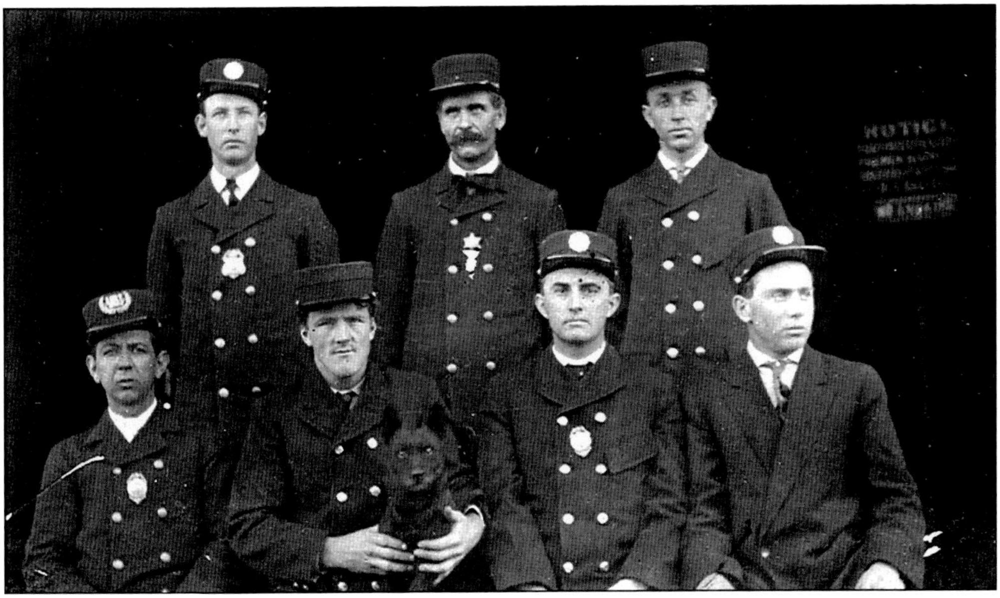

FIREMEN. These are the men of the Fire Department of Warrensburg, some decorated, with their faithful canine companion. We can't make out the notice to the right. (JCHS Collection.)

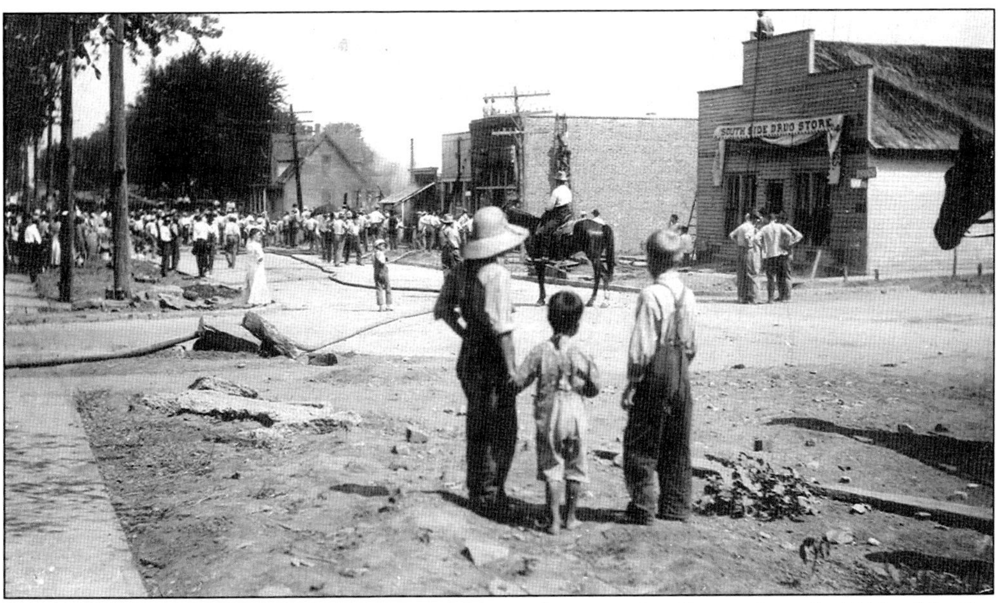

FIRE NEAR THE CORNER OF MAGUIRE AND CLARK. On September 4, 1913, this fire destroyed several businesses, including Williams Grocery, VanMeter Barbershop, and M.J. Riggle's barn. Three boys curiously watch the goings-on as the fire is being brought under control. Also affected by the fire was South Side Drugs, to the far right, at the corner of Clark and Maguire Streets, a.k.a., "Buente Town." (JCHS Collection.)

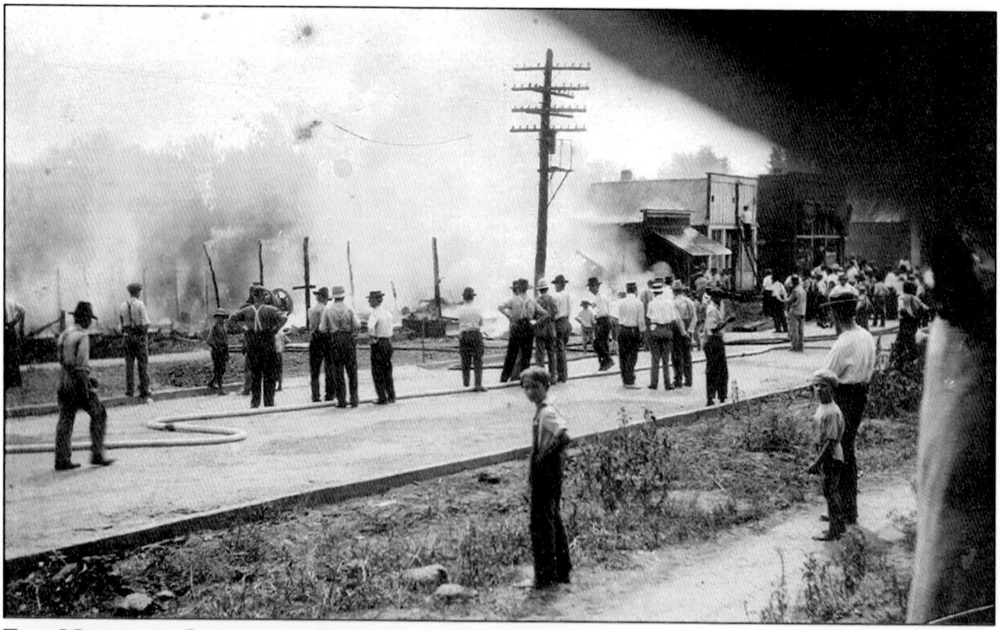

Fire Near the Corner of Maguire and Clark. Crowds of people, drawn by the fire and smoke, anxiously watch the battle to subdue the blaze. The cause of the fire was unknown, but careless smoking was suspected. (JCHS Collection.)

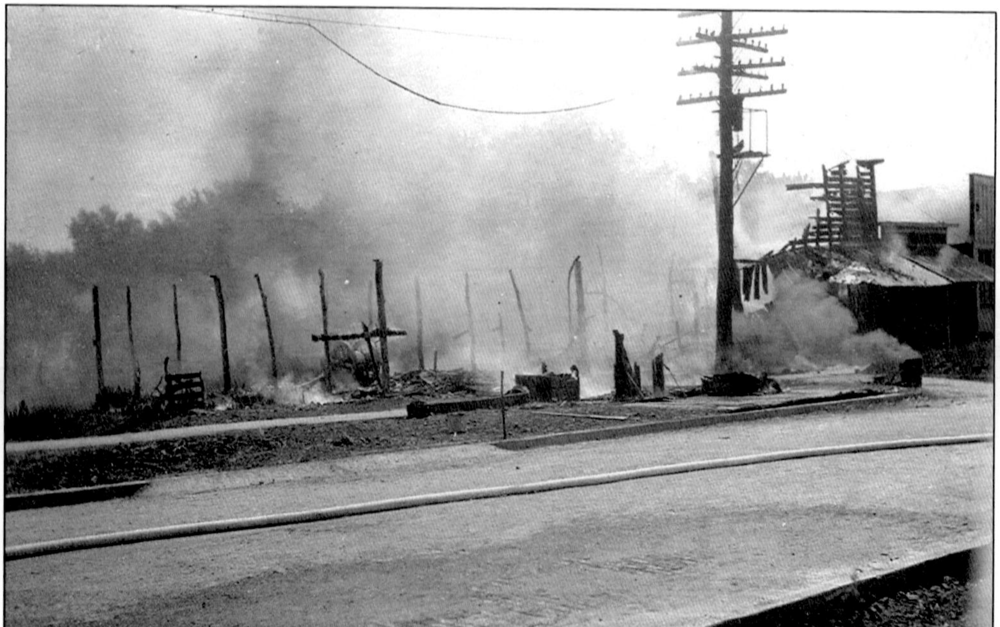

Fire Near the Corner of Maguire and Clark. The lingering clouds of smoke signal that the fire is essentially extinguished. There was little wind that day, which helped prevent an even worse disaster. (JCHS Collection.)

Seven

Neighbors

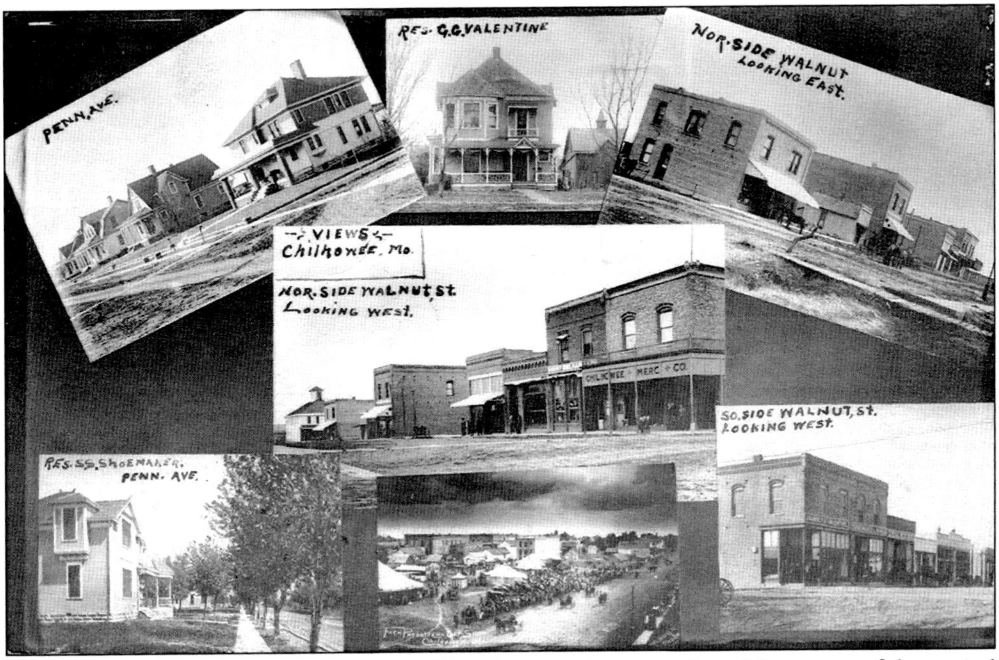

Multiview of Chilhowee Streets. The photographer was advertising some of the period postcards available, such as residences of G.G. Valentine & S.S. Shoemaker, a residential street scene, downtown buildings, and the Colt Show. The card has a 1913 postmark.

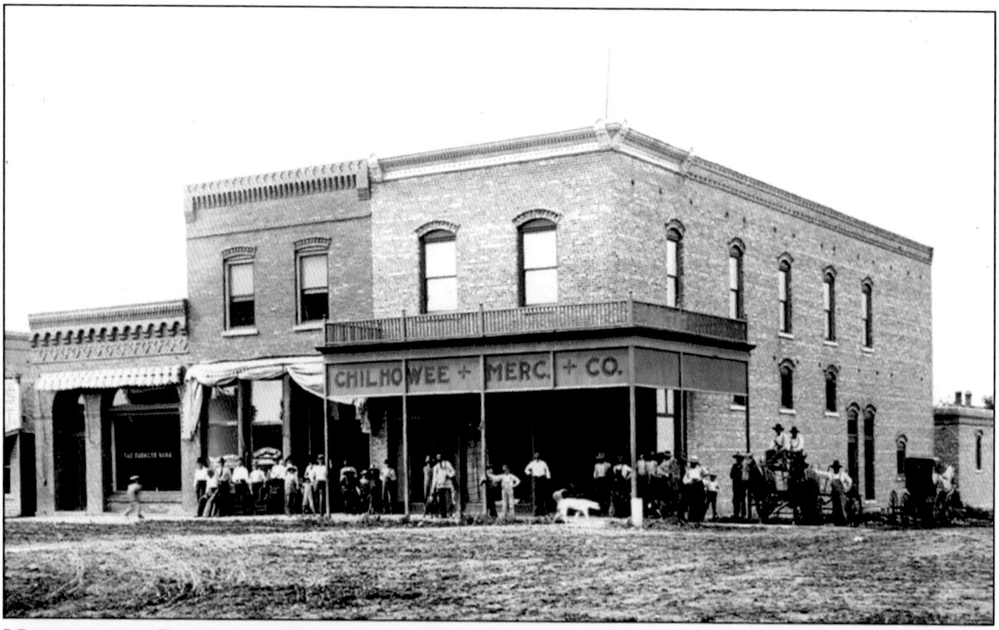

NORTHWEST CORNER OF WALNUT & PENNSYLVANIA. This *c.* 1910 view shows storefronts that are much the same today. The Chilhowee Mercantile Co. is now Chilhowee Stores Inc. The Farmer's Bank became the post office for a period of time, and is currently the Chilhowee Café. The small structure standing behind the Chilhowee Merc. Co. building was for storage. Only the foundation remains.

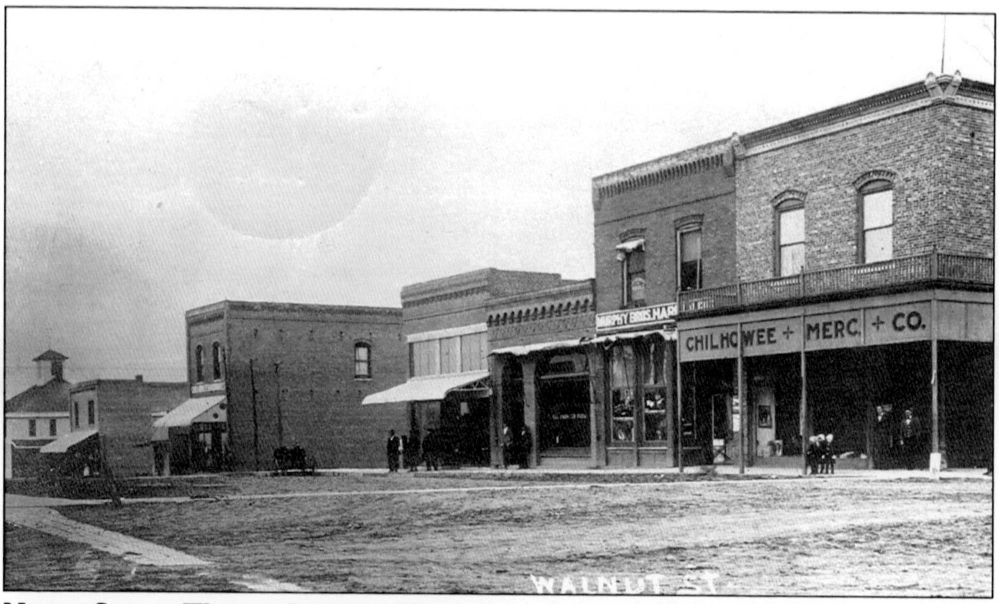

NORTH SIDE OF WALNUT LOOKING WEST. A new brick building occupies the lot west of the bank in 1912. NYP Corporation is its present occupant. The name Murphy Bros. Hardware can be seen on the next building and the Chilhowee Hardware store is farther west. In the far left background is the Big Store, which was constructed in Old Chilhowee, by Jonas A. Young in 1876, and moved when the town was relocated. It burned in 1912.

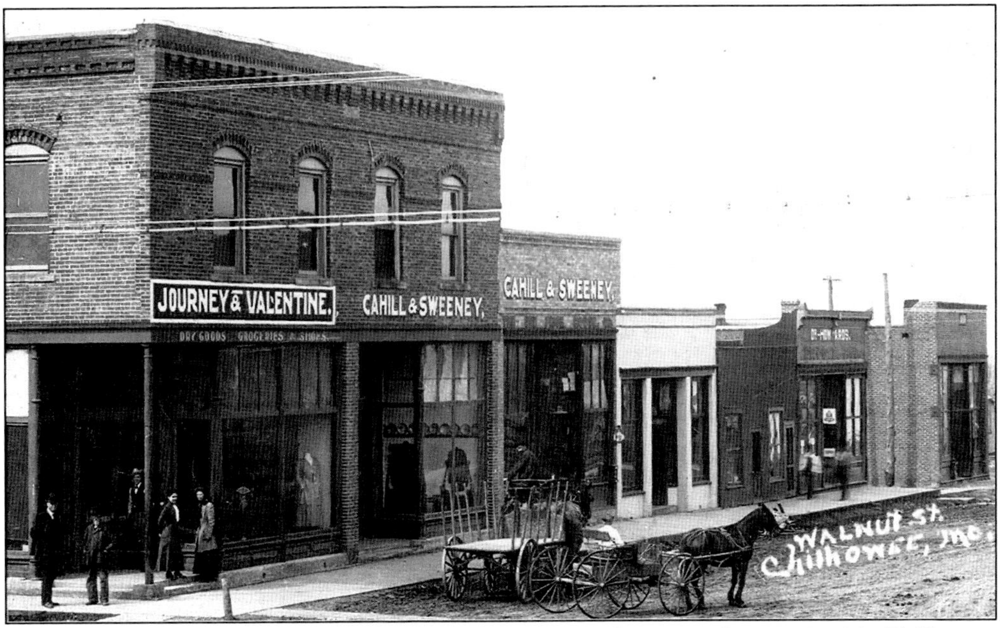

SOUTH SIDE OF WALNUT LOOKING WEST. Seven store fronts can be seen in this Chilhowee photo. Postmarked 1910, this card shows a Bell Telephone sign on the front of the Dr. Howard's drugstore. The date at the top of the Journey & Valentine and Cahill & Sweeney two-story buildings is 1907. The brick building at the extreme right no longer stands, but a frame building, Justsusans beauty salon, serves customers there today.

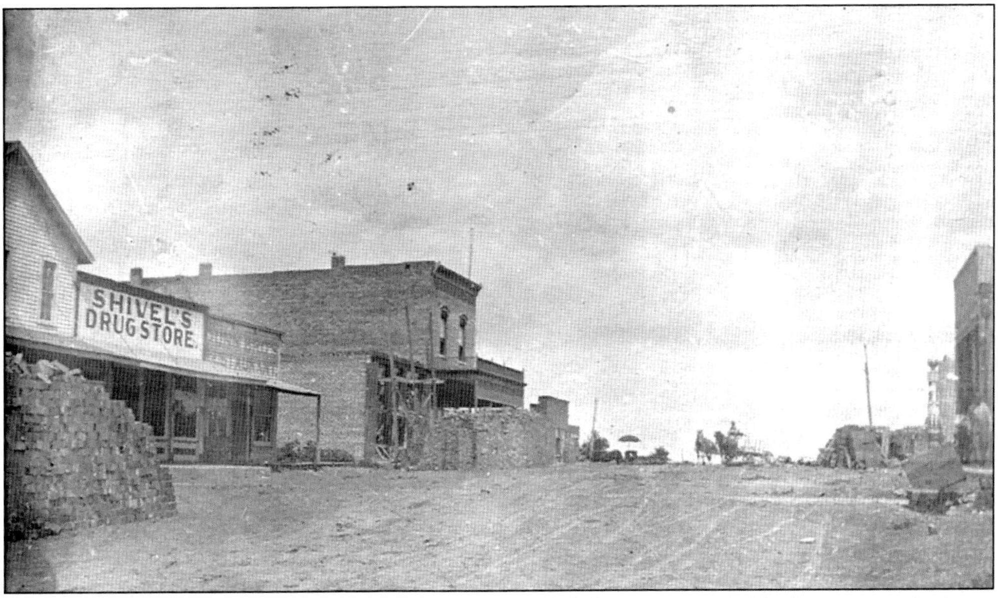

NORTH SIDE OF WALNUT LOOKING EAST. Mailed August 23, 1907, this postcard shows Walnut Street viewed to the east. A stack of bricks (extreme left) are probably those for the construction of the Chilhowee Hardware. Next is an unidentified two-story frame building, followed by Shivel's Drugstore, John Bros. Restaurant, and the first floor of a two-story brick building under construction.

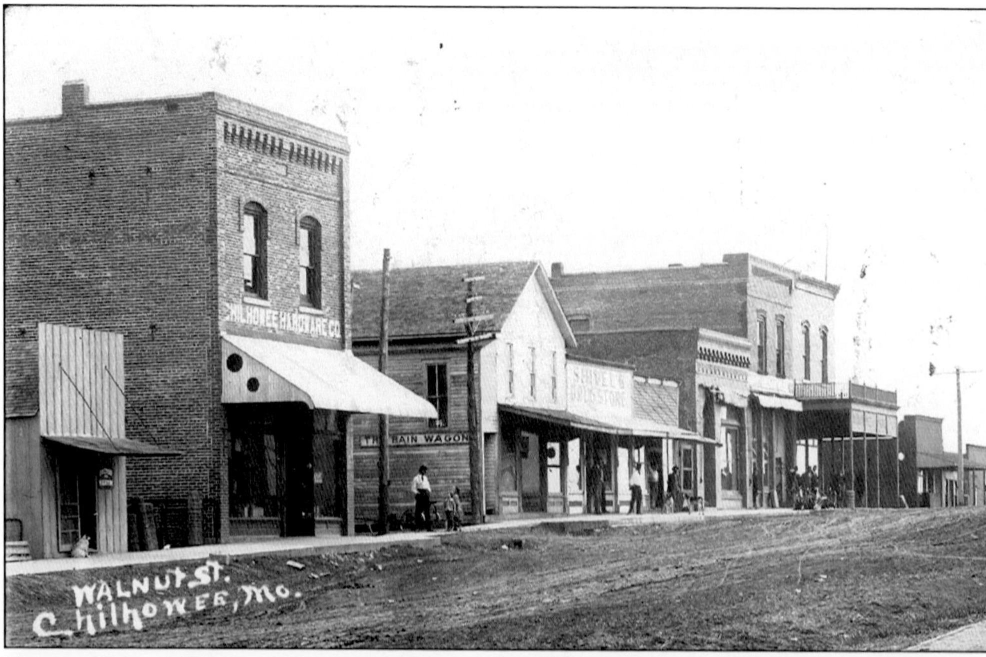

North Side of Walnut Looking East. In 1910, the Chilhowee Hardware is complete, the Murphy Bros. Hardware building now has its second floor, and the Farmer's Bank has been built. At left is a tiny frame office for Dr. Martin, where a dog "patiently" waits at the door.

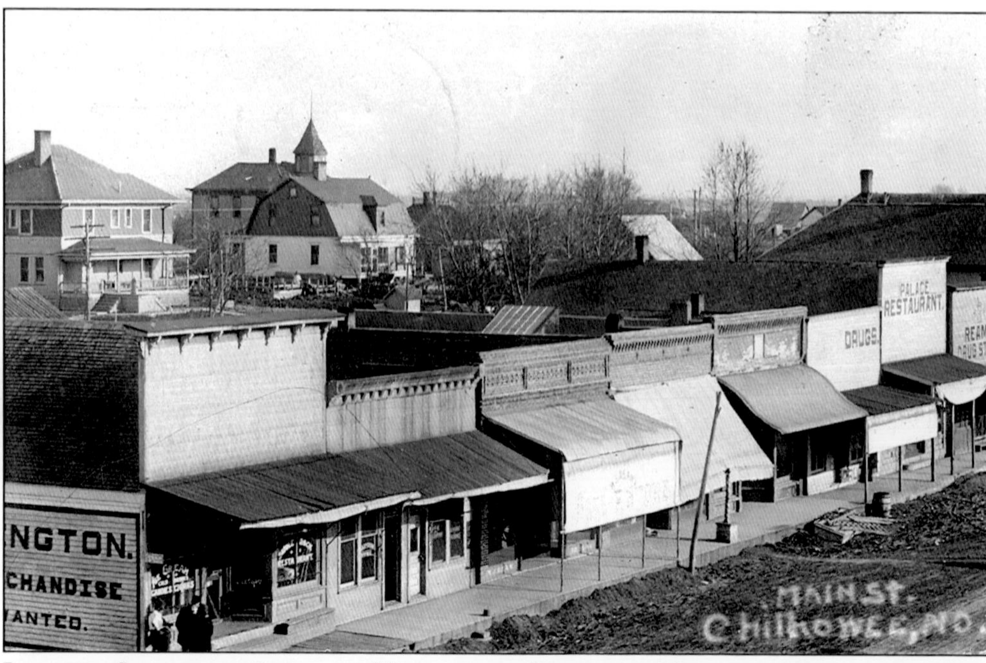

Looking Southeast From the Northwest Corner of Main and Walnut Streets. This *c.* 1910 Chilhowee view from the top of the Big Store shows several stores along Main Street, some homes on Pennsylvania Avenue, and the first school in town (the building with the bell tower).

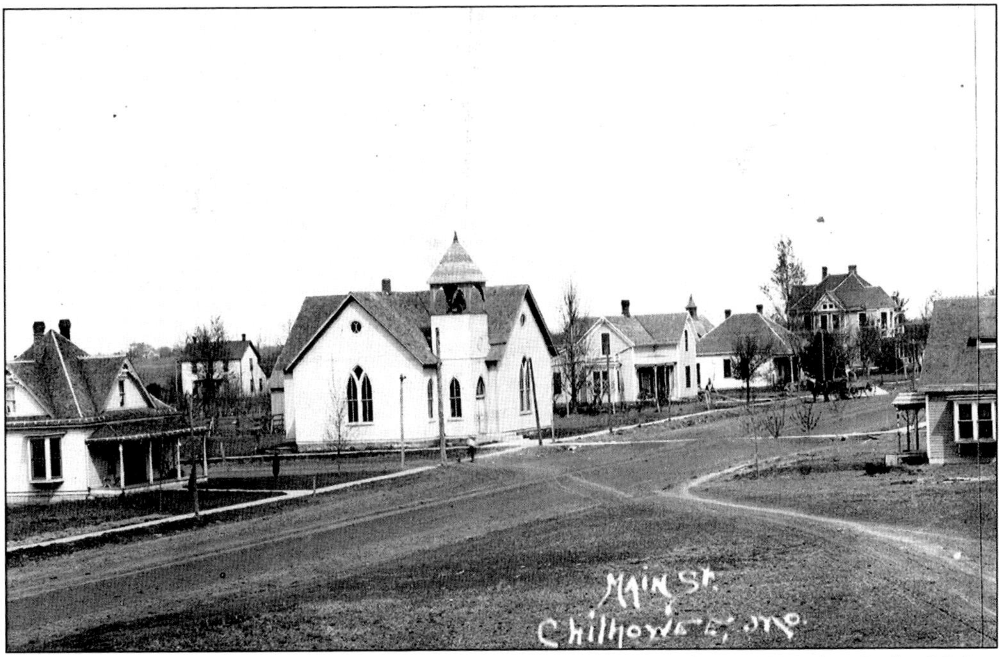

Chilhowee Union Church. The "Center of Attraction" in this *c.* 1910 shot is the Union Church. While the building no longer exists, some of the windows can still be seen in a building on a farm at the south side of Missouri Highway 2 as you travel east of town.

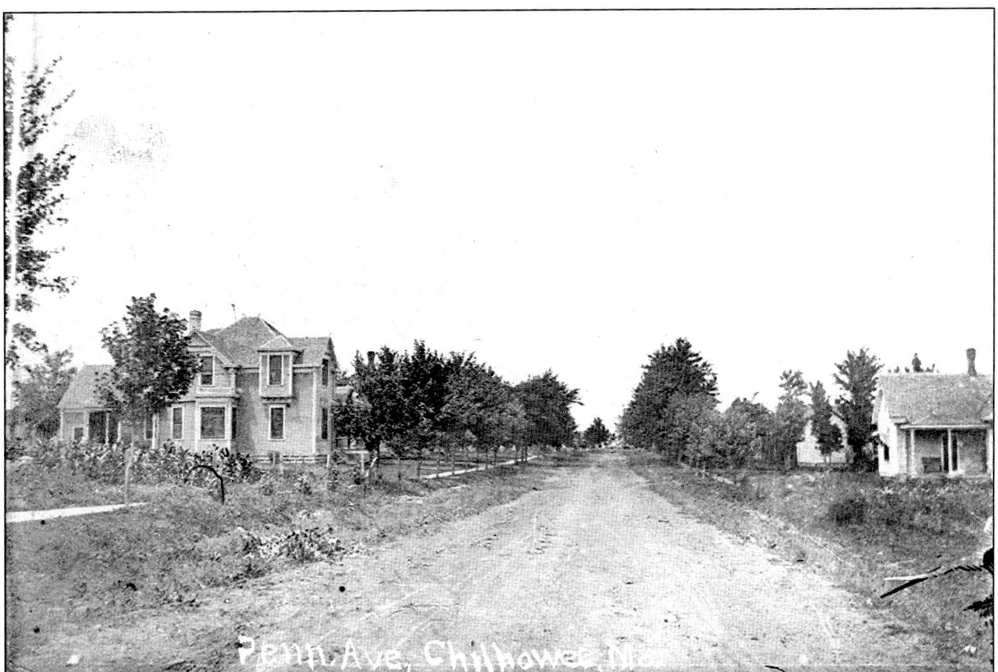

Pennsylvania Street Looking North. Chilhowee resident Sell Shoemaker's newly constructed home is on the west side of Pennsylvania Avenue. This is how it might have looked from the corner of Walnut Street around 1908.

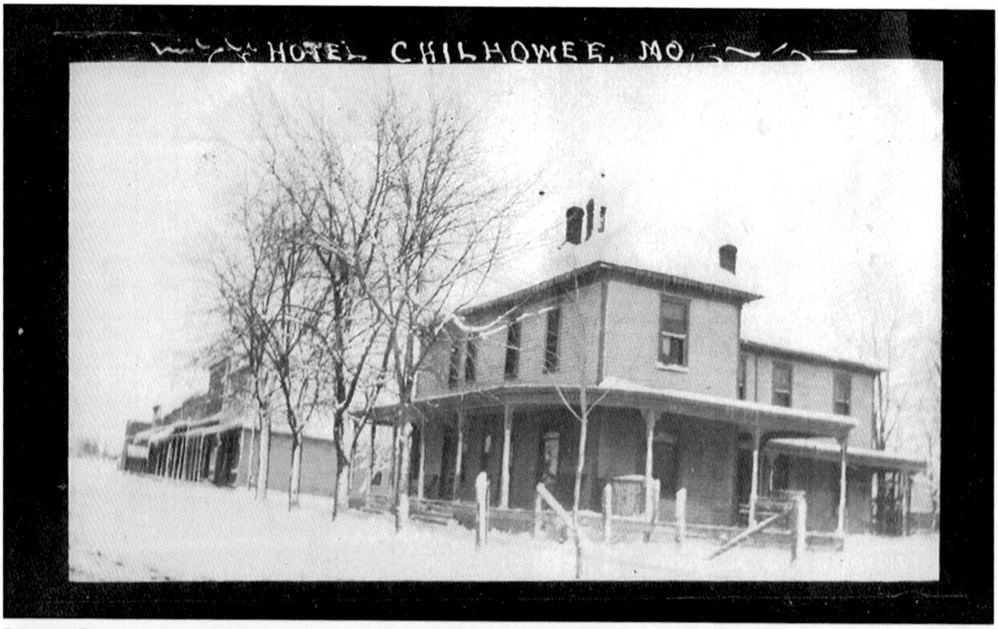

MAIN STREET LOOKING NORTH. In 1915, if you arrived via the Katy you were just a half block from the Chilhowee Hotel on Main Street. Within the next block were restaurants, drugstores, mercantile stores, grocery stores, and hardware stores, as well as doctors' offices and a bank.

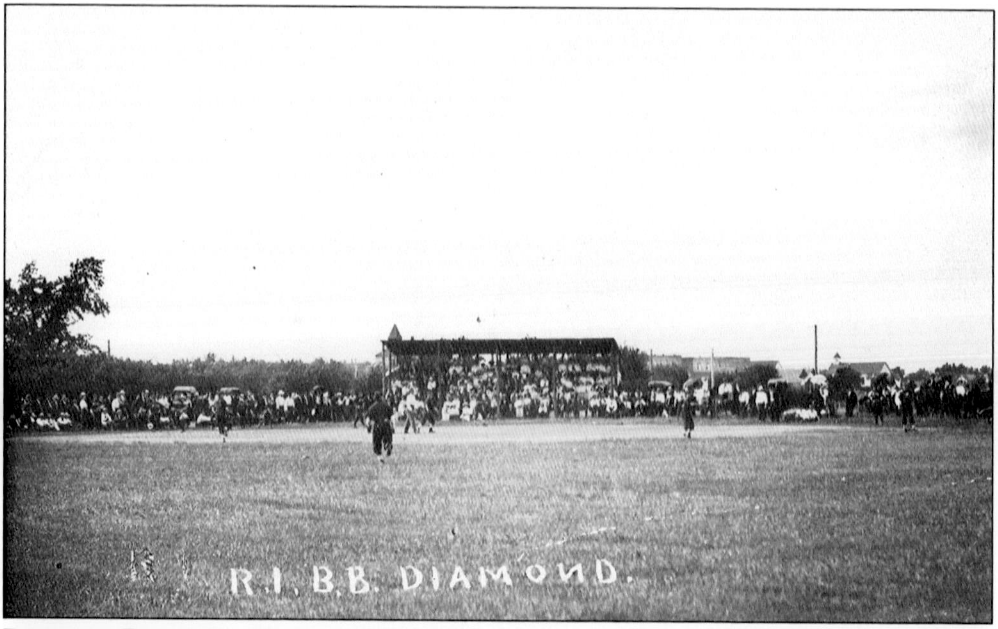

BASEBALL DIAMOND. The Rock Island baseball diamond was a popular recreation spot. The town is a few blocks to the northwest as evidenced by the school bell tower, the city business buildings, and the Methodist Episcopal Church. This is one of the few postcard photos to which an exact date can be affixed—June 5, 1908. The back of the card reads. "Chilhowee Mo. June 10-08 This is us playing ball June 5. Score Urich 6, Chilhowee 5, 14 innings." What a game!

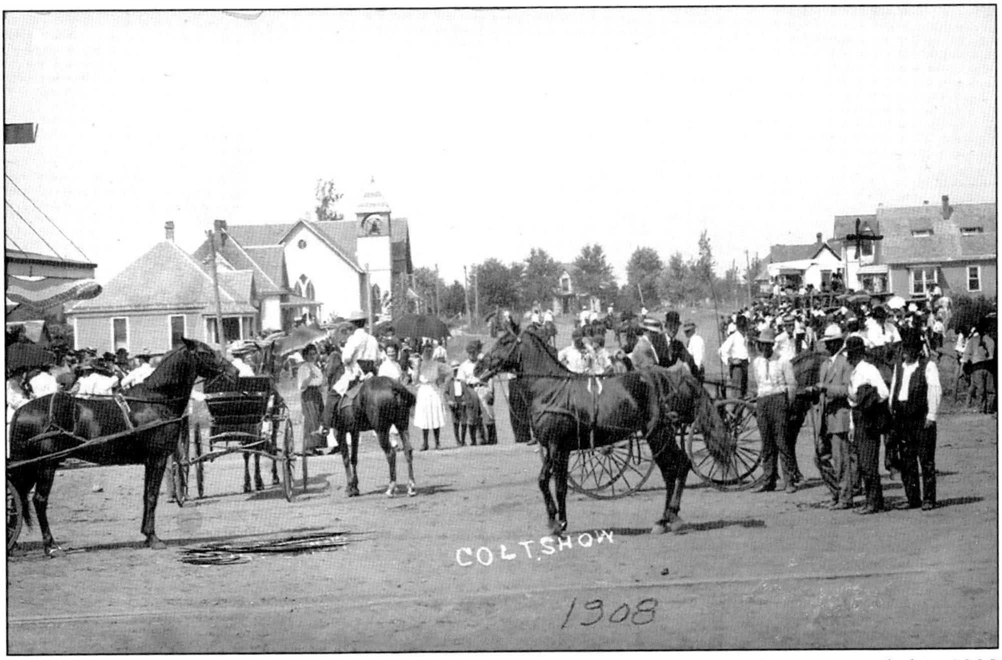

Colt Show 1908. Today revelers enjoy the Chilhowee Fair, just as they enjoyed this 1908 Colt Show. Main Street was abuzz with many visitors. The September 18, 1908, edition of the *Chilhowee News* saw it this way, "The display of farm products, while not on a very extensive scale, was of the very best. As to corn we never witnessed a better display anywhere."

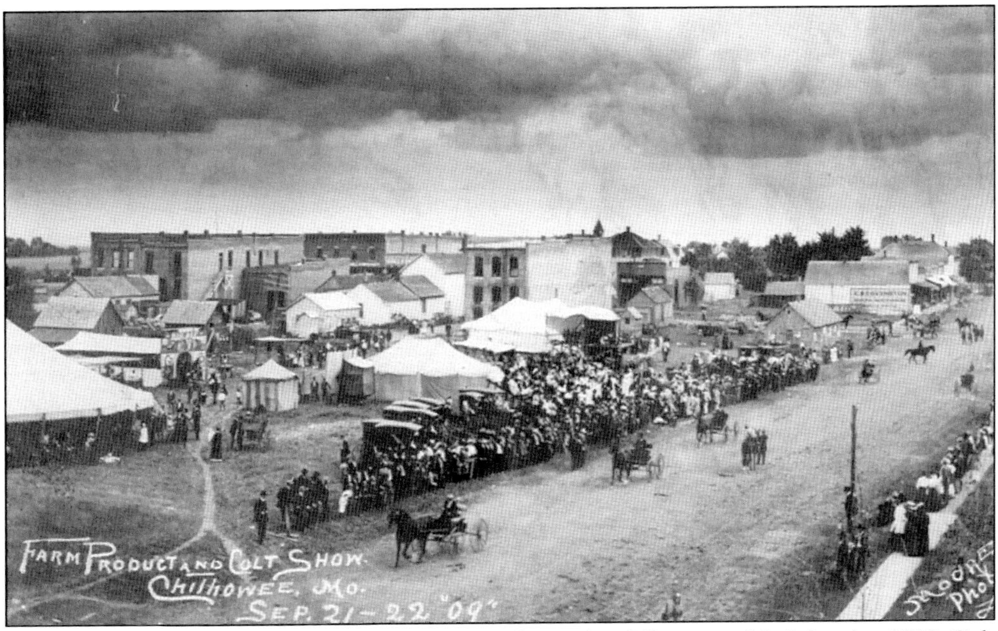

Colt Show 1909. The lowering sky looms above the folks assembled for the 1909 Colt Show in Chilhowee. People line the streets to observe what appears to be a parade of sorts. The Chilhowee Fair, though itself only a little over 50 years old and still going, mimics this earlier day. (JCHS Collection.)

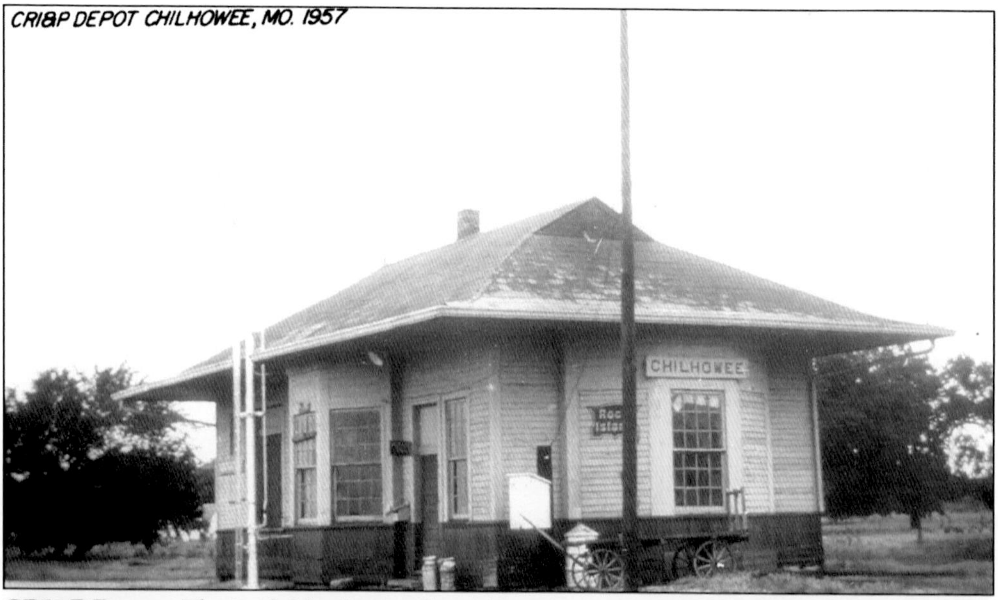

CRI&P DEPOT. The Rock Island was still a viable railroad in 1957 and saw at least freight service through Chilhowee for another 20 years. This view shows the *c.* 1923 depot with the semaphore, a Western Union sign, a baggage cart, and two cream cans. By this time there was no longer a full-time depot agent. Rock Island built the railroad through Chilhowee in approximately 1904. The first depot, built in about 1905, was struck by lightning and burned down in 1923.

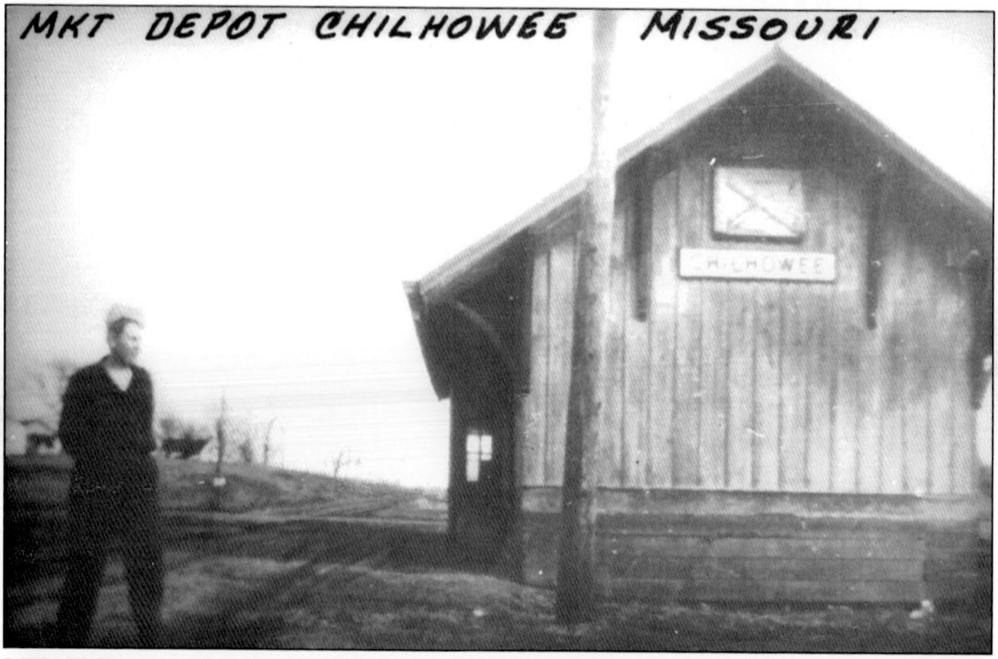

MK&T DEPOT. The Katy laid the tracks through Chilhowee in approximately 1895. This railroad and the discovery of coal were the major influences that prompted the town to relocate here from a mile north. This photo of the depot and agent is early 1900s. The Katy ceased operations through town and pulled the tracks in about 1958.

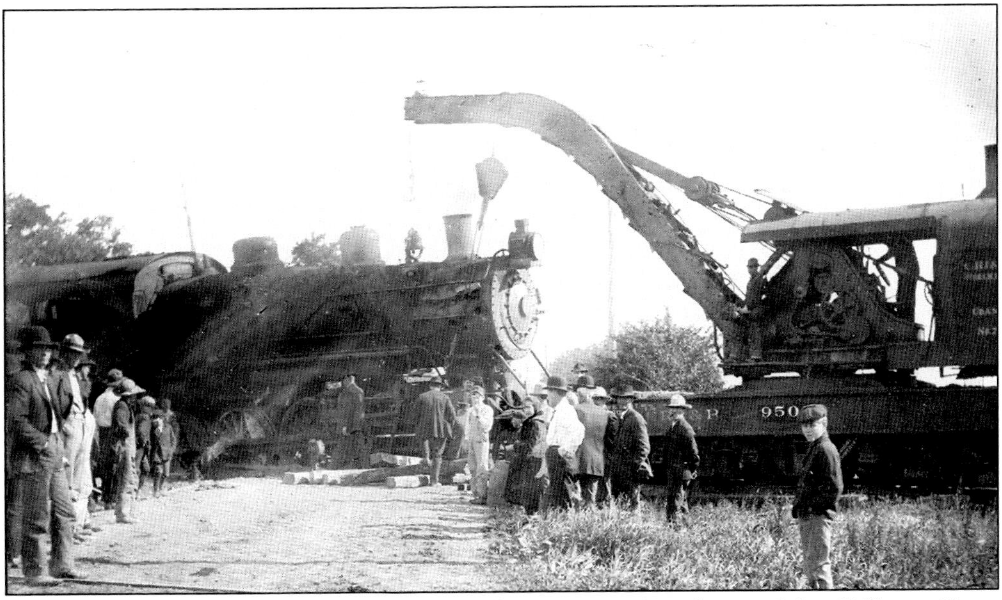

CRI&P Train Derailment. According to the June 4, 1909, edition of the *Chilhowee News*, "No. 96, the east bound freight, was tied up here from Sunday noon until Monday noon by the engine and tender getting off the track while switching." The article also states, "Our photo man made some nice post card pictures of the big wrecking crane at work." This card, postmarked July 8, 1909, is probably one of those nice cards.

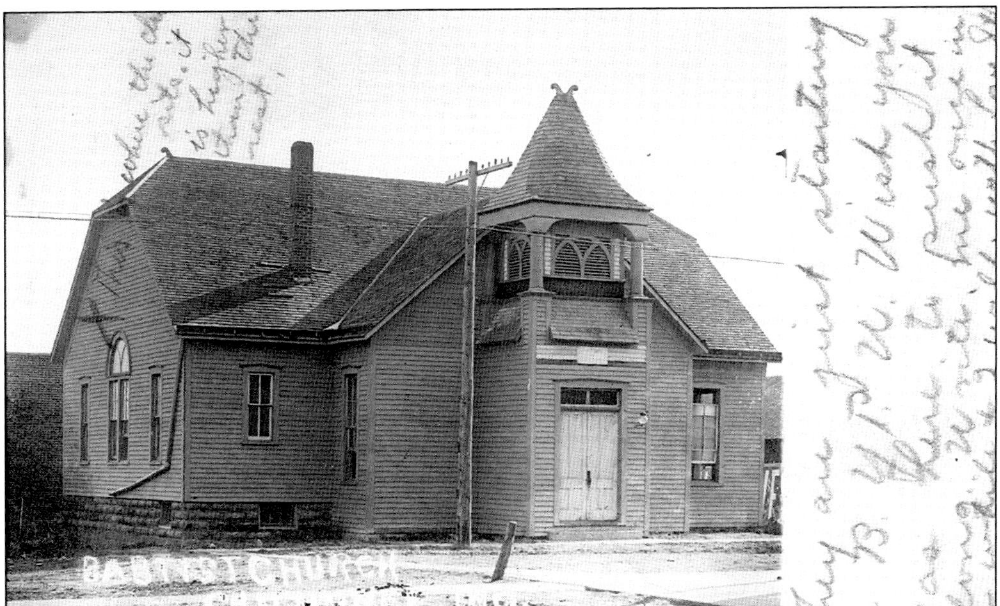

Chilhowee Baptist Church. The "Babtist Church" (note the spelling by the photographer), seen here, existed from 1907 until it was replaced in 1985 by the modern structure seen today at the southeast corner of Walnut Street and Pennsylvania Avenue. This card has a 1913 postmark.

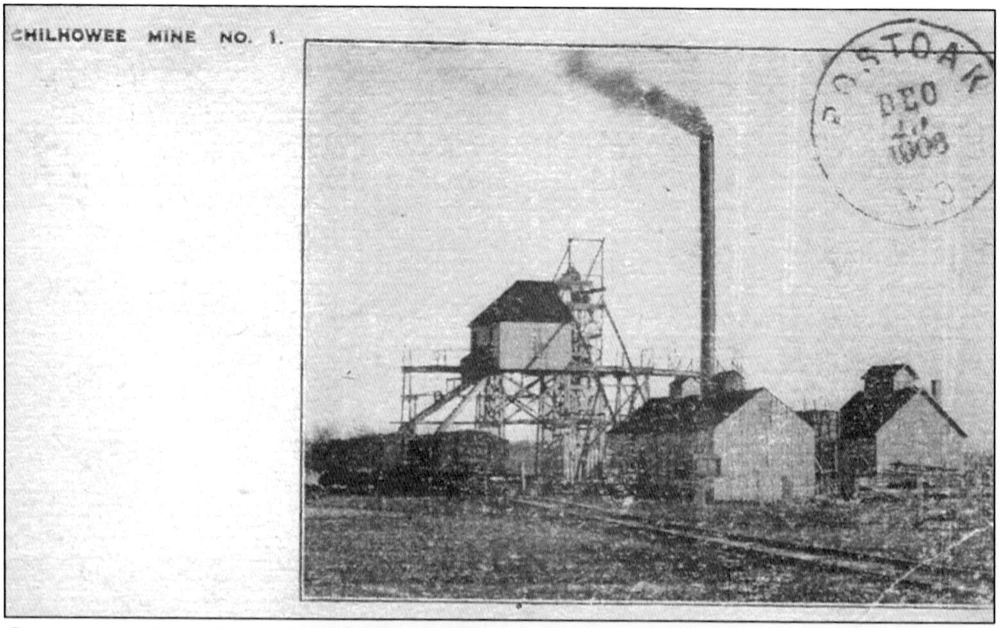

CHILHOWEE COAL MINE NO. 1. The Chilhowee Coal Co. had sunk three shafts, No. 1 and No. 3 about a mile west of Chilhowee and No. 2 at Denton, Missouri. The second day of the 1908 Colt Show was to celebrate the opening of Mine No. 3. No. 1 was apparently the only one to become an operating coal mine. This card is back stamped PostOak, Missouri, December 1906. The photo was taken looking northwest.

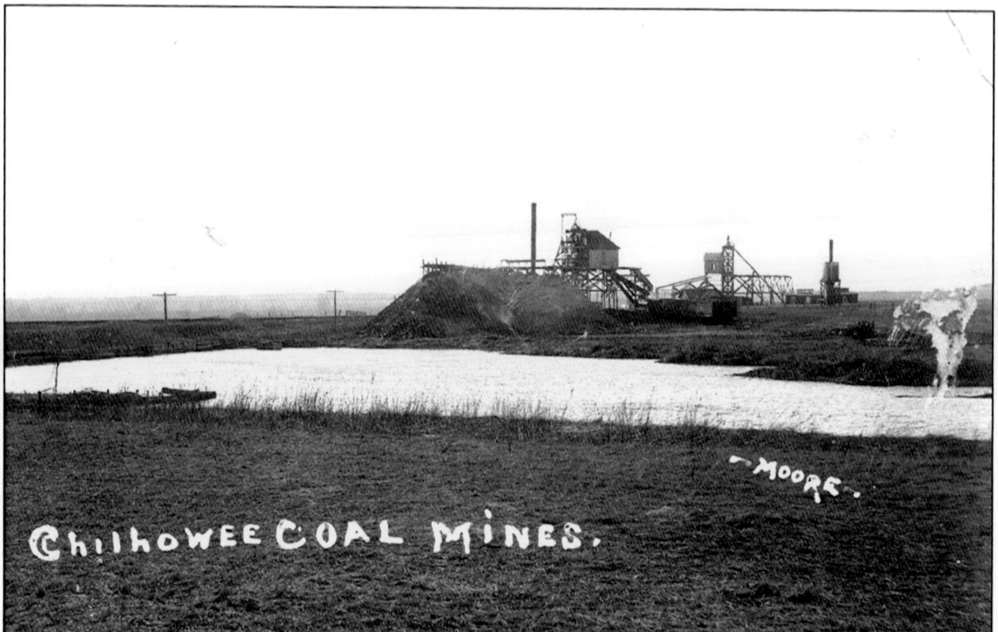

CHILHOWEE COAL MINE NO. 1. A 1909 photo by Moore shows Mine No. 1 looking southwest. It was adjacent to the Rock Island Railroad. In October of 1909 the mine closed.

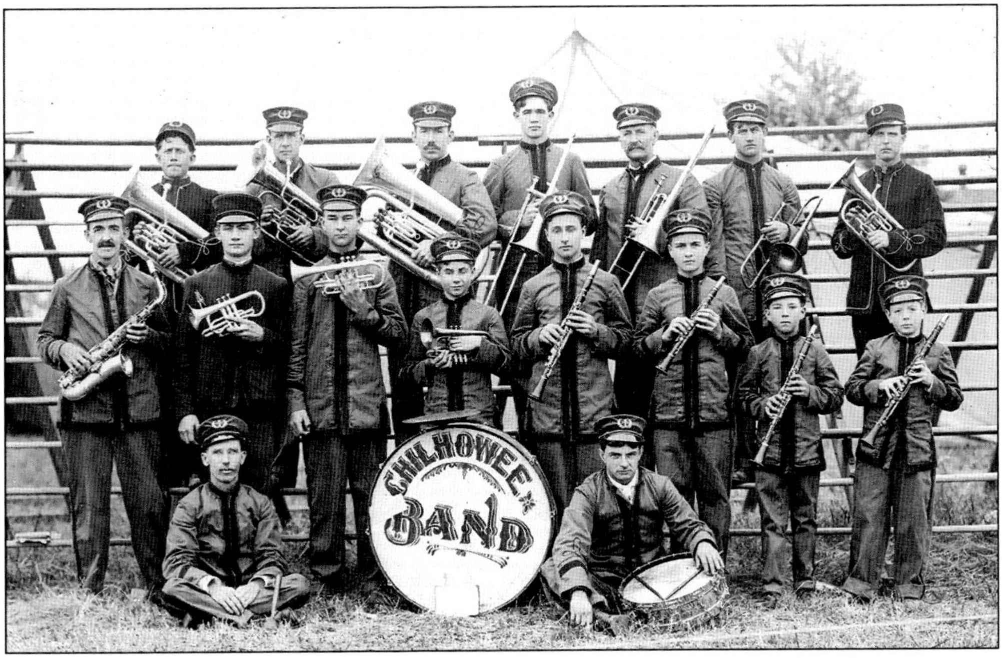

Chilhowee Band. Ready to perform, the Chilhowee Band is a rather diverse group, although their uniforms are "uniform." "The band boys did their purtiest to bluff that rain Wednesday and kept up their fight right in the teeth of the rain. The same spirit is what pulled off the colt show successfully this year," states the September 24, 1913, issue of the *Chilhowee News*. (JCHS Collection)

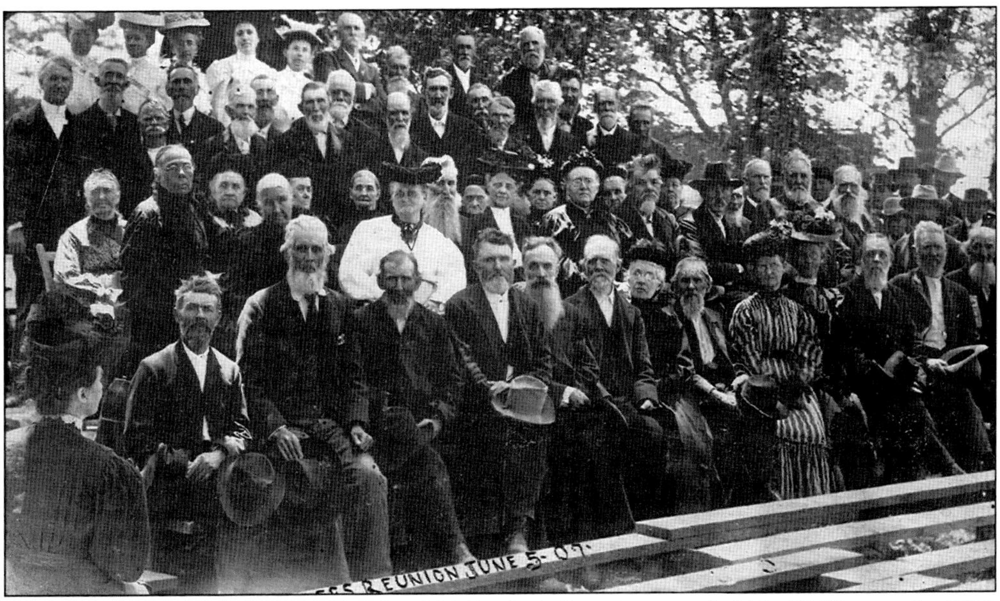

Old Settler's Reunion 1909. The Old Settler's Reunion was held in Chilhowee in 1909. Many of the original pioneers of the county, some who had weathered the North/South conflict here, some in other locales, came together to remember old times. (JCHS Collection.)

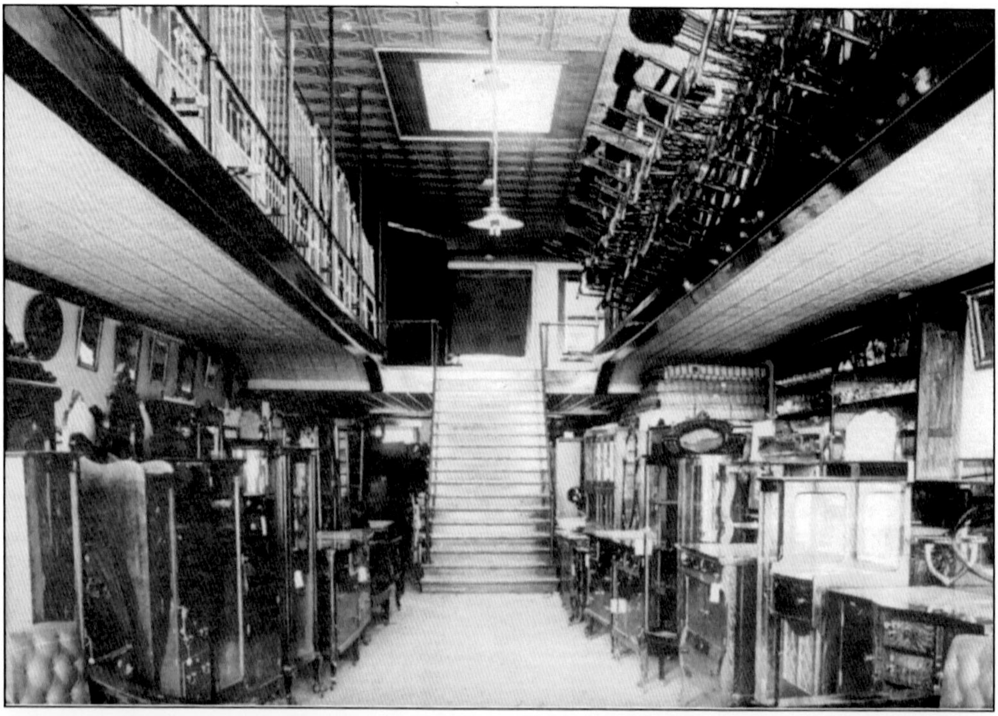

Sweeney Store. Shown here is the interior of S.R. Sweeney's store, at 113 East Walnut Street, Chilhowee, *c.* 1910. He started his house furnishings and undertaking business on August 27, 1907. O.L. Cook bought a half interest in the business in 1927. In 1934, Sweeney sold his interest to Cook, whose son, J.W. Cook, later took over the business. NYP Corporation maintains a computer software business there today. (JCHS Collection.)

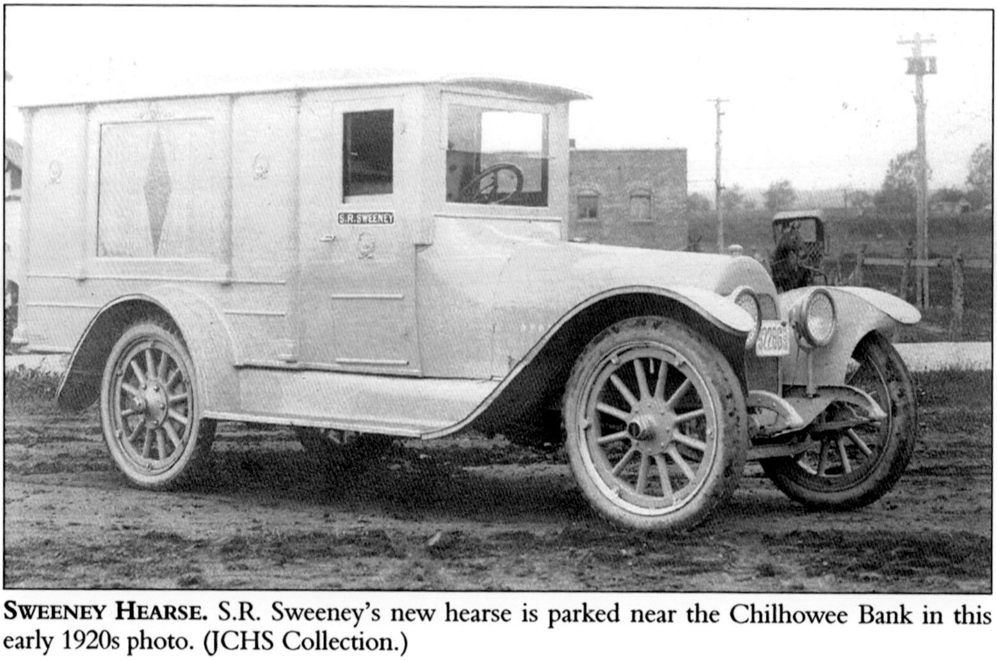

Sweeney Hearse. S.R. Sweeney's new hearse is parked near the Chilhowee Bank in this early 1920s photo. (JCHS Collection.)

Sweeney Store. In about 1908, three dray wagons are seen in front of S.R. Sweeney's store. The brick building to the left was Chilhowee Hardware, where Heet Gas Co. is now. (JCHS Collection.)

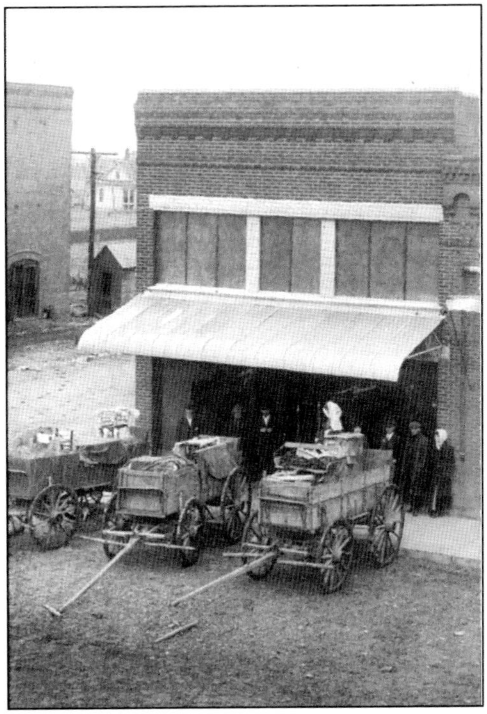

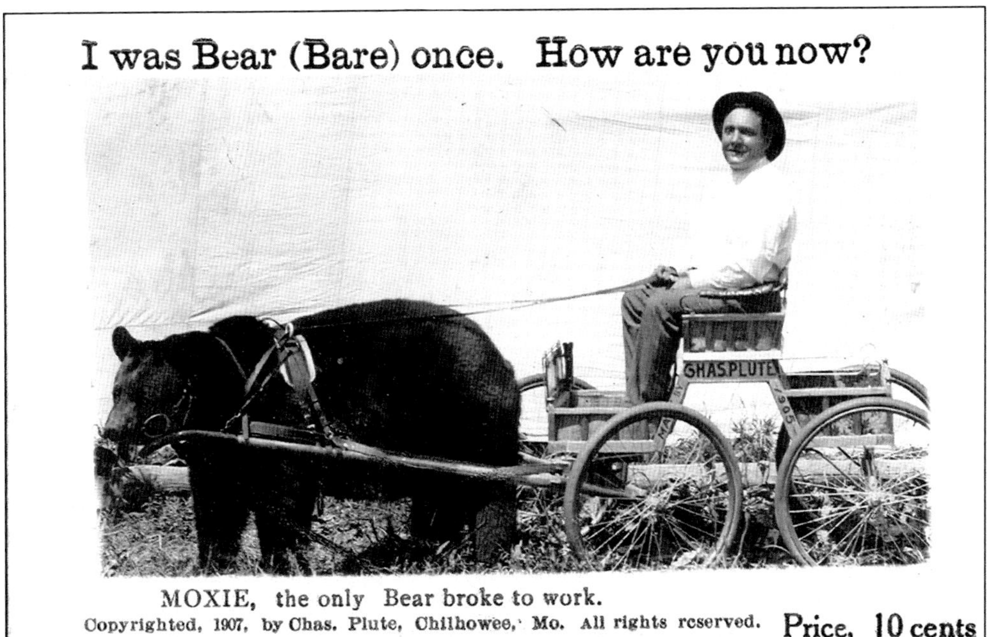

Moxie the Bear. In this 1907 photo, Charles Plute sits in the carriage he built with his trained bear, Moxie, hitched to it. Charlie was a local blacksmith, confectioner, and general store proprietor, and enjoyed showing off his astounding animal. Quite a celebrity, Moxie, a gentle, declawed, and trained bear, took children for rides in the cart and would wrestle anyone willing to come forward. A tragic fire in May 1908 cost Moxie his life.

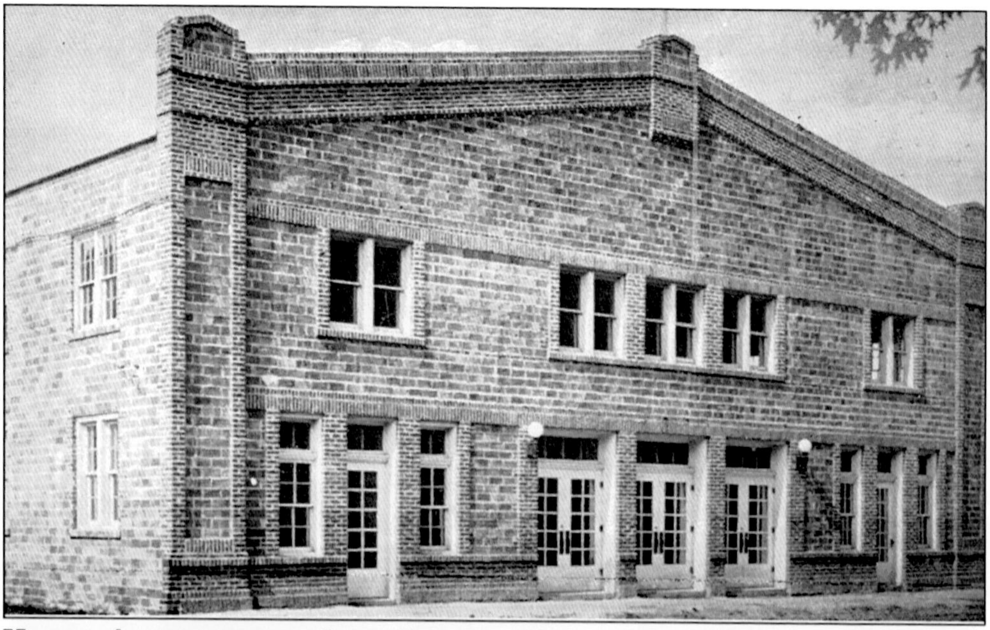

HOLDEN AUDITORIUM AND SALES PAVILION. While this nice building was constructed in 1922 for a different purpose, it was sold to Bagby Bros. of Sedalia at a trustees sale in 1929 to be used as a hatchery. At some point in time it became known as Missouri Poultry Yards and continued operations under this name until 1956 or 1957.

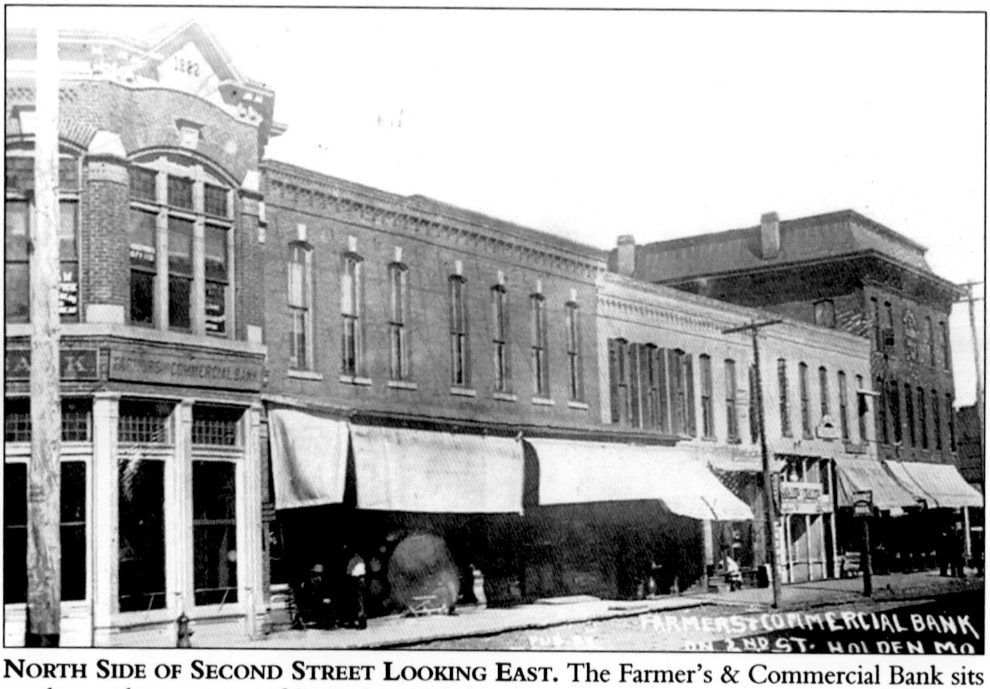

NORTH SIDE OF SECOND STREET LOOKING EAST. The Farmer's & Commercial Bank sits on the northeast corner of Second and Market Streets. It is the most prominent building in this *c.* 1900 shot from Market Street in Holden.

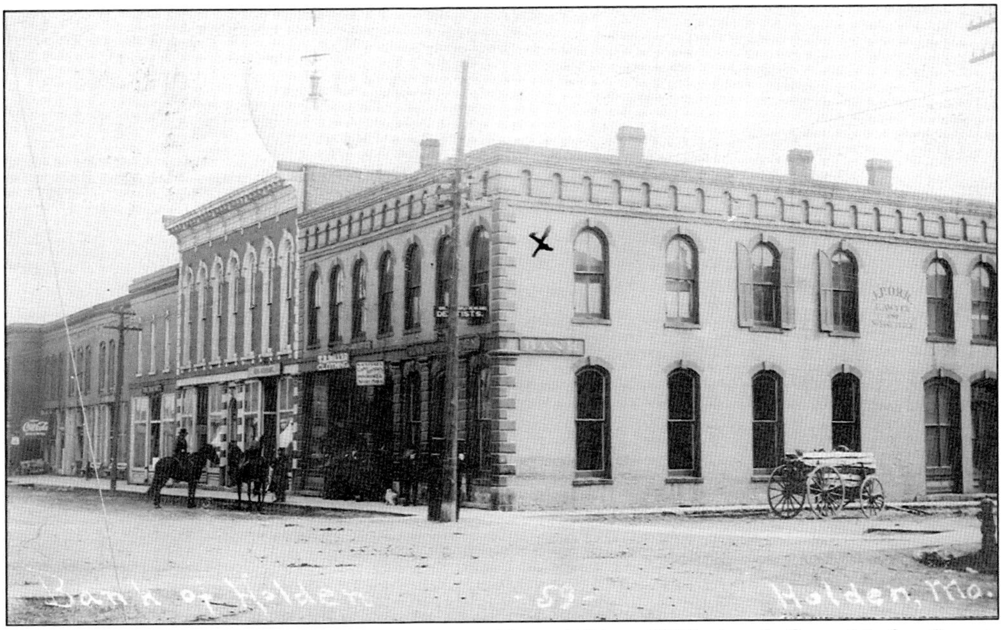

SOUTH SIDE OF SECOND STREET LOOKING EAST. This *c.* 1900 view is from Market Street. The Bank of Holden, organized about 1870 and reportedly the oldest bank in Johnson County, is shown here on the southeast corner of Second and Market Streets.

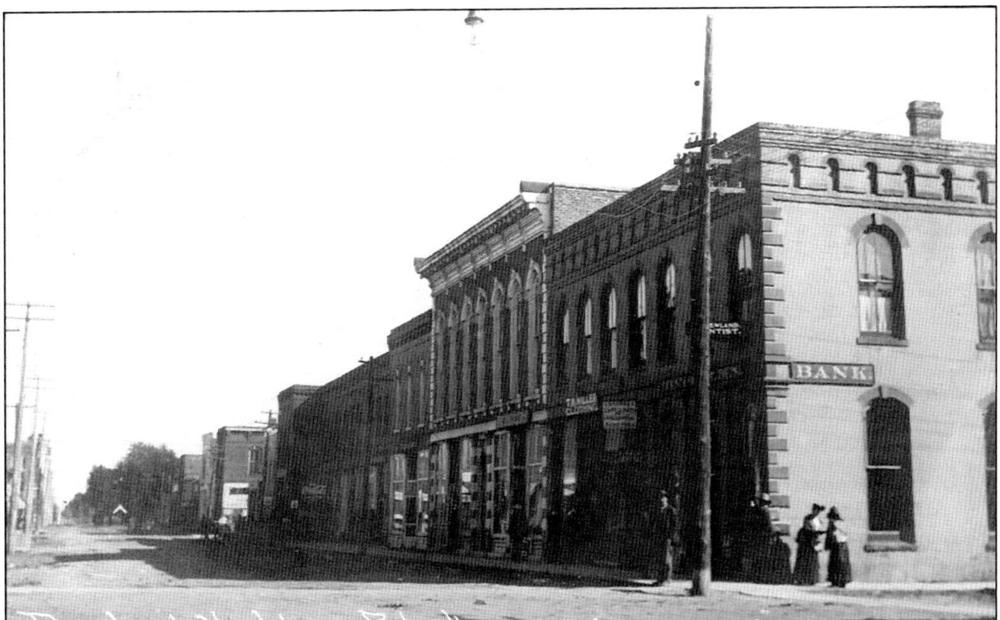

SOUTH SIDE OF SECOND STREET LOOKING EAST. Another *c.* 1900 view from Market Street. One can see businesses farther down the street in this photo. An article in the July 1, 1880 issue of the *Holden Enterprise* proclaimed, "Holden is destined to become the Indianapolis of Missouri."

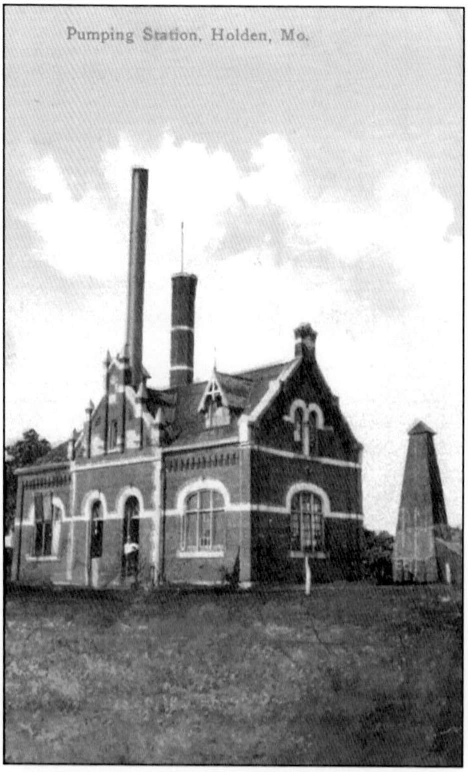

PUMPING STATION. Some records indicate that it was located at 101 West Third Street, others suggest it was near the city lake about one-and-one-half miles east of town. Whatever the case, this is how the pumping station might have looked in approximately 1900. It was destroyed by fire in 1913.

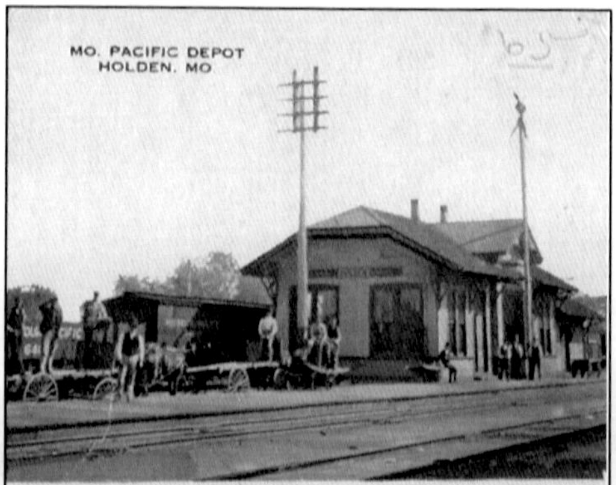

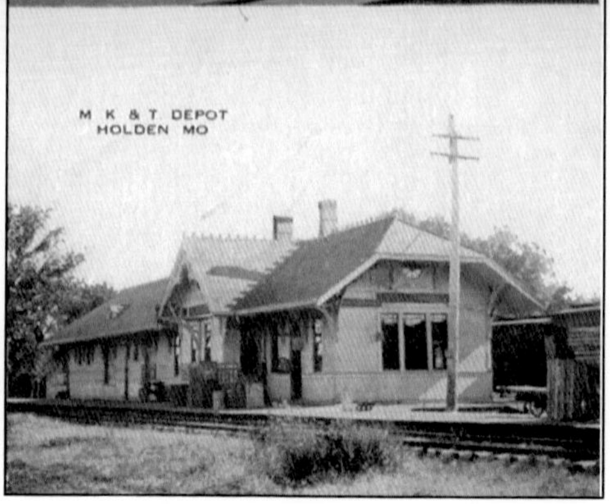

MISSOURI PACIFIC AND MK&T DEPOTS OF HOLDEN. The Missouri Pacific track was laid from St. Louis to Sedalia by January 1861, continued westward in early 1864, and reached Warrensburg by summer. Construction ceased until 1865, when it was finished to Kansas City. The Holden Depot was built about this time. The Katy Railroad was completed through Holden in about 1872. The MK&T Depot was built *c.* 1881 and abandoned in 1958.

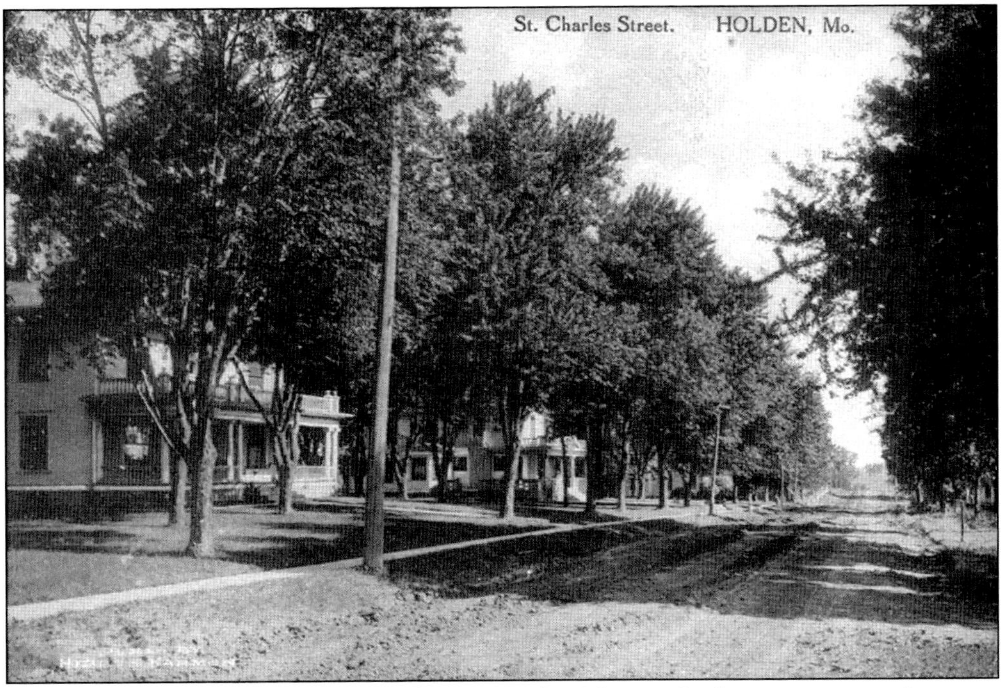

ST. CHARLES STREET IN HOLDEN. This is a residential street in the western part of town.

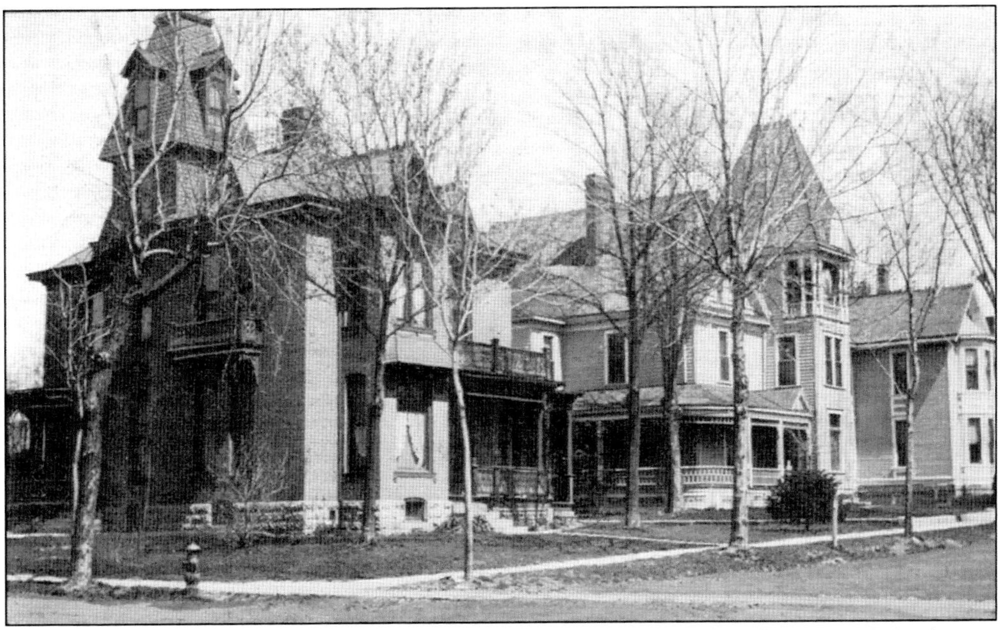

OXFORD PLACE. A *c.* 1910 view. The Oxford Sanitarium was listed in the 1912–1913 Johnson County directory at 411 South Market Street in Holden as, "a first class hospital with modern equipment, offering unexcelled service to all surgical and medical cases. Open to all physicians in good standing. Doctor W.G. Thompson, manager." Yet another discrepency—the 1914 plat map shows the sanitarium at the northeast corner of Fifth and Main Streets.

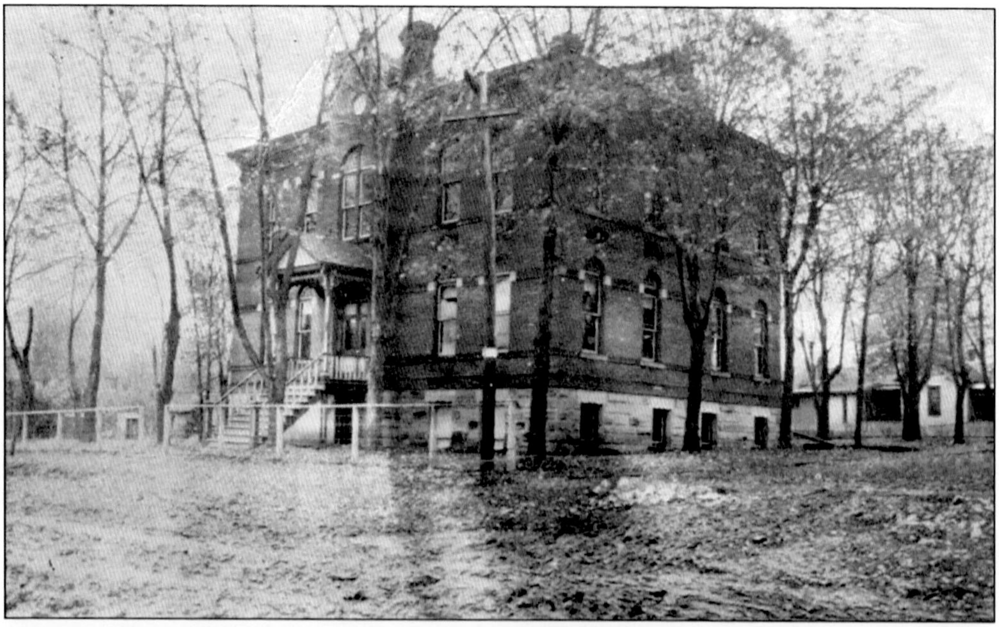

HOLDEN HIGH SCHOOL. In 1898, the high school, at the corner of Fifth and Lexington Streets, offered a two-year course, but in 1902 expanded into a four-year course. The *Peptimist* became the school newspaper. The school song, "Blue White," was written by Roy Rogers (a local celebrity, not Trigger's boss).

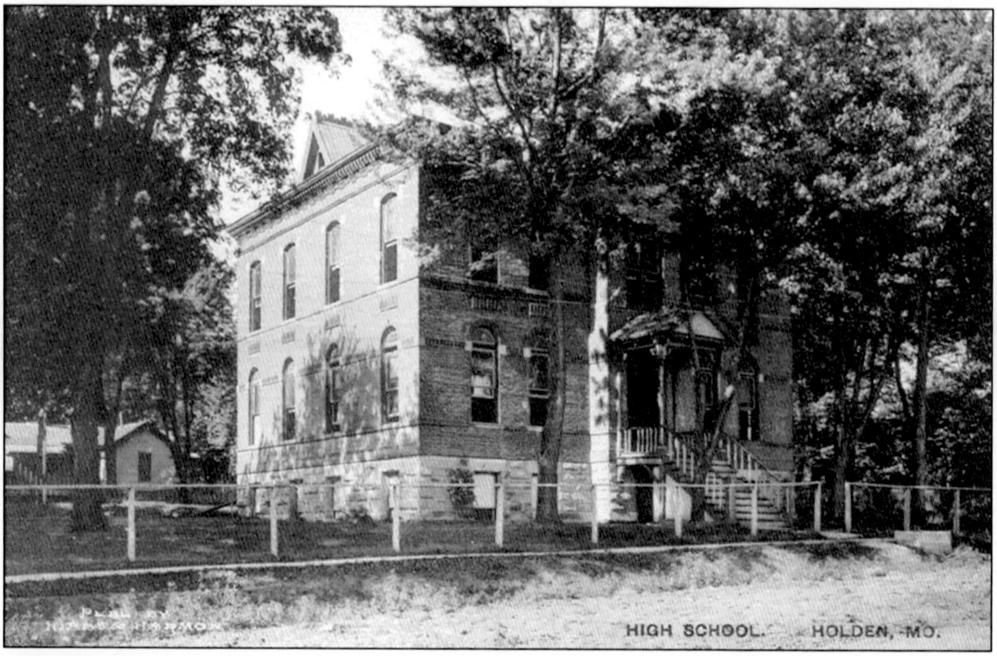

HOLDEN HIGH SCHOOL. The school burned on November 6, 1927, but was rebuilt in 1928–1929.

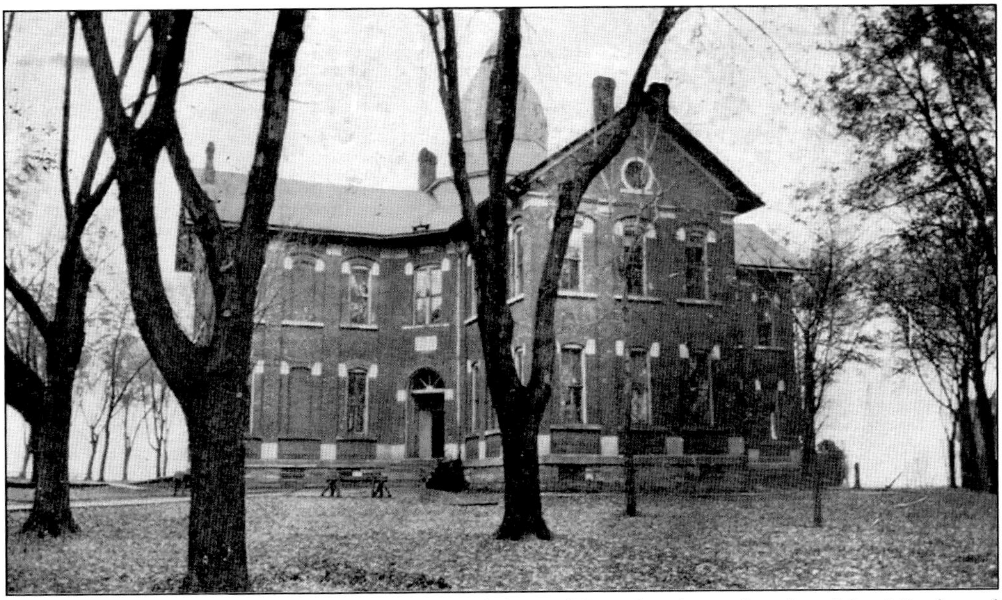

HOLDEN PUBLIC SCHOOL. The campus of the public school was bordered by Ninth and Tenth Streets on the north and south, and by Olive and Market Streets on the east and west. A two-story brick building with eight rooms, each capable of accommodating 80 pupils, was built in 1882.

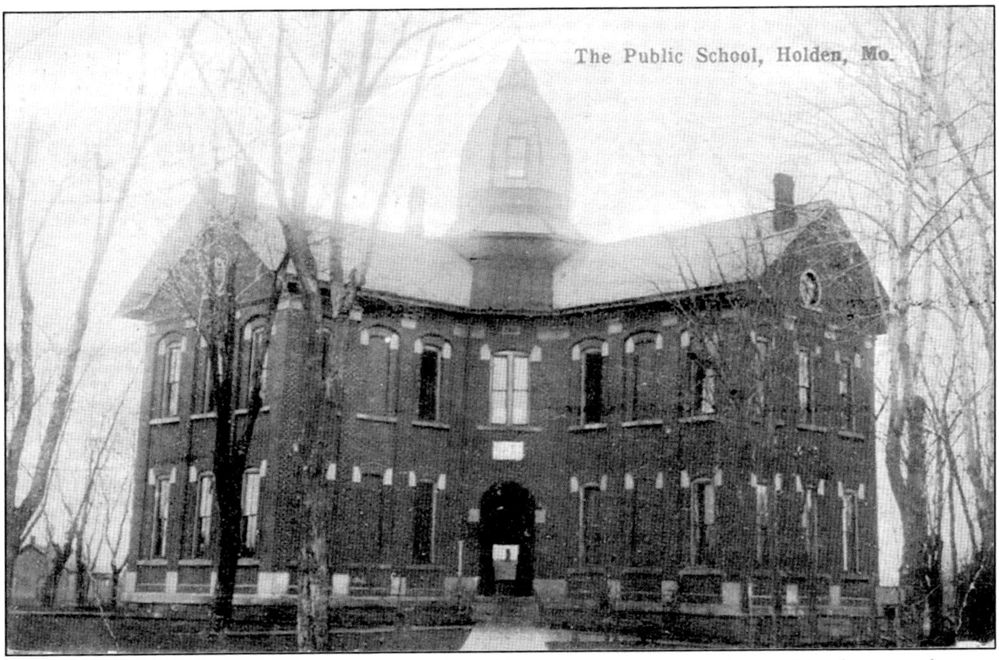

HOLDEN PUBLIC SCHOOL. This school building was constructed in an "X" shape and sat at an angle to the street. The 1914 Johnson County plat map shows the layout very well.

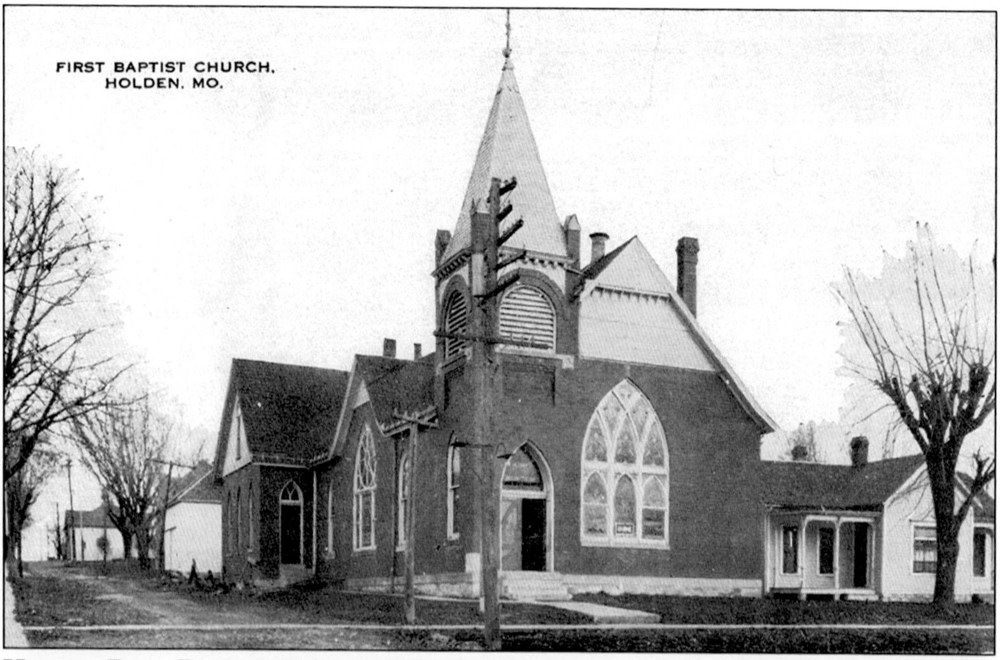

HOLDEN FIRST BAPTIST CHURCH. The First Baptist Church was organized in 1878 and the congregation met in Daniel's Hall until it burned in 1897. The building shown here was built *c.* 1900 at the corner of Sixth and Market Streets.

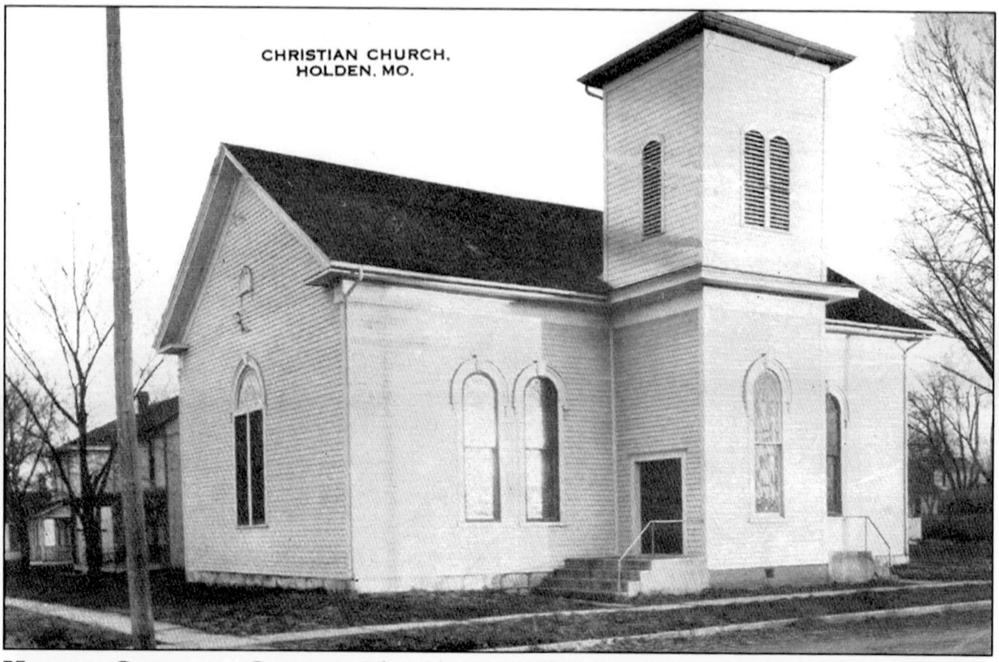

HOLDEN CHRISTIAN CHURCH. The Christian Church was organized in 1865. The first church was erected in 1870 and is still in use today. It is located at the corner of Third and Main Streets and is the oldest church in Holden. David Nation, husband of Carrie Nation, was the first church clerk.

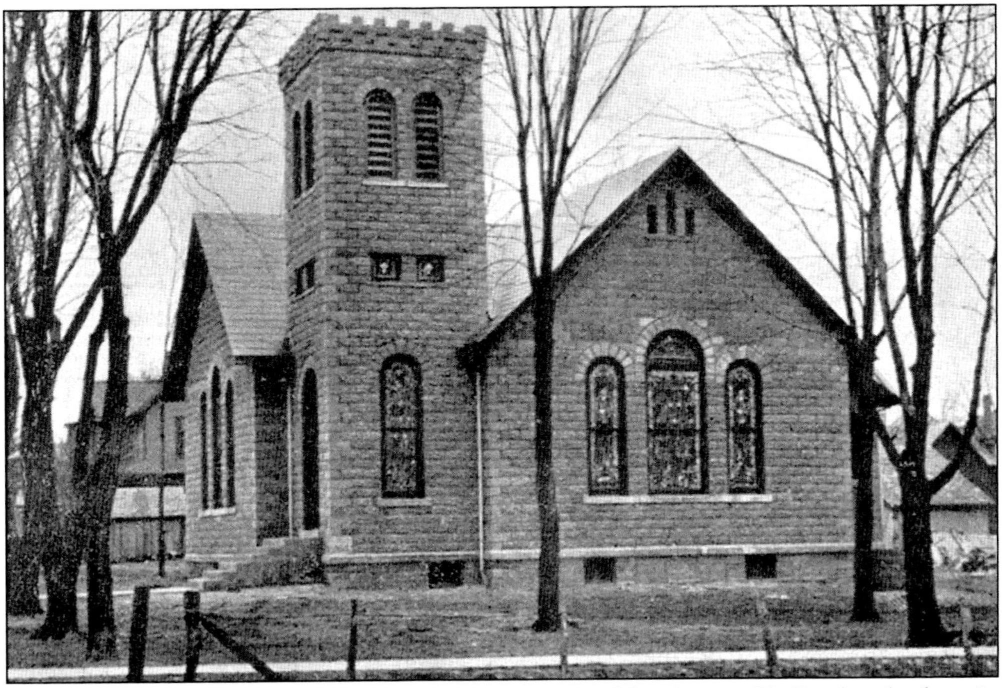

HOLDEN METHODIST EPISCOPAL CHURCH. Organized by George H. Reed and others in 1867, the first church was built in 1869. The present church was constructed in 1907 and located at 400 North Main Street. (*c.* 1907.)

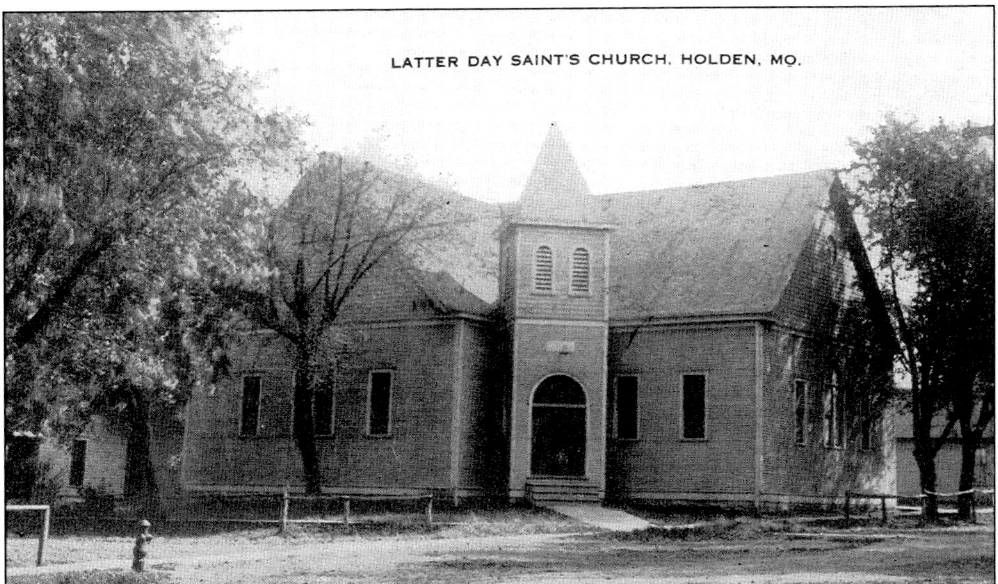

HOLDEN LATTER DAY SAINTS CHURCH. This church was first organized in 1873 by Henry Scarcliff and Kom Johnson. The present-day congregation originated in 1886. Early meetings were held in homes, a store building at Second and Main Streets, and over a blacksmith shop at Third and Main Streets. The unoccupied Episcopal church at Fourth and Main Streets was used in 1901. The current building at Fourth and Pine Streets was completed in 1908.

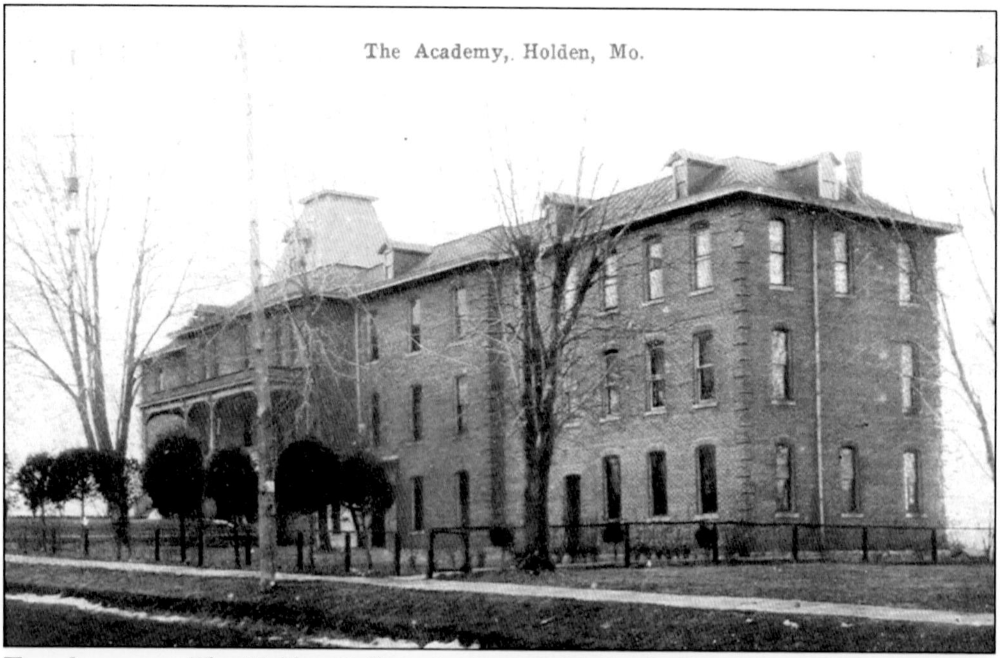

The Academy. The Holden College, in the 800 block of Olive Street, began classes on September 12, 1881. It burned January 19, 1887. A new building soon arose, but by 1888 it was sold and became Lester Seminary. It operated under this name for a year, then Sisters of Charity, a catholic organization, established St. Cecelia Seminary in 1889. This *c.* 1900 photograph shows the building.

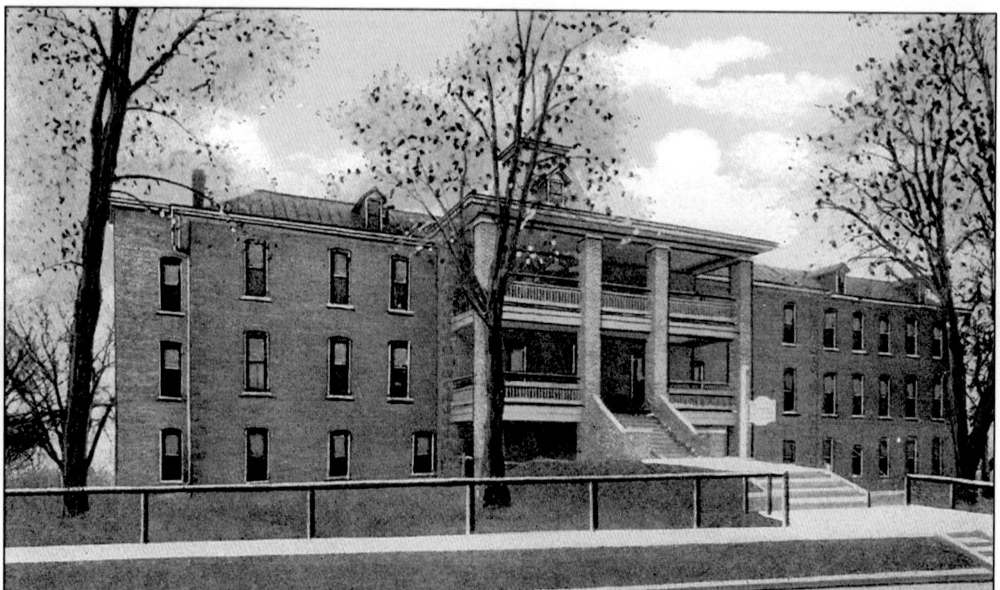

Holden Latter Day Saints Home. The Catholic St. Cecelia Seminary operated until 1908. It was purchased by Latter Day Saints in 1917 to serve as a home for the aged. It was used in this capacity until the late 1930s.

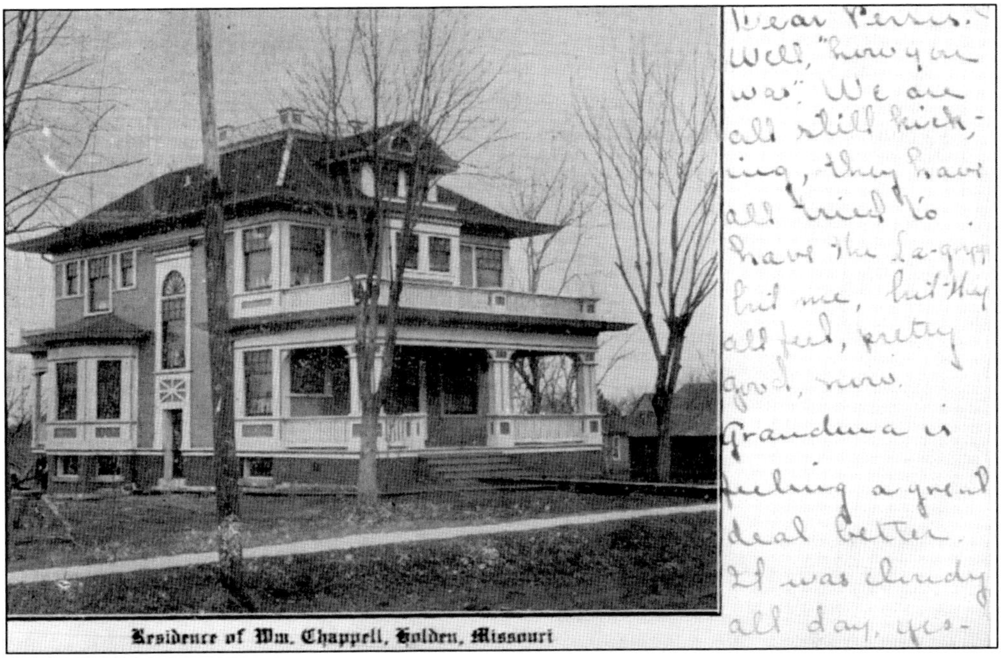

WILLIAM CHAPPELL HOME. A 1900–1901 Johnson County directory lists William Chappell as owner of a lumber yard. This became the Johnson County Lumber Co. According to a 1905 article in the *Holden Progress*, the "most notable social event of the season" was an apparent open house at William Chappell's new home. This photo is from the early 1900s.

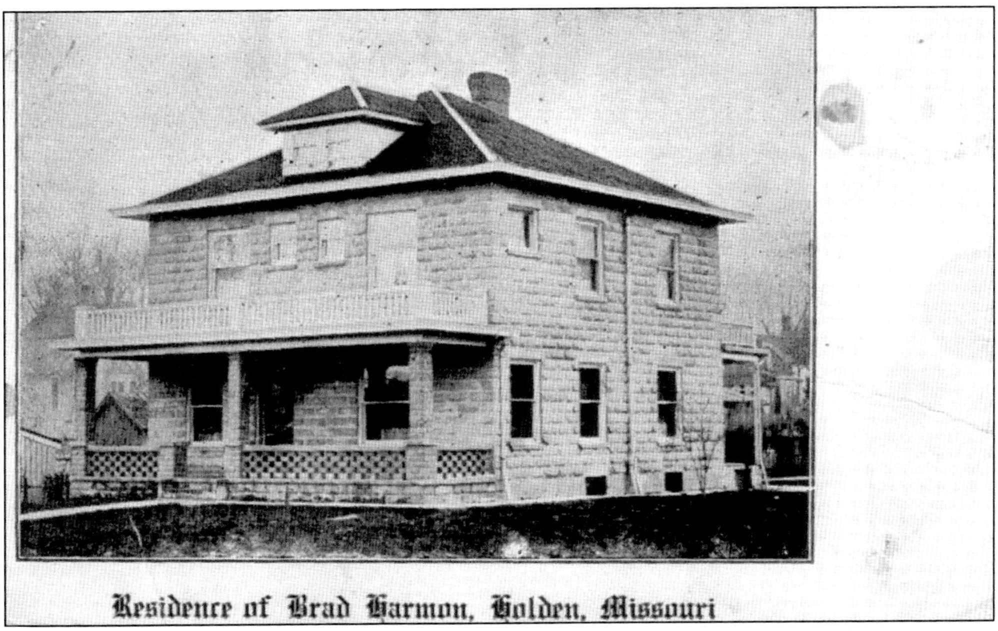

BRAD HARMON HOME. A *c.* 1900 shot shows Brad Harmon's home at 410 South Main Street. Born in 1869, Brad Harmon, known as "Uncle Brad," was a druggist with his father-in-law at Hibbs & Harmon Drugs, located at 115 East Second Street. Mr. Hibbs died in 1901 and the business became Harmon Drugs.

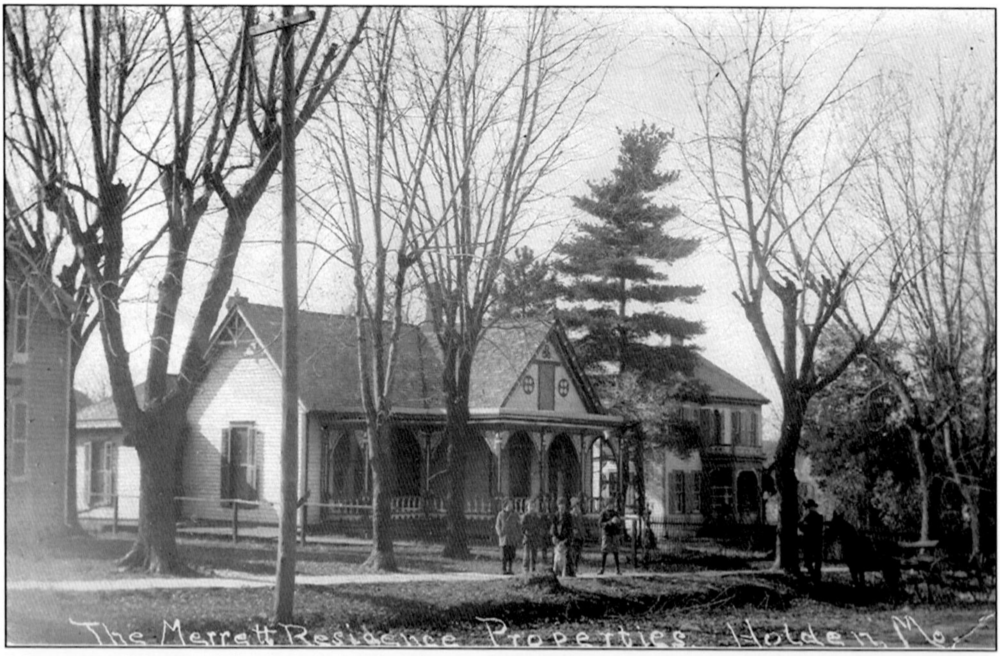

MERRETT HOME. The Merrett Residence Properties merited attention on this postcard. Though it is uncertain whether the same family, Mr. and Mrs. Lewis C. Allie (L.C. & A.) Merret ran a Furniture, Undertakers, and Embalming business at 100-102 West Second. In the 1912 Directory, 213 West Second Street in Holden was their home address. (JCHS Collection.)

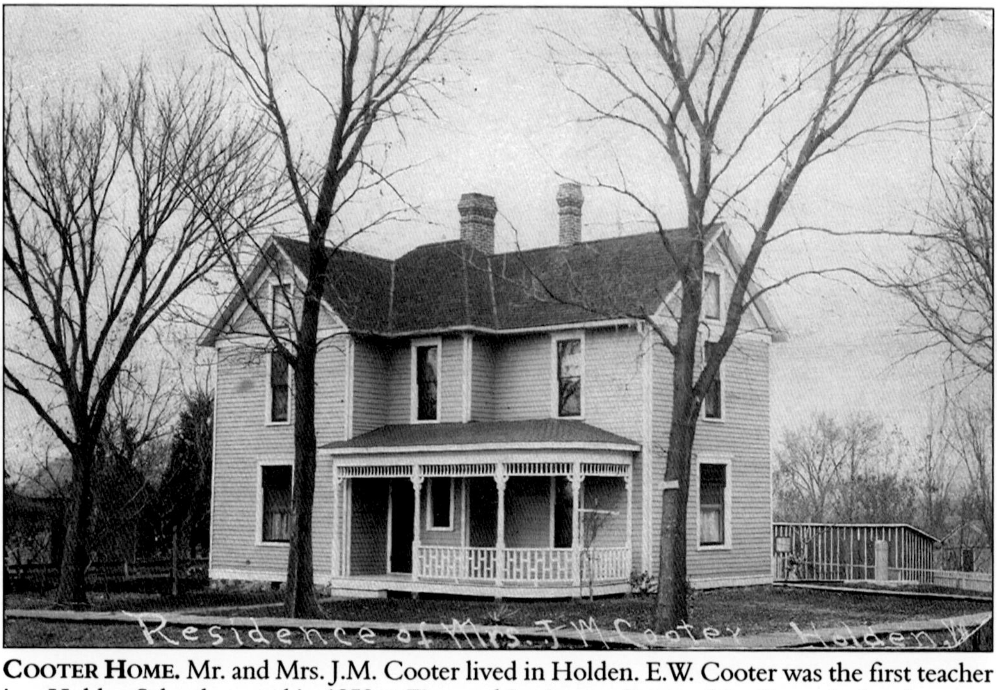

COOTER HOME. Mr. and Mrs. J.M. Cooter lived in Holden. E.W. Cooter was the first teacher in a Holden School erected in 1859 at First and Lexington Streets. Mr. Cooter's daughter was the first child born in the city limits of Holden. (JCHS Collection.)

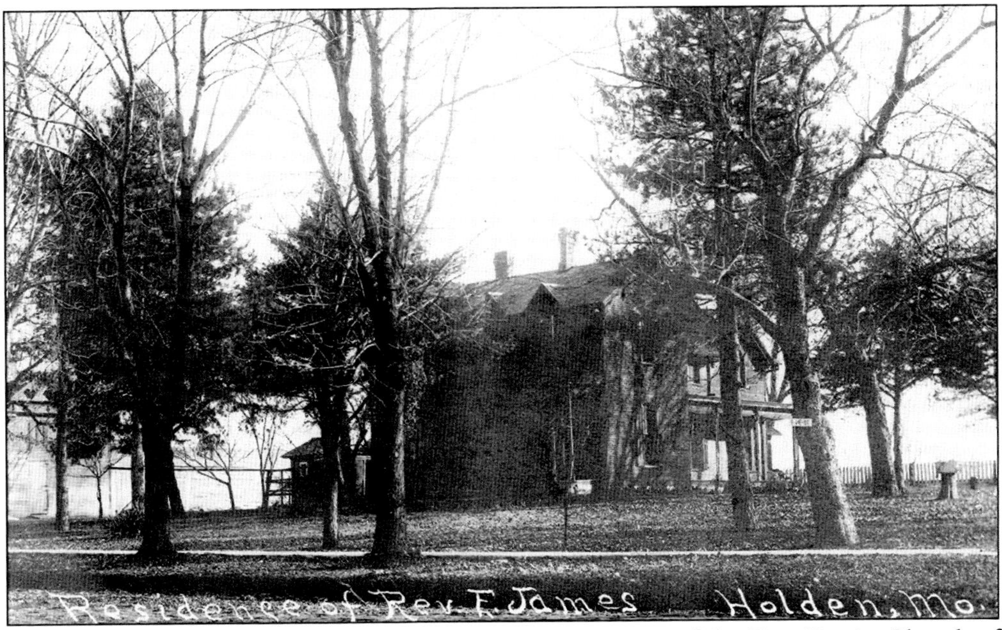

REV. EDWARD JAMES HOME. Rev. Edward Rea James, pastor of the First Baptist Church of Holden, was born in Ireland in 1850. He died in 1928, six years after he was elected mayor of Holden. The *c.* 1900 home shown here was located on four-and-one-half acres on South Market Street in Holden.

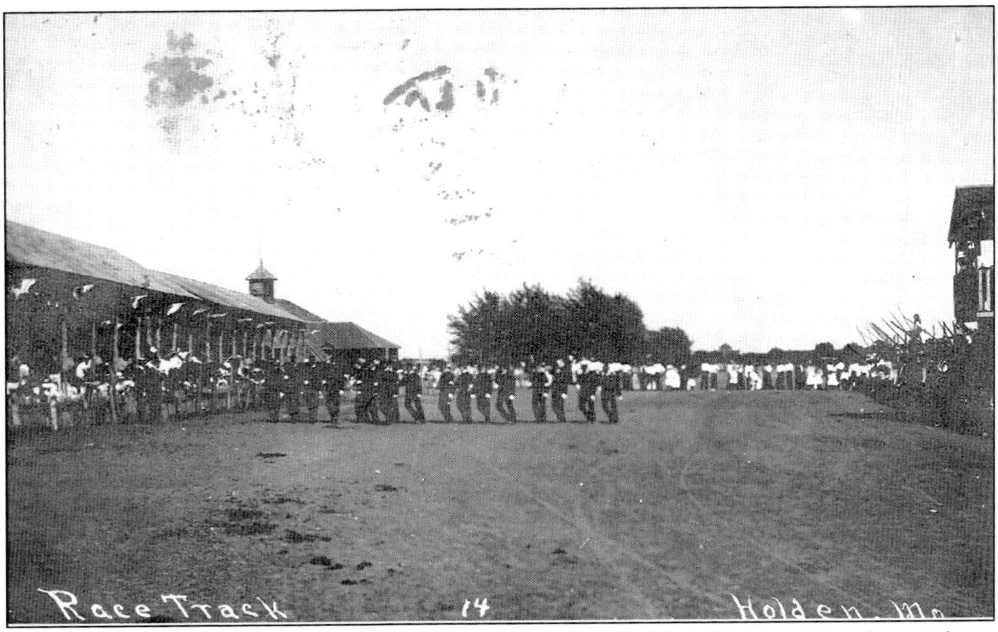

HOLDEN RACE TRACK. This facility was located on the Holden fairgrounds at the southeast edge of town. Holden was home for the Johnson County Fair in the late 1800s. The half-mile long race track saw races run every afternoon of fair week during the 1892 Johnson County Fair. Trotting and pacing events were popular, but the horse races produced the real excitement. Given to author Lisa Irle by Minnie Loveall, this card belonged to Loveall's Uncle Will Shinkle.

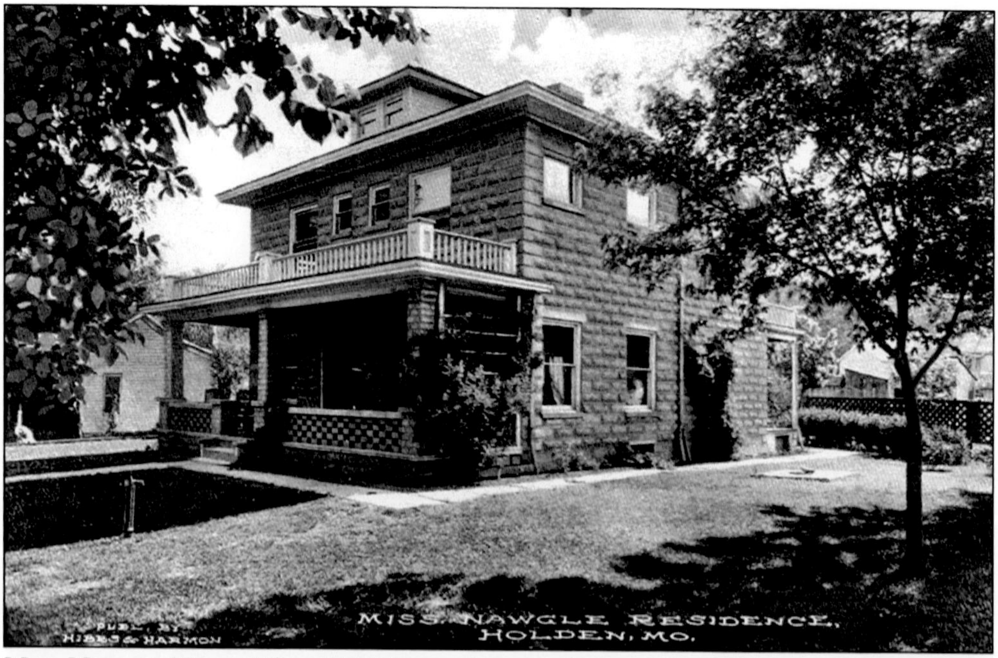

MISS NAWGLE HOME. The 1912 Johnson County directory lists Miss Rose E. Nawgel and Miss Laura M. Nawgel living at 705 South Main Street in Holden. Note, there seems to be a difference of opinion as to the spelling of the surname. This view is probably *c.* 1910.

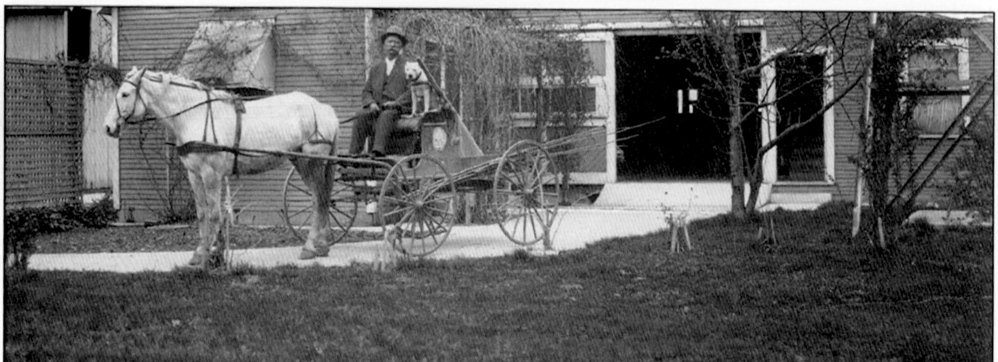

MR. COOTER. The Cooter Collection of photographs at the Johnson County Historical Society features this partial card, showing Mr. Cooter heading out on a fishing expedition—or at least the poles on the wagon might indicate that. (JCHS Collection.)

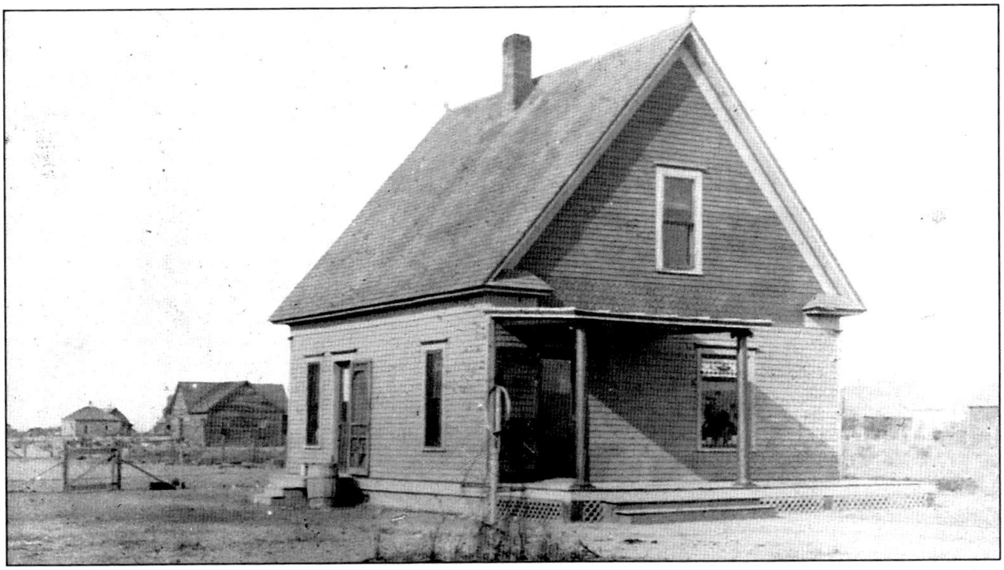

J.M. SUMMERS HOME. "Dear Uncle and Aunt, ...Lela and her family were here yesterday her baby is big and fat. This card is a picture of my house I built my self. Just completed about a year before Mary died. Your nephew, J.M. Summers." The location of the house is undetermined, but the return address is in Holden, Missouri on March 22, 1909. This is from a postcard album prepared for Lela Lanning Irle by T.E. Lanning.

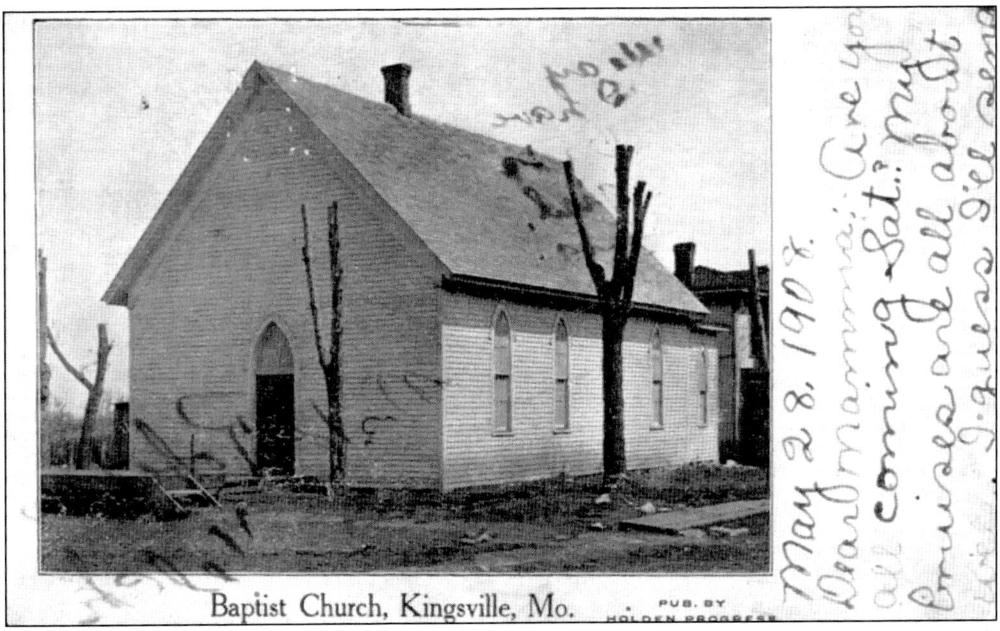

KINGSVILLE BAPTIST CHURCH. This is the Kingsville Baptist Church in 1908. The church was originally organized on March 10, 1860. Andrew Worth and Rufus Wise were the first deacons and Rev. George Minton was the first pastor. The church, like many others in the region, disbanded during the War Between the States, "suddenly scattered abroad by the ravages of civil war." (JCHS Collection.)

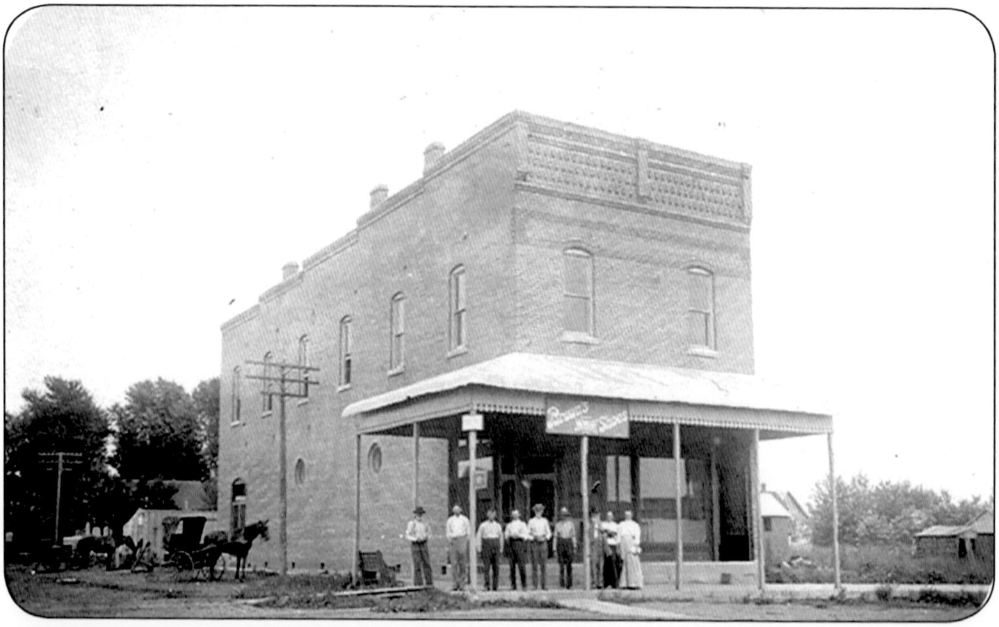

Brown's Shoe Store. The Brown's shoe store in Leeton was captured in this postcard. Pictured are, Mr. Bailey, Marsh Bronaugh, Arthur Wyatt, Abe Hall, Frank Wise, Lester Wyatt, Jamie Wilson, and Mrs. Reynolds. (JCHS Collection.)

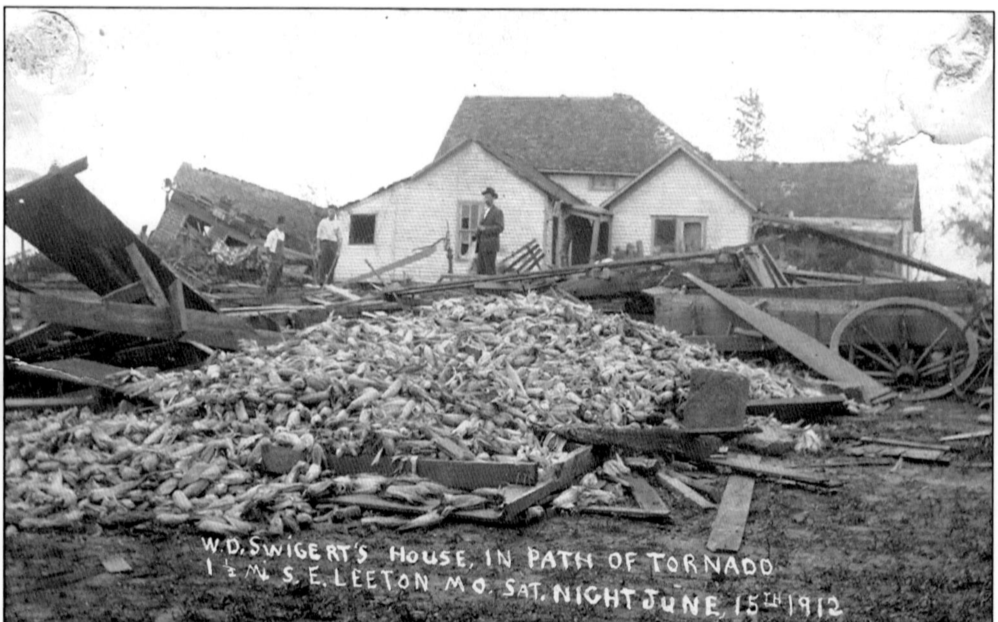

Leeton Tornado Damage to Swigert Home. When the tornado hit Leeton in 1912, a photographer hit the streets in its wake to record the damage. At the Swigert's home a corn crib burst and a wagon nearby was crushed as well. (JCHS Collection.)

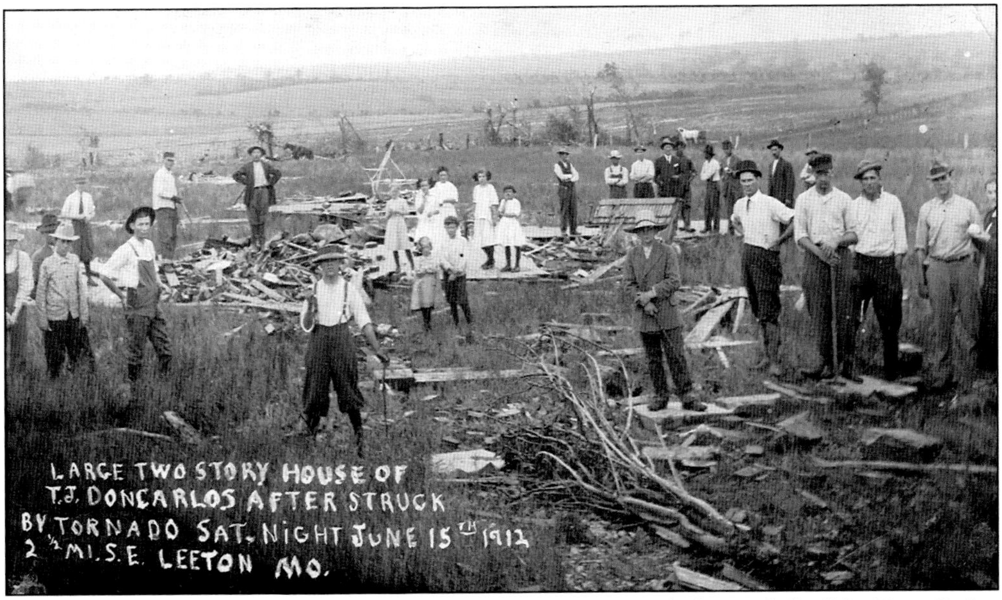

LEETON TORNADO DAMAGE TO DON CARLOS HOME. Very little was left of the Don Carlos family's home, better known as the Mayfield Place. The four-county Windsorite reported that four years after they built their beautiful farm "not a vestige of house, barn, or any outbuilding being left save the foundations." This view is down the hill where the wood siding had blown. The elder Don Carlos and his wife were killed in the storm. (JCHS Collection.)

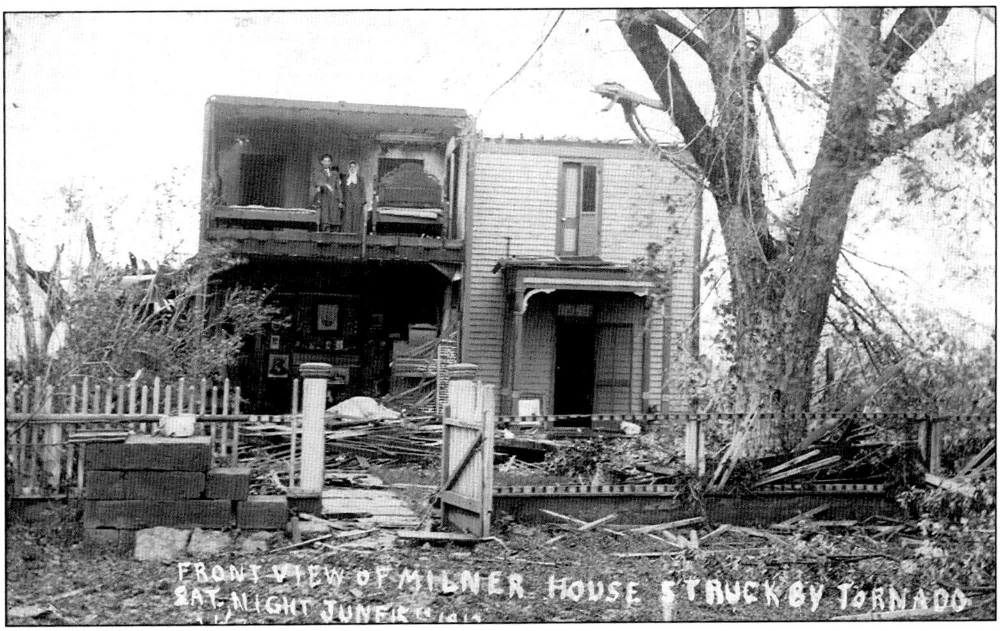

LEETON TORNADO DAMAGE TO MILNER HOME. Only the wall was torn off and the residents, with some of their belongings, appear as though on stage in this image. Two deaf sisters slept soundly as the storm approached. The housekeeper heard it, woke the sisters and all made it to safety. Following the storm, the sisters saw that the chimney had fallen on the bed where they had slept. Waiting for help to arrive, they sang hymns for comfort. (JCHS Collection.)

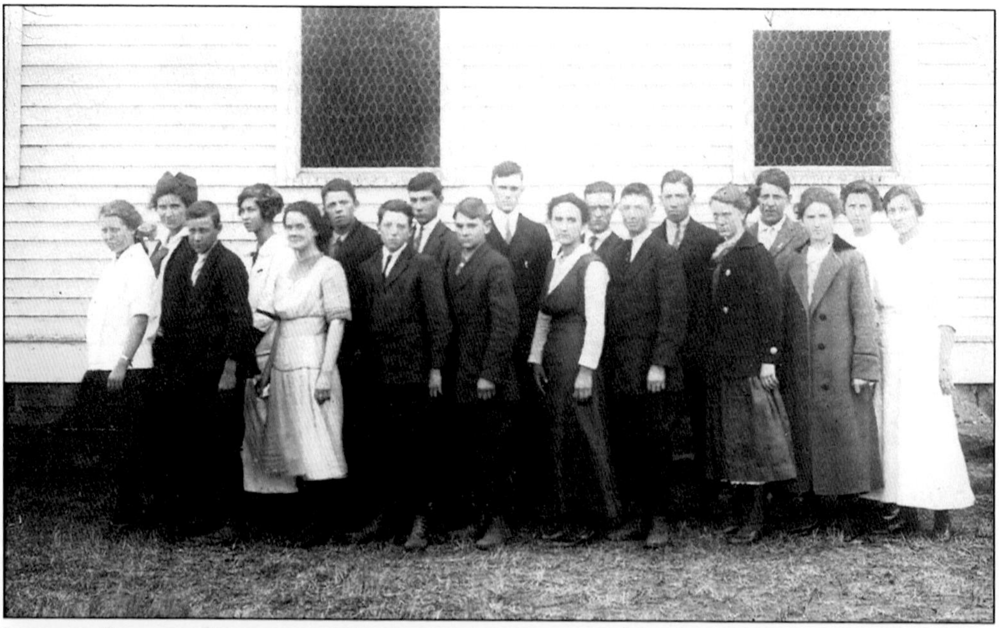

LEETON SCHOOL STUDENTS. The frame school, attended by this 1915 class, was fronted on Wall Street and the school grounds occupied the entire block between Fewel and Kelly Streets. A new brick school was constructed in 1916.

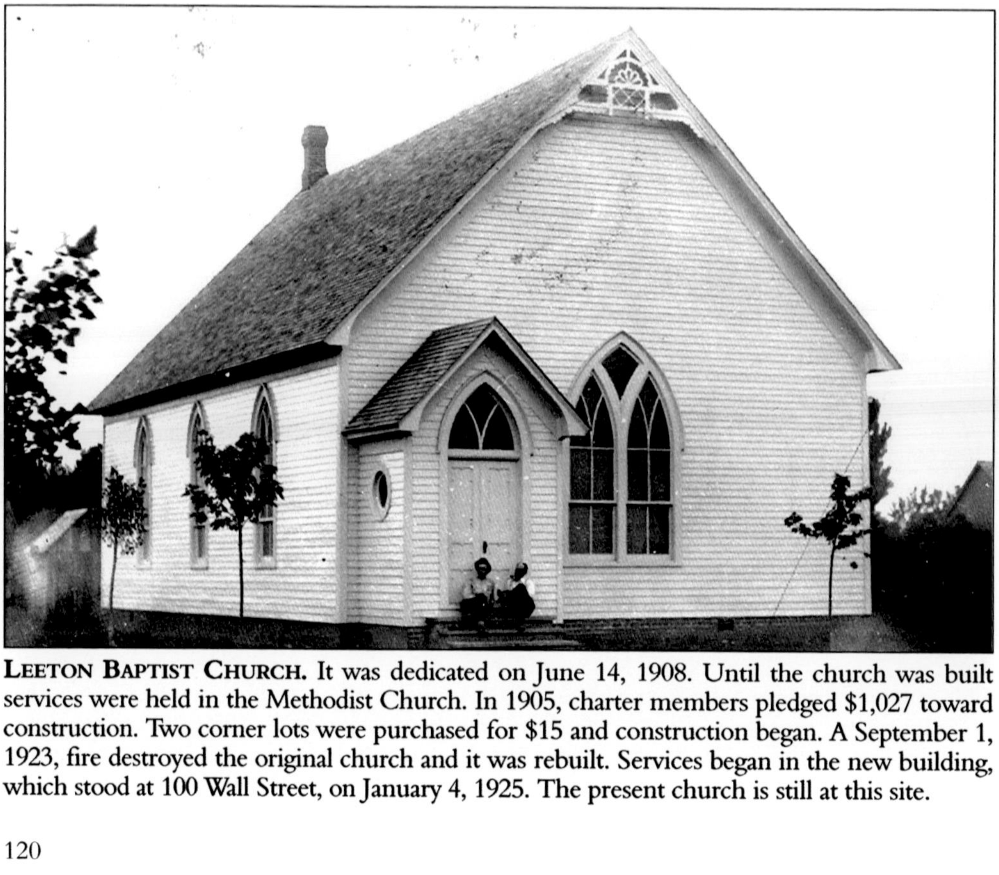

LEETON BAPTIST CHURCH. It was dedicated on June 14, 1908. Until the church was built services were held in the Methodist Church. In 1905, charter members pledged $1,027 toward construction. Two corner lots were purchased for $15 and construction began. A September 1, 1923, fire destroyed the original church and it was rebuilt. Services began in the new building, which stood at 100 Wall Street, on January 4, 1925. The present church is still at this site.

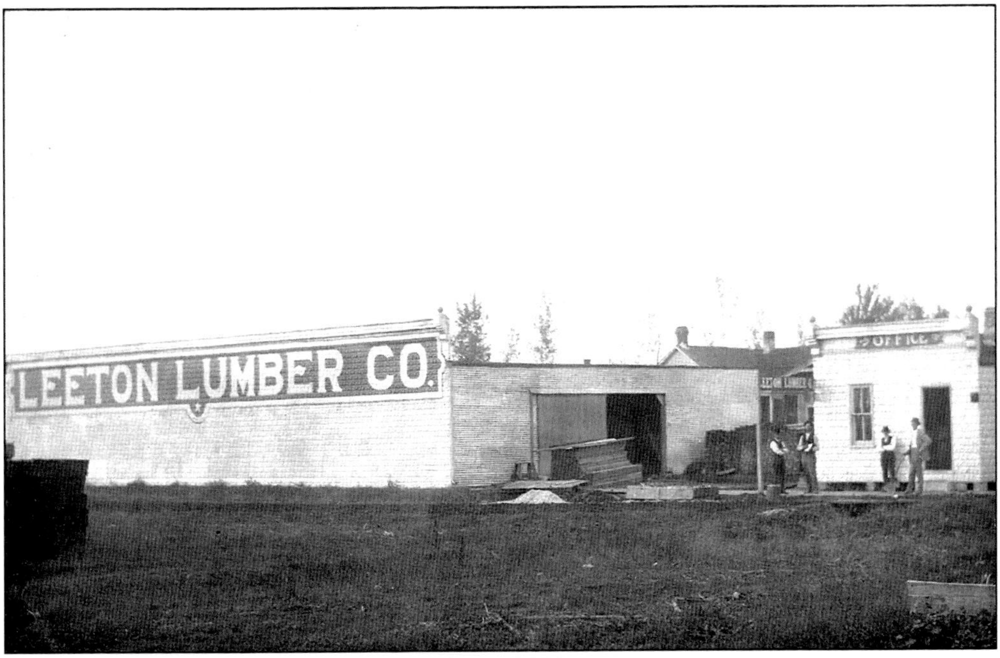

LEETON LUMBER CO. This photo was taken *c.* 1920.

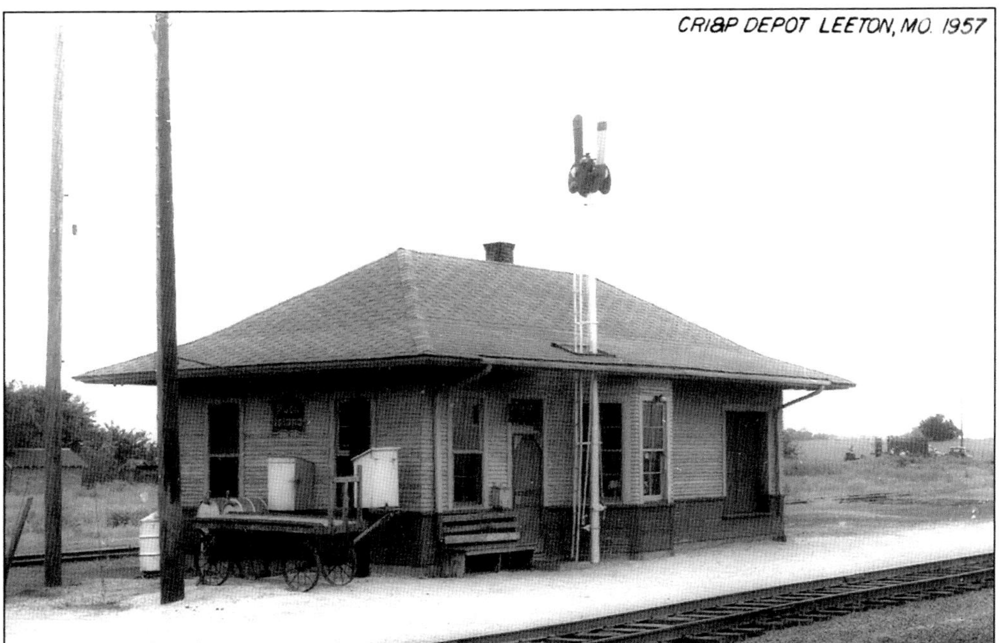

LEETON CRI&P DEPOT. This photo was taken of the Leeton depot in 1957. Running parallel to the Katy tracks, the CRI&P was the last of the four railroad lines in Johnson County, and completed in 1906. Often referred to as the Rock Island Depot, it was built farther west than the Katy Depot. The original Rock Island Depot burned down and was rebuilt. The depot no longer stands and much of the railroad right-of-way is overgrown with brush and weeds.

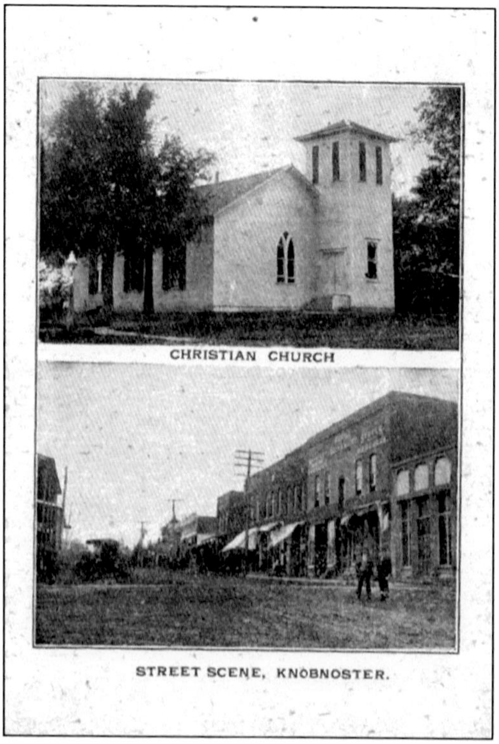

KNOB NOSTER CHRISTIAN CHURCH. Knob Noster is represented in this collection (as are many of the smaller communities) by a single postcard. The Christian church, shown above, has always occupied its present location at the corner of South Monroe and McPherson. The first church was started in 1870. The present church was built in 1911. Many of the buildings, shown in the lower part of the photo, still line the street today. (JCHS Collection.)

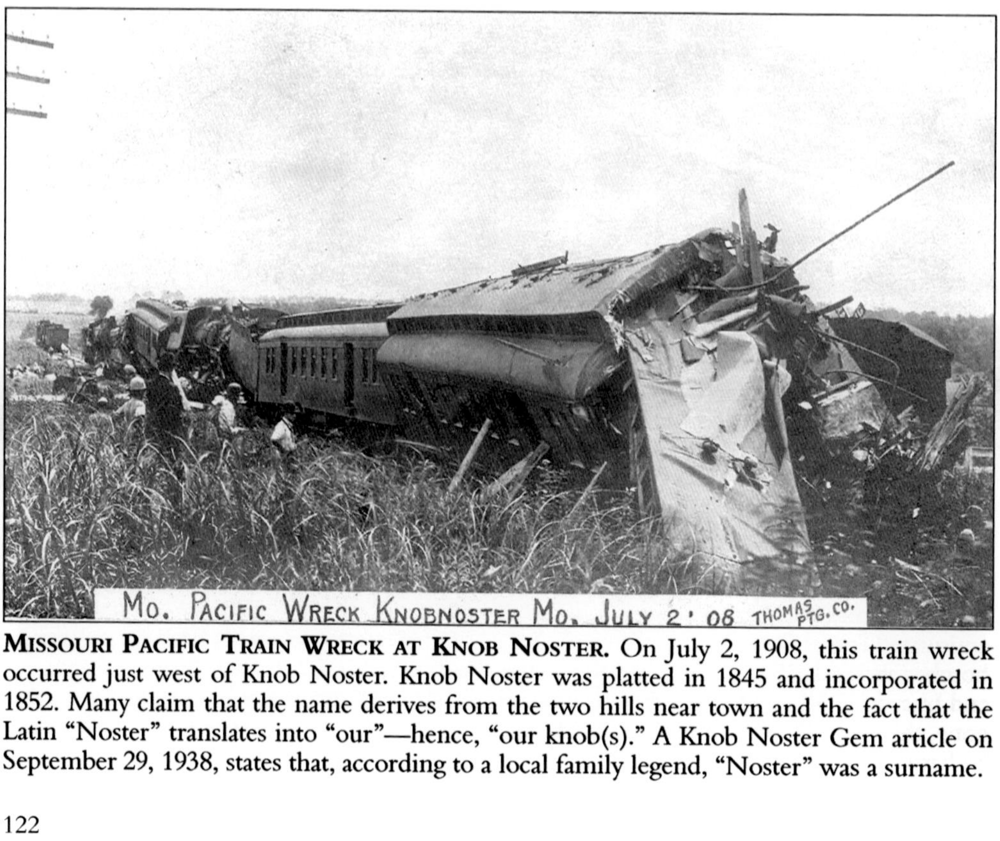

MISSOURI PACIFIC TRAIN WRECK AT KNOB NOSTER. On July 2, 1908, this train wreck occurred just west of Knob Noster. Knob Noster was platted in 1845 and incorporated in 1852. Many claim that the name derives from the two hills near town and the fact that the Latin "Noster" translates into "our"—hence, "our knob(s)." A Knob Noster Gem article on September 29, 1938, states that, according to a local family legend, "Noster" was a surname.

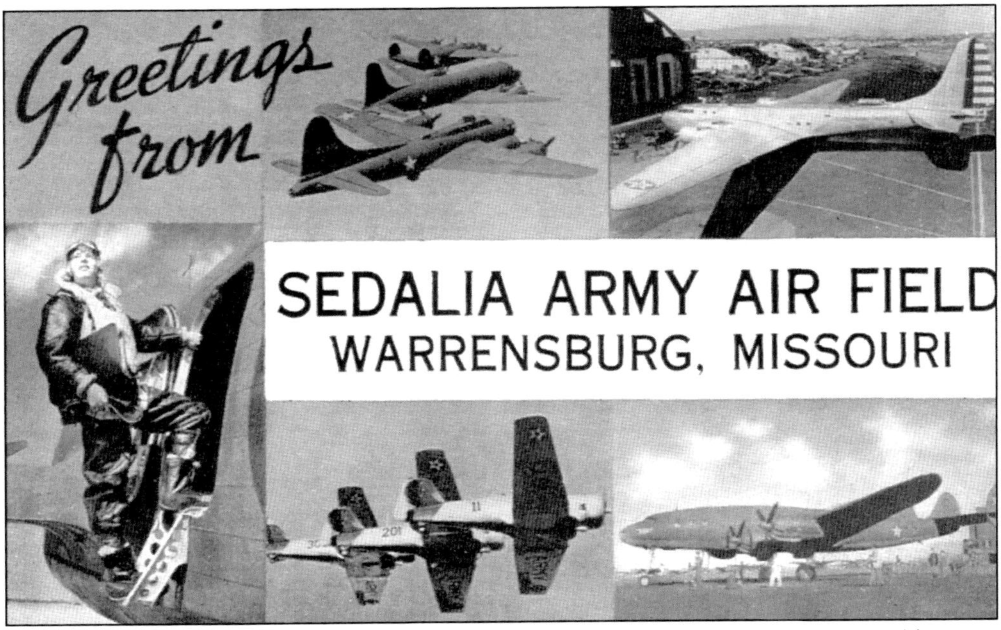

Air Base. Symbols of the armed services, an airman and a variety of vintage World War II aircraft, appear on this Sedalia Army Air Force, Warrensburg, Missouri card. It was eventually renamed in honor of the first airman killed at Pearl Harbor, George Whiteman from Sedalia.

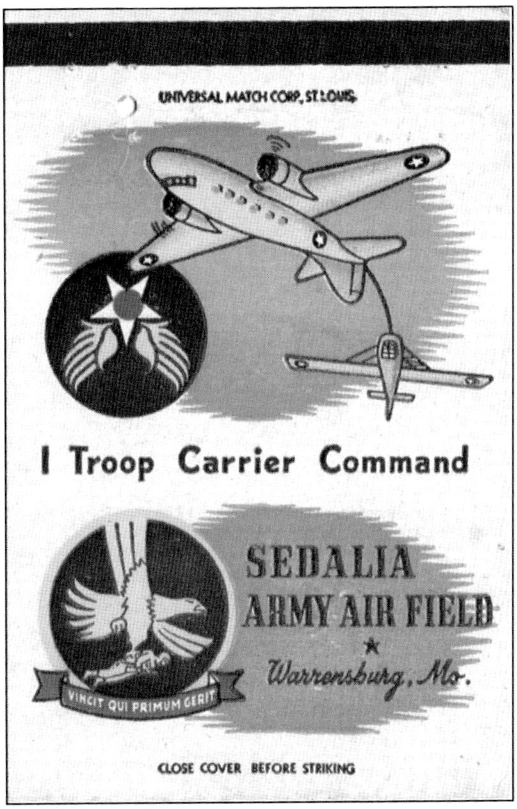

Matchbook/Postcard. "Sedalia Army Air Field, Warrensburg, Mo." is actually near Knob Noster. A C-47 towing a CG-4A glider on this match cover reminds us that the aircraft of World War II is very antiquated compared to the B-2 stealth bomber and A-10 Warthog of the Gulf and Iraq wars. When the matches were gone, this World War II matchbook could be flattened and used as a postcard.

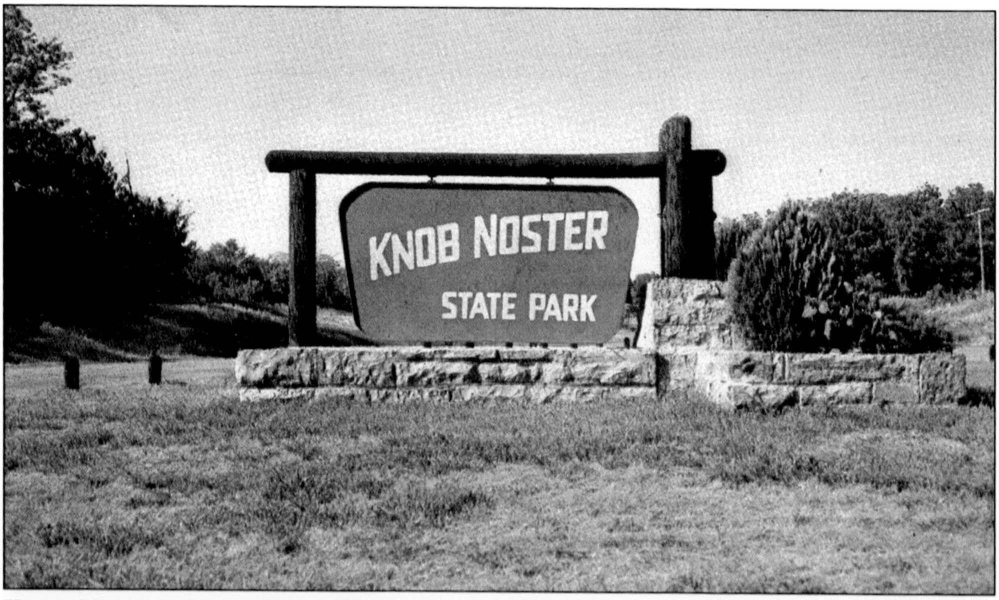

Knob Noster State Park. The entrance to Knob Noster State Park and a lovely picnic spot, it was once known as Montserrat Park Recreational Demonstration Area. The park has trails, public campgrounds, and two group camps—Shawnee and Bobwhite, both with modern facilities. Some of the structures built by the CCC in the 1930s still exist and the park is listed on the national register of historic sites. (JCHS Collection.)

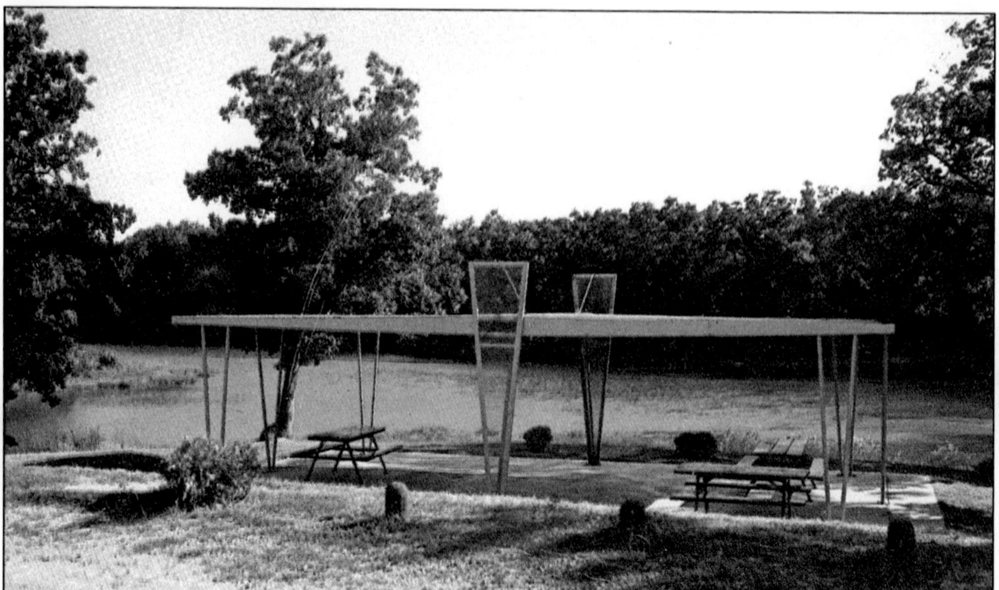

Knob Noster State Park. This is Lake Buteo. Perhaps not all know that Buteo is a specific name for the type of hawk known all around these parts as the "Redtail Hawk." Other lakes are named Clearfork, for the stream, and Morel, for the much sought after mushroom. The trails are called Raccoon, Possum, and other names inspired by the great Missouri outdoors. (JCHS Collection.)

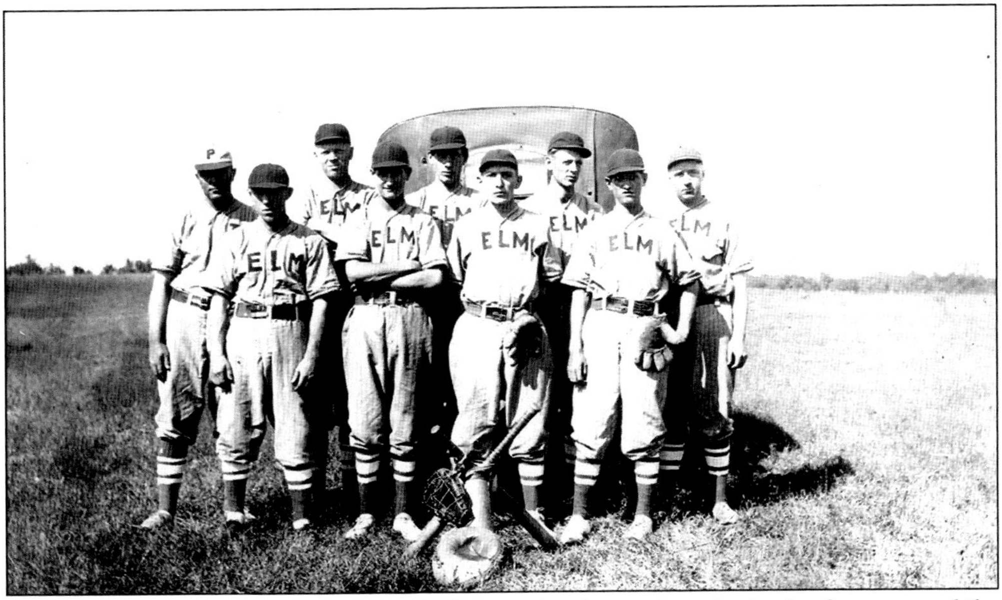

Elm Baseball Team. The Elm Baseball team, leaning against the back of an automobile. (JCHS Collection.)

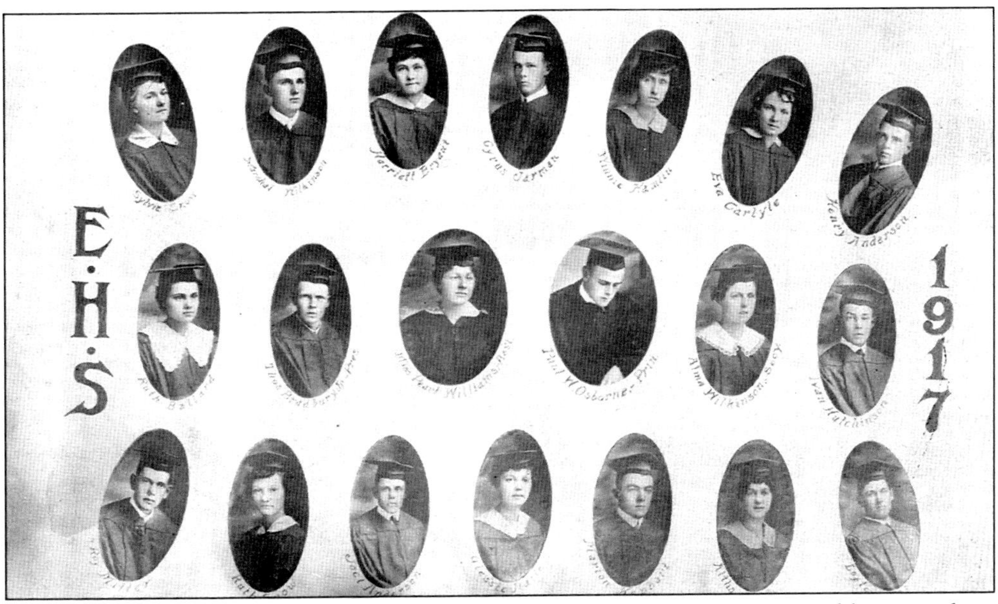

Elm High School Graduates. Elm High School graduates of 1917 were able to purchase postcards of their graduating class in caps and gowns. (JCHS Collection.)

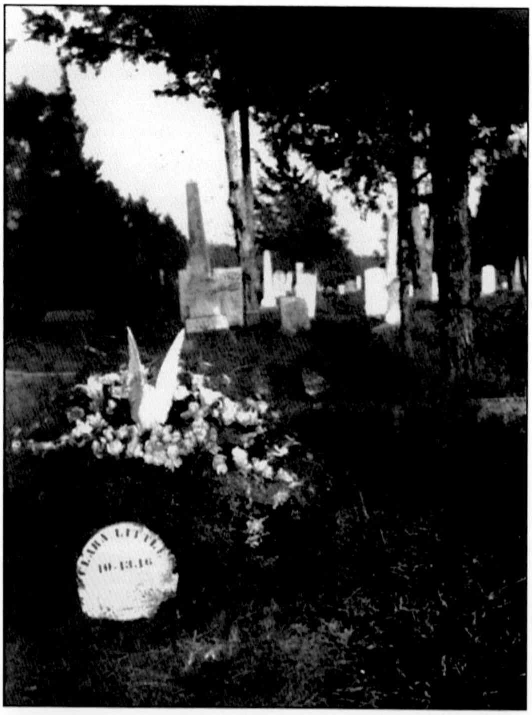

Centerview Cemetery. The only postcard that the authors could locate from the Centerview area is this image of the gravesite of Clara Little, who was buried in the Centerview Cemetery. The large bird that adorns her resting place is a sign of great love and sorrow. She died on October 12, 1916, at the age of 58. (JCHS Collection.)

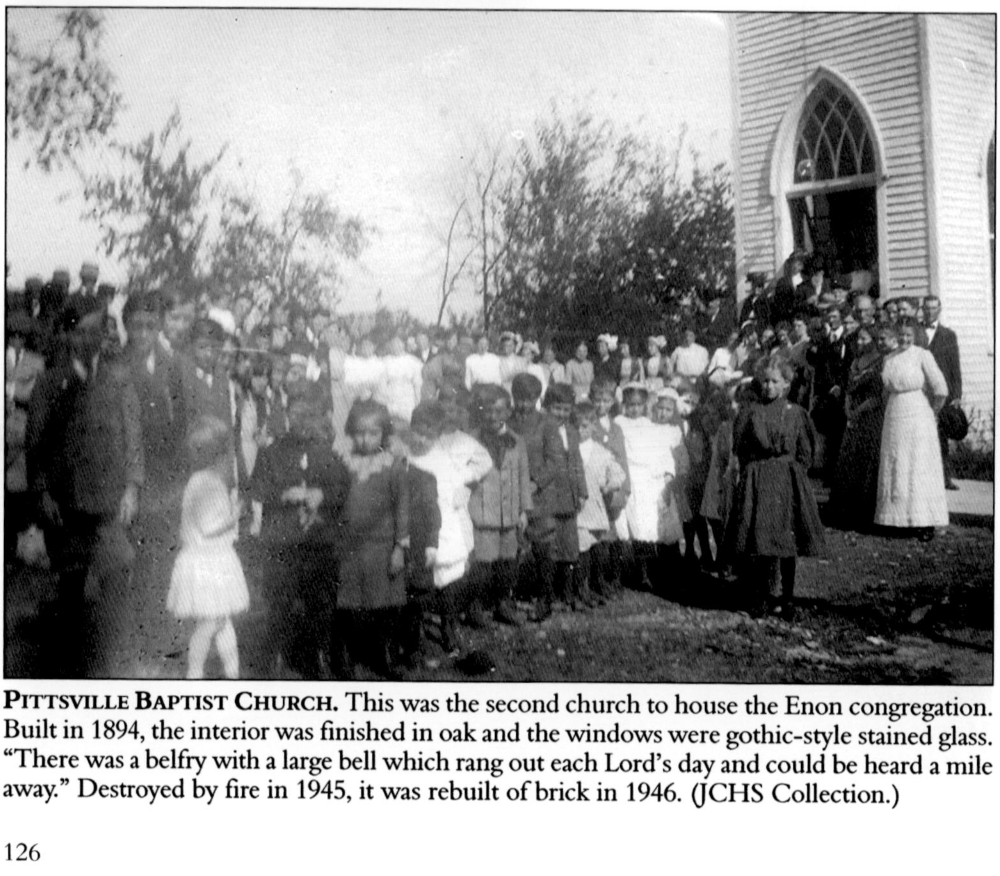

Pittsville Baptist Church. This was the second church to house the Enon congregation. Built in 1894, the interior was finished in oak and the windows were gothic-style stained glass. "There was a belfry with a large bell which rang out each Lord's day and could be heard a mile away." Destroyed by fire in 1945, it was rebuilt of brick in 1946. (JCHS Collection.)

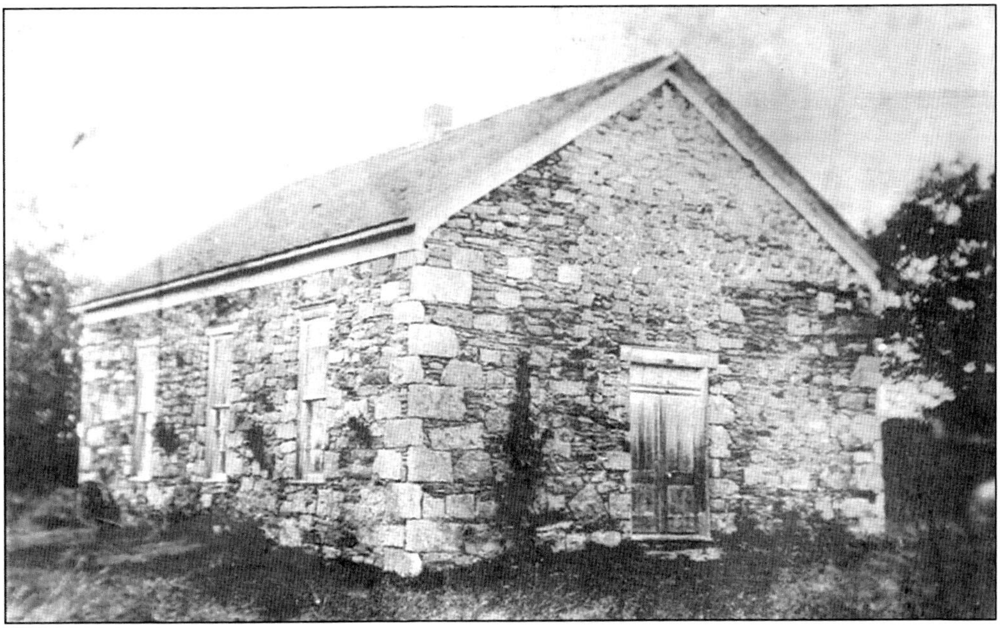

Rock Springs Church, Johnson County. This church was located north of Holden, just off Missouri Highway 58. Originally a log church, the native stone church was erected in 1856. It was gutted by fire early in the Civil War. A small church of this approximate design stands on the same spot today. (JCHS Collection.)

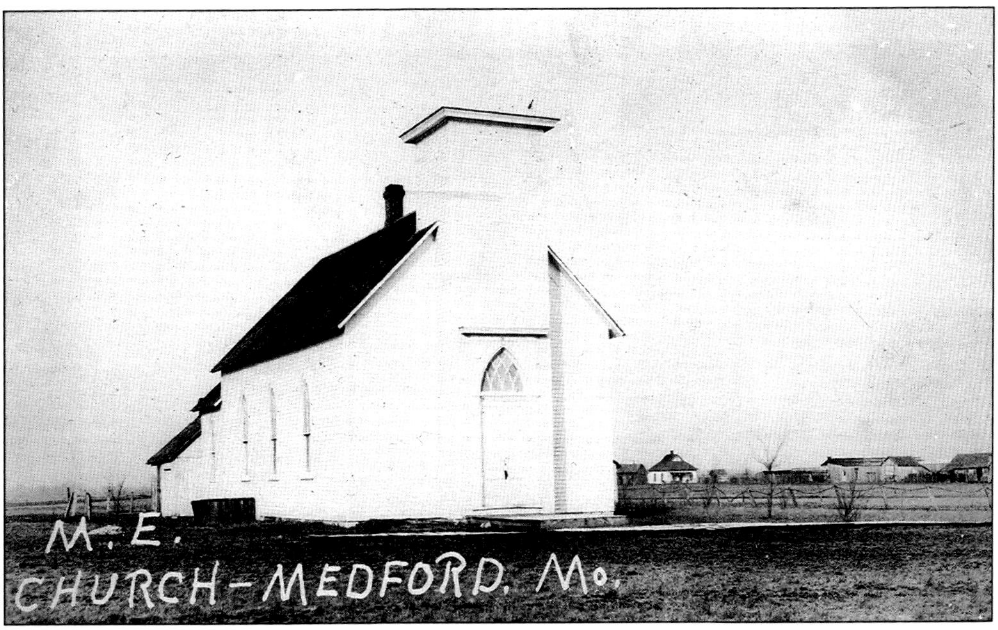

Methodist Episcopal Church at Medford. Dedicated May 12, 1907, the building was 26 ft. x 44 ft. Its cost, along with two lots, was $1,800. Not until 1978 was a bell tower placed atop the original square tower. (JCHS Collection.)

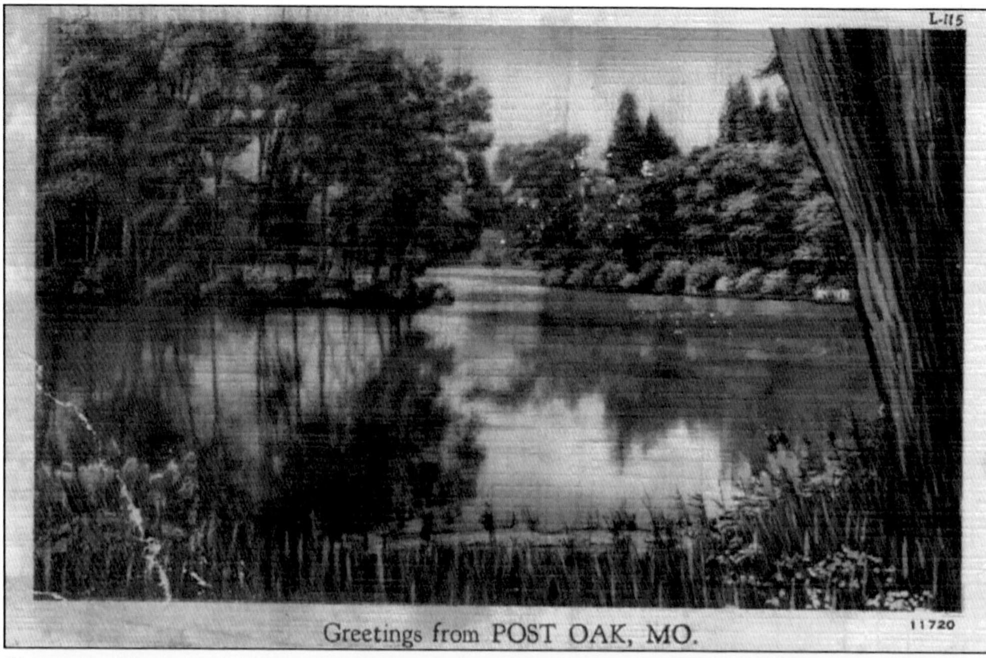

GENERIC GREETING CARD FOR POST OAK. This generic greeting card advertises Post Oak, Missouri. The town was platted as "Lingo" or "Lingo City" in the late 1800s, named for J.H. Lingo, a landowner in the area. It was listed as "PostOak" in the 1914 Johnson County plat book, another town that sprang up on the Katy Railroad.

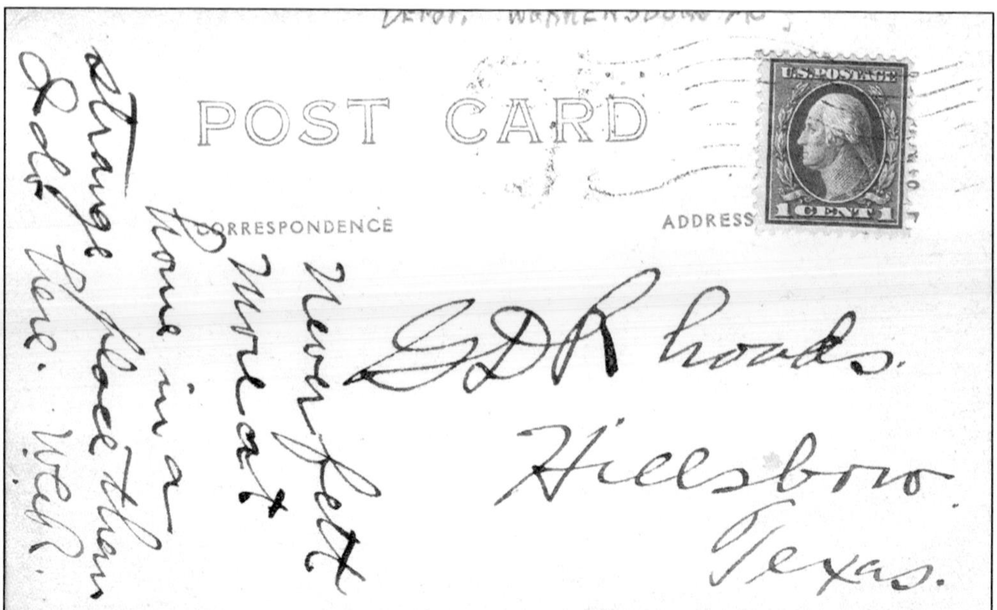

BACK OF A POSTCARD. "Never felt more at home in a strange place than I do here." This could have been said by anyone about any of the towns in this book. Hope you had fun!